# WRITING ABOUT PLACE

## THE ESSENTIAL GUIDE FOR ARCHITECTS, PLANNERS, AND OTHER PLACEMAKERS

### CHARLES EUCHNER

*For Isabel*

# CONTENTS

Part VI
ANALYSIS

# EXTENDED TABLE OF CONTENTS

# FOREWARD

## CROSS TRAINING FOR WRITERS AND PLACEMAKERS

Perhaps because I am a lover of both cities and words, I have always thought about them in the same way. They're both about creation, about building something worthwhile.

In both realms, you start with an idea and materials. Once you understand the project's purpose, you sketch some designs. Then you gather materials and start building. You begin with a strong foundation. As you work on the project, you adjust your plans; even the best ideas need to be tweaked. By the end, you produce something that doesn't just meet functional needs but also expresses some larger value.

I drew inspiration from lots of sources when writing this book. But the greatest inspiration comes from the architect Christopher Alexander's classic *A Pattern Language*.

As the title suggests, it's a "pattern book" for the challenges of architecture and planning. Alexander begins with a simple truth: Over our lives, we do relatively few things. We eat, sleep, work, play, socialize, care for family, make and enjoy things, and ... well, can you think of anything else?

In *A Pattern Language*, Alexander identifies 253 distinct patterns. With them, he shows how to design all the spaces that we use—from the level of the community (towns and roads, work spaces, transportation networks, clusters of buildings, town centers, streets and promenades, workplaces, social places and shopping areas, and more) down to the level of the single building (windows and doors, rooms, roofs and ceilings, balconies, seating, and more).

The magic of *A Pattern Language* lies in its simplicity. Alexander explains each pattern in three or four pages, with simple language and drawings and photographs. Anyone can read any one of the book's 253 sections and learn how to approach a specific challenge. Alexander's prescriptions are not rigid. He invites users to adapt each pattern to their particular needs and desires.

When I started teaching writing—first in political science classes at Holy Cross, then, years later, in writing classes at Yale—I searched for a book that brought Alexander's approach to writing. Surely, I thought, some book, somewhere, identified all of the basic strategies and skills of writing. If we could provide a how-to guide for each skill, with helpful case studies, we could give writers everything they need to write well.

Finding no such work, I set out to create it myself. I started by identifying the essential skills or techniques for writing in all fields.

My first iteration of this project was called *The Elements of Writing*, which explains 79 simple "elements" of writing. Each one—like Alexander's patterns —is simple and intuitive. Each one comes with a case study, which shows how real-world writers use that element in their work.

Now I have adapted these 79 elements to professionals in "place making"—planning, architecture, preservation, real estate, the environment, and so on.

### Cross Training

I think of this guide as a form of cross training.

In sports, athletes often train not just for their specific sport, but for a broad range of athletic skills. Many train for more than one sport so they can gain greater range as athletes. Many baseball players, for example, practice yoga, run, swim, lift weights, rock-climb, surf, ride bikes, and golf. These skills may not be directly useful on the baseball diamond, but they improve the ballplayer's flexibility, strength, attention, endurance, and other capabilities.

In this book, you will learn all the writing skills you need to compose clear and lively prose, whether you're writing a report, review, proposal, memo, web copy, or email. With the case studies, you will also learn about some of the great issues involved in architecture in planning.

At the same time, the case studies also teach about placemaking.We explore authors and practitioners like Christopher Alexander, Kevin Lynch, Jane Jacobs, Corbusier, William Whyte, I.M. Pei, and many more. We also explore histories, modern projects, academic works on the experience of place.

### Placemaking and Writing:
### Metaphors for Each Other

Many of the principles of writing offer metaphors for architecture and planning … and vice versa. Learning principles in one realm, then, makes it easier to learn principles in the other realm.

Consider the following five "elements of writing" and how they might be adapted to architecture and planning:

**"Start strong, finish strong"**: In every sentence, paragraph, section, and whole piece, start and end with a bang.

*Architecture/planning parallel*: Make sure that users of space—whether it's a building, a street, or a park—know how to move from every possible starting point to every possible destination.

**Create a "throughline" for every character**: Give all major characters a powerful desire that governs every aspect of their lives.

*Architecture/planning parallel*: Give every project a clear *parti*, or "big idea," that informs all decisions about the space. Use that big idea to develop the project's program.

**Use "beats" to pace stories and analysis**: In every scene, create a number of specific actions that change the trajectory of the story. If an action does not drive the story forward, eliminate it.

*Architecture/planning parallel*: Create orienting devices along pathways—streets, pathways, corridors—to orient and direct the user.

**Use details that surprise the reader**: Choose the details that enhance the reader's understanding. Do not emphasize the details that the reader already knows. Highlight the details that make the reader sit up and take notice.

*Architecture/planning parallel*: Give purpose to every element of space—doors, hallways, windows, pathways, centerpieces, and more. Use details that enliven those elements, rather than extraneous details that confuse or detract the user.

**Give every sentence a clear "action blast"**: Make sure the reader understands —right away—what happens in a sentence. Do not ramble or get lost in setup details. Say who does what, as soon as possible.

*Architecture/planning parallel*: Give every space "legibility." Make sure people understand all the uses of a particular place. Make sure people can see, clearly, how to use every element of a place.

I do not want to overstate the point. Writing and making places are different activities. But mastery of one can help you to understand the other.

### Five Kinds of Writing

In the course of your education and careers—as they produce emails and memos, case studies and evaluations, RFPs and proposals, and more—architects and planners must produce five distinct kinds of writing.

**Profiles of People**: Placemaking begins with people. Who are we serving when we design or plan a building or a complex, a park or a plaza, a campus or a streetscape? What are their motivations and needs? So we need to understand what makes people tick.

**Descriptions of Places**: Once we understand people, we can move to place. What makes places succeed? How do people move in and around place? What features—of a building, park, street, school, office, factory, whatever—bring people together?

**Depictions of Action**: People don't just *occupy* places; they also *act* in places. So we need to show how people do different things in places. How do students act in a classroom? How do residents, businesses, and visitors act in a street? How do workers perform their jobs in an office or a factory floor or warehouse?

**Explanations of Processes**: Action is just the beginning. In even the simplest places, a wide range of actions are happening at the same time or in sequence. To understand how people use a park, for example, we need to understand how different systems—traffic, maintenance, services, and more—feed into each other. So we need two describe processes, the way different streams of activity feed into each other.

**Analysis of Issues and Challenges**: When working on projects, we need to understand the larger processes—the abstract forces—at work. What causes what? What variables matter? What's the best way to understand complex relationships? What models offer useful guidance?

### Onward!

Placemaking is one of the most important processes in all societies. Great places—buildings, streets, parks and plazas, public buildings, museums and recreational spaces, subways and bus and bike lanes, waterfronts—make so much else possible. Beautiful and functional places not only please us. They also make us better.

We need placemakers to play an active role in our political and social debates. For that to happen, they need to express themselves, in words as well as in pictures and the physical places they help to create.

My modest hope is that this book will help our architects and planners to gain the voice they need to improve our civic debate, even more than they already have.

# I

## THE CORE IDEA

Imagine, if you will, a world in which people followed a simple eleven-word imperative.

This imperative is universal. Religions and ethical systems across the world embrace this ideal. It is so simple that even small children understand it. And when followed, even imperfectly, it guides people to live well and and to take care of each other.

I am talking, of course, of the Golden Rule: "Do under others as you would have them do unto you."

The power of the Golden Rule lies in its appeal to empathy. When trying to decide whether to commit some act, just imagine how you would *feel* if someone else did the same thing. When I think of the Golden Rule, I think of the jazz great Louis Armstrong. Responding to critics who said his song "What a Wonderful World" was naive, Armstrong explained:

> All I'm saying is, see, what a wonderful world it would be if only we'd give it a chance. Love, baby, love. That's the secret. Yeah! If lots more of us loved each other, we'd solve lots more problems. And then this world would be a *gasser*.

Under the Golden Rule, we don't have to *love* everyone—just *respect* everyone. That should be easy enough, right?

Now imagine an even simpler imperative to guide writers. This one is just eight words long. It has two parts, each four words. Those two parts are really just statements of the same idea from different angles.

- Make everything a journey.
- Start strong, finish strong.

This imperative—which I call the Golden Rule of Writing—will not solve all your problems. You still need to understand your topic, gather ideas and evidence, figure out what to say, and find just the right words to say it. These and other writing skills take time and effort.

But the Golden Rule of Writing offers an approach that—if you use it— provides the focus you need to develop your skills as a writer. If you apply this simple little rule—every time you compose and edit sentences and paragraphs, and then organize those pieces into sections and whole pieces—you can't fail.

Here's how to do it …

1

# THE GOLDEN RULE OF WRITING

Elegance is achieved when all that is superfluous has been discarded and the human being discovers simplicity and concentration: the simpler and more sober the posture, the more beautiful it will be.

— PAOLO COELHO

To go someplace, you need to know your starting point and your destination.

The first time I visited Paris, I arrived to a steady drizzle and a transit strike. I took a cab to the Left Bank but didn't know where to go; I had left my friend's contact information at home. So I schlepped around, getting soggy while carrying two bags. I studied the maps in my *Plan de Paris*, hoping I would recognize the name of my friend's street. But I didn't. I was lost.

Finally, I found help in a travel agency. An agent found a hotel and told me about nearby restaurants and sights. After I called home to get my friend's contact information, the agent unfolded a map and pointed to my hotel and my friend's apartment. I was just a block and a half away.

Once I knew where I was—and where I was going—everything worked well.

Writing works like that. If you know where to start and finish, you will never get lost or disoriented. Neither will your readers. But if you don't know where to begin and end, you will struggle.

Too often, writers wander without direction, like me on that first day in Paris. Struggling to get their bearings, uncertain what ideas and evidence matter, they wander. If asked where they want to take the reader, they recite ideas that excite them. But they do not state, clearly, where they want to take the reader.

So here's a simple rule to guide your writing: *Make everything a journey, at every level of writing.* In every sentence, paragraph, section, chapter, article, report, and book, take your reader from one point to another, different point. Be clear about this journey. What do the readers know at the beginning? What do you want them to know by the end? How do you want to get from one place to the other?

If you can answer these questions, every time you write something, your job as a writer will be clear.

Of course, I'm not the first to understand writing as a journey. Jincy Willett talks about the "orderly march of words across the page." David Lambuth talks about "writing as a trip from a definite starting point to a definite destination." What's different here, I think, is the idea of making *every level* of writing —sentence, paragraphs, sections, and whole pieces—whole journeys unto themselves.

Now let's figure out a simple way to plot the journey. Consider this simple corollary: *Start strong, finish strong.* At every level of writing, start with a bang and end with a bang. Put your most important material at the beginnings and endings of sentences, paragraphs, and pieces.

I call this the Golden Rule of Writing. If you apply the Golden Rule to all of your challenges, you will succeed as a writer.

∾

### Element 1
### Make Everything a Journey

MAKE EVERYTHING A JOURNEY? Really? That might seem extreme. Sure, stories matter. But is *everything*—every sentence, paragraph, section, even email or report—really a journey?

Think of it this way. We write in order to show readers something new—an observation, an image, a moment, an idea, a theory. We write, in other words, to take readers to a new place. A critic takes the reader to insights about a movie or play. A scientist takes the reader to a new understanding of how variables interact. A reporter takes the reader to a new knowledge of the day's news.

Always, the writer takes the reader on a journey from one place—or one understanding of the world—to another.

Imagine meeting a friend for a trip. When you get together, you share some background and expectations about the trip. Maybe she has taken this trip before; maybe this is her first time. To be the right kind of travel companion, you need to know. You need some idea of what she knows at the start. You also need to know the destination. When you know the starting point and the destination, you can park out the path. You might move quickly through some areas. In other areas, you might wish to stop for a while to explore. It's all fine, as long as you get back on the road.

As a writer, you need to do the same thing. Let's get a little more specific.

• **The beginning of the journey**. Ask yourself, what's the best place to meet. Do you want to begin with something exciting, that catches the reader's attention? Do you want to start the goal of the journey? Do you want to introduce key ideas, questions, and situations? There are no limits to how you start your journey. You must, however, orient the reader. Your job is to offer a worthwhile journey, which offers something of value for your reader. Make sure your reader gets engaged and focused on the trip ahead.

• **The end of the journey**. Where are you going? What do you want your reader to have at the end? What kind of experience do you want to offer? Do you want to tell a story? If so, what kind? Do you wish to convey facts and ideas? If so, what are the most important ideas—and do you have a single, overarching idea you want to convey? Do you want to make an analysis or argument? What do you want the reader to know or understand at the end?

• **The middle of the journey**. Now that you know the beginning and end, you can chart a path. Imagine a series of stepping stones. Each stone represents some information you need to get from the beginning to the end. How will you organize those stones? Most writing clusters bunches of related facts and ideas. So your path must organize those facts and ideas into sections.

Sequence matters. Before you introduce a new idea or experience, you need to make sure the reader will understand it. If you know your audience, you will know what ideas will be familiar and unfamiliar to your readers. Unfamiliar ideas require setup—definitions, background information, explanations about why they matter.

Every story, every journey, involves *change*. Whoever the characters, setting, or issues, something changes by the end of the story.

If everything in writing is a journey, then we should be able to map out that journey. Just as I can map out my journey from my home in Connecticut to a meeting in Manhattan—drive to New Haven's Union Station, jump on the 8:53 Metro North train to Grand Central Station, take a subway to Greenwich Village, walk five blocks, and so on—I should be able to map out the journey of every unit of writing.

To map a passage, simply draw pictures of the journey. Get out a clean piece of paper. Write down, on one side, the starting point for the journey.

Then write down, on the other side, the endpoint. Between those two places, mark the steps you need to get from one place to another. If the journey is simple, a straight line will do. If the journey is more complex—if you take detours or shift your approach—show how the journey twists or veers off course.

Pick up a book or story of any of the best writers you know. Get Ernest Hemingway or Scott Fitzgerald, Virginia Woolf or V.S. Pritchett, Truman Capote or Tom Wolfe or Joan Didion. Plot the movement from beginning to end. You will see a clear journey—often with some zigs and zags, tension and struggle, along the way—from one state of being to another.

## Case Study
## Nathaniel Rich's 'When Parks Were Radical'

Few people have shaped America's urban landscapes more than Frederick Law Olmsted, who designed and oversaw the construction of New York's Central Park and Prospect Park, Boston's Emerald Necklace, San Francisco's Golden Gate Park, and hundreds of other parks, lawns, campuses, and natural spaces.

But Olmsted's natural spaces were far from natural. Like a sculptor, Olmsted worked to shape and tame the great outdoors. He looked for a sweet spot, neither too natural nor too tamed. Olmsted wanted parks to *appear* natural, but he carefully designed and built them. Here's now Nathaniel Rich describes Olmsted's approach:

> An unmistakable irony creeps vine-like through Olmsted's landscape theory: It takes a lot of artifice to create convincing "natural" scenery. Everything in Central Park is man-made; the same is true of most of Olmsted's designs. They are not imitations of nature so much as idealizations, like the landscape paintings of the Hudson River School. Each Olmsted creation was the product of painstaking sleight of hand, requiring enormous amounts of labor and expense. In his notes on Central Park, Olmsted called for thinning forests, creating artificially winding and uneven paths, and clearing away "indifferent plants," ugly rocks, and inconvenient hillocks and depressions—all in order to "induce the formation ... of natural landscape scenery." He complained to his superintendents when his parks appeared "too gardenlike" and constantly demanded that they "be made more natural."

Rich provides a rich journey from the idea of irony to Olmsted's demand for an unnatural nature space. Let's map Rich's paragraph. (See the next page for my version.)

However you draw it, the map should show the critical choices Olmsted faced. He started with natural, unkept spaces in the middle of Manhattan. To design Central Park, he used a number of "slights of hand." He also used abundant outside labor and materials. He did not go down two possible roads —the overly idealized gardens of the British or the wild and untamed spaces that he found.

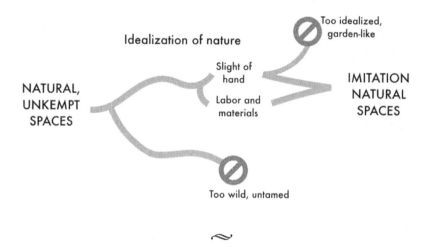

~

**Element 2**
**Start Strong, Finish Strong**

Chances are that you do not want to map everything you write. You might want to map larger, more complicated journeys. But to write great sentences and paragraphs, you need a simpler approach. Hence, Part II of the Golden Rule: *Start Strong, Finish Strong.*

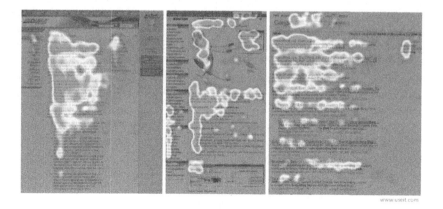

Look at the "heat map," which shows where readers' eyes go when scanning webpages. Readers almost always look at the left side of the page, where the sentences begin. The eyes then leap to the ends the page. Only occasionally do eyes track all the words in a sentence.

The eyes tell you what you need to know. If readers pay the greatest attention to the beginnings and endings, where should you put your most important material? Obviously, at the beginnings and endings.

Think about your own experiences in life. Most of us remember best the first and last parts of any experience. We remember the beginnings and endings of songs, books, movies, and events. What happens in the middle matters too, of course. But the beginnings and endings frame the whole experience.

Or consiedr tihs sohrt paargraph. You can udnrestnad the paassge eevn touhgh I hvae srcmblaed all the mddile ltteres of the wdros. To udnrstnead even splime wrdos, we uallusy jsut need the bgnneigns and ednngis of tsohe wrdos. Azamnig!

Let's explore the three parts of all journeys.

**Start Strong**: In the beginning, we invite the reader into our journey. To engage the reader, it's best to start with strongest material.

Usually, that means telling the reader, right away, *who does what*. When the reader knows the subject right away—the focus, the point of it all—she can understand whatever follows. So we might say:

> Reagan looked out at the crowd …
> Macbeth expressed doubt …

These simple passages bring the reader into the middle of the action, right away. The reader knows exactly what's happening, who does what, without any delay or confusion.

All too often, we writers wander before getting to the point. We provide background information, define terms, and explain possible objections—before saying a word about who does what. Pick up a newspaper, magazine, or book —right now. Find a dozen random passages. How long does it take the writer to get to the subject and verb? I wouldn't be surprised if some sentences wandered for a dozen or more words before getting to the point. I have seen sentences meander for 40 or even 50 words before stating who does what. That's usually too much.

Of course, starting every single sentence with a subject and verb might get tedious. Also, sometimes "starting strongly" means providing a brief setup for the subject and verb. So you might "start strong" like this:

> Before uttering his historic lines, Reagan looked out at the crowd
> …
> Appalled by the murder he was about to commit, Macbeth
> expressed doubt…

These openings offer important context, so we can understand the meaning of the action.

**Finish Strong**: We need closure, a sense of completion, when we finish reading something. We need to know how something "turns out." We feel unease when a writer fails to clinch the point. So at the end of every sentence, paragraph, and piece, give the reader closure. Whenever possible, complete your thought. So:

> Reagan looked out at the crowd and challenged Gorbachev to "tear down this wall."
> Macbeth expressed doubt about killing Duncan, prompting Lady Macbeth to question his manhood.

These sentences end with a bang—Reagan's challenge to Mikhail Gorbachev and Lady Macbeth's challenge to her husband. Each comes like a thunderbolt. Each demands a response.

You can "finish strong" in two other ways: By raising a question or offering an intriguing image. Questions and images activate the reader's mind—and help propel the piece forward, to the next sentence, paragraph, or section. Look at these two possible conclusions:

> Reagan looked out at the crowd at the Berlin Wall, not knowing whether Mikhail Gorbachev would make good on his promise of reform.
> Macbeth expressed doubts, stammering and pacing before his stern wife.

Both of these endings create suspense, making the reader want to read on.

**Bridges and Brackets in the Middle**: If the beginnings and endings frame the journey, the middle material offers the pathway. The middles offer two kinds of information, which I call *bridges* and *brackets*.

Let's start with bridges. Bridges take the reader, step by step, from the beginning to the end of the passage. See how these two sentences offer a pathway for the reader's journeys:

Reagan looked out at the Berlin crowd, gauging the mood of the crowd and pausing for effect, then challenged Gorbachev to "tear down this wall."

Macbeth expressed doubt about killing Duncan—professing his love of the king, his qualms about the witches, and his fears of a bloody civil war—prompting Lady Macbeth to question his manhood.

Now, consider brackets. Sometimes we need to provide notes, side information that helps us to understand the situation. We might want to provide the source of the information. Many readers don't care about the sources. But specialists and skeptics do care; they want to know whether the information is credible. See how these two sentences "bracket" sources in the middle:

> Reagan looked out at the crowd feeling upbeat, according to aides who sat nearby on the podium, and challenged Gorbachev to "tear down this wall."
>
> Macbeth expressed doubt about killing Duncan in Act I, Scene 7, prompting Lady Macbeth to question his manhood.

The brackets here—"according to aides" and "in Act I, Scene 7"—provide the sources of information. Most readers glide over this material. But for readers who want to assess the passage's credibility, the middle chunks provide a place to go. Many readers skim over the middles. Some don't care about source information. Others don't care about the steps from the beginning to the end. In fact, you could delete the middles from most well-built sentences and still convey the main idea. But for readers who do care about this information, it's there.

Strong starts and finishes are essential for every level of writing. With them, you have the bones of a good piece of writing. Without them, you are doomed.

## Case Study
### Stewart Brand's *How Buildings Learn*

Starting and ending strongly is a core principle of both writing and design. "There is every reason why the beginnings and endings of streets should be well marked, as part of the street, to introduce us to them and to take us elsewhere," Jane Jacobs writes. In other words: *Start strong, finish strong.*

Stewart Brand, the creator of the iconic *Whole Earth Catalogue* as well as an author on planning and technology, follows this edict in this passage about so-called "granny flats," the small apartments sometimes attached to houses:

> A few years back I lived inexpensively in a tiny cottage in an extremely affluent place called Belvedere, California.
>
> Two local women were pressuring the City Council to register and tax all of the town's "second units" (also called accessory apartments, granny flats, mother-in-law units) and outlaw all new ones.
>
> Most of the innumerable second units have been added quietly over the years without permits or official notice by the city.
>
> The council was about to pass the new ordinance when front-page coverage in the local paper brought the biggest crowd in memory to a City Council meeting.
>
> The two women sat rigid as the whole town explained in detail that second units were the salvation of Belvedere.
>
> They gave families the flexibility to stay in their homes, because there was a place for the aging parents, the au pair, the growing teenager.

They provided affordable housing for city staff, local nurses, local
   shop employees—the town's whole support population.
Rent from the second units reduced the cost of primary homes.
A financially and socially brutal community was made broader
   and more adaptive by second units.
Don't outlaw them, help them.

All but one of these sentences starts, right away, with the subject ("Two
local women," "Most of the innumerable second units," "The council," etc.);
the other starts with context ("A few years back"). Each of the sentences ends
by completing the thought ("in Belvedere, California," "outlaw all new ones,"
"official notice by the city," etc.).

The middles all help to fill out the sentences. But if we cut the middles, we
would still get the point of the sentences. A few examples:

I lived ... in Belvedere, California.
Two local women were pressuring ... to outlaw all new ones.
Most have been added ... without official notice by the city.
They gave families ... a place for the aging parents, the au pair,
   the growing teenager.
They provided affordable housing for ... the town's whole
   support population.
Rent ... reduced the cost of primary homes.
A financially and socially brutal community was ... more
   adaptive by second units.

At every level of writing—sentence, paragraph, section, and whole—Brand
takes the reader on a journey. He guides the reader from one place to another,
different place. By starting and finishing strong, he gives his prose clarity and
power.

~

### Element 3
### Take the Landscape View

WHAT IF I offered you a simple system that would help you follow the Golden
Rule, without muss or fuss, for everything you wrote?

To apply the Golden Rule of Writing, use a simple technique that I call the
Landscape View. Here's how:

- Use the landscape (horizontal) format for all your documents.
- Write one sentence per line.
- Single-space your document.

• Skip a space between paragraphs.

I developed the Landscape View when I was teaching writing at Yale. Over the course of one semester, my students and I explored the Golden Rule. We parsed sentences, paragraphs, essays, and books. The students vowed to "start strong, finish strong" at all levels of their writing. But then they slipped back into old habits. They didn't start or end strongly.

One day, desperate for a simple way to guide their writing, I came up with the Landscape View. I required students to do an assignment using the format. Their writing improved dramatically, right away. In fact, from that point, my students never wrote a sentence that I struggled to understand. Not only that, they wrote with greater energy and creativity than ever.

Why does the Landscape View work so well? We discovered five benefits:

**1. Checking starts and finishes**: With the Landscape View, you can easily check to see whether you start and finish strongly. Just run your finger down the left side of the page, line by line, to see if you start strongly. Run your finger down the right side to see if you end strongly. Finally, look down the middle of the page for bridges and brackets.

If you start or end weakly, you know what to do. Sometimes you need to recast the whole sentence. But if you know what you want to say, that usually takes little effort. Sometimes, you need to delete the sentence. Sometimes you need just a minor fix, like clarifying the subject or verb.

Can't we check sentences in the standard blocks of text? Yes, but we don't. Finding the beginnings and endings of sentences in paragraph blocks takes too much effort. Most people simply stop trying after three or four paragraphs. The brain, as researchers tell us, is *lazy*. If you ask the brain to do too many things, it will falter. So give your brain a shortcut. Make it easy to check the beginnings and endings of sentences with the Landscape View.

**2. Controlling sentence length**: The landscape format helps you to monitor sentence length. Using the TimesRoman font, with 12-point type, gives you about 20 to 24 words per line. Research shows that readers best comprehend sentences that average 17 to 19 words. Inevitably, your sentences will vary in length; some will be more and some will be less than the average. If your sentence runs onto a new line, that's OK; it's fine to write sentences of 30, 40, or even more words. If a sentence runs long, just make sure you *need* all those words to make your point. Make sure that one long sentence conveys your ideas better than two or three shorter sentences would.

Remember old-fashioned typewriters that sounded a bell at the end of every line? The end of every line should ring a bell in your head, signaling you to ask: *Should this sentence be so long? Or should I recast it or break it up?*

**3. Varying sentence length**: The Landscape View also shows, instantly, whether you vary sentence length.

Why does this matter? Reading a piece with all short sentences feels like water torture. And reading a piece with all long sentences feels like hacking through a forest with a machete. So to keep the reader engaged, make an effort to vary your sentence lengths.

Varying sentence length also helps you to pace your writing. Short sentences create a sense of action, movement, and suspense. Longer sentences offer a more relaxed, reflective mood, where the reader can explore the different aspects of an issue without rushing.

**4. Focusing on sentences, line by line**: The one-sentence-per-line rule does something even more powerful. It forces you to pay attention to each sentence. It gives every sentence *integrity*.

When my students turned in their first papers using the Landscape View, a student named Jessica smiled and said: "It looks like *poetry*." And it does. In poetry, of course, every line matters. The line-by-line system forces us to pay attention to each sentence as if it's a line of poetry. If you can write a great sentence, you can write anything. This process helps you to do just that.

Academic researchers actually discovered the power of the line-by-line approach more than a century ago. In a 1901 study of the rhythm and format of language, research subjects read poetry and prose. When they read passages with the line-by-line format, they thought they were reading poetry. When they saw those passages packed into standard paragraphs, they thought they were reading prose. The students lingered—and paid more attention—to the line-by-line format.

**5. Checking paragraphs**: Can the Landscape View help us write better paragraphs, too? And better whole pieces? Yes and yes.

Since we can easily spot the first and last phrases of the paragraphs, we can check whether the "journey" begins in one clear place and ends in another, different place. And we can assess whether all the middle lines offer the brackets and bridges we need—sources and attribution, steps and context—to get from the beginning to the end.

The Landscape View offers a simple, effective mechanism to test the basic elements of writing. Once you write a draft, you can easily check whether you start and end strongly—not just sentence by sentence, but also paragraph by paragraph.

### Case Study
### Applying the Landscape View

Take a look at the image at the end of this section. See how easy it is to check whether you start strong? And whether you finish strong? And whether the material in the middle offers a bridge or bracket from beginning to end? And see how quickly you can tell whether you vary sentence length? And whether your sentences run longer than 20 words?

Finally—most important—do you see how easy it will be to fix what ails your sentences and paragraphs? When you find a clunker at the beginning of a line, you know right away. If you know what you want to say, you will know how to fix it right away. That's the power of the Landscape View. Use it and you will never write a bad sentence again.

The Landscape View offers the perfect tool for checking your writing, line by line and paragraph by paragraph—instantly. But for most readers, you want to format your test in standard paragraph blocks.

When you have finished your draft, you can easily switch the format back to the standard paragraph format. Just go to the beginning of the lines and hit the BACKSPACE bar. That backs one line into the previous line.

Here's how you do it all at once:

- Type two spaces at the end of each line (sentence) and in every space between paragraphs.
- Go to Edit in your toolbar, then scroll down to Find and then Replace.
- In the top bar (Find), type two spaces and then the paragraph mark (^p).
- In the lower bar (Replace), type two spaces.
- Then hit the Replace All button. Voila! You have reformatted your piece.
- Finally, change it to the Portrait view.

If you want to shift from the block format to the Landscape View:

- Make sure to type two spaces at the end of every sentence.
- Go to Edit, Find, and Replace (as above).
- In the top bar (Find), type two spaces.
- In the lower bar (Replace), type two spaces and the paragraph mark (^p).
- Then hit the Replace All button. Voila! You have reformatted your piece.
- Finally, change it to the Landscape view.

Easy peasy. Seems complicated, but it isn't. Just make sure to put two spaces after every sentence. Then you can do all the reformatting when you've finished editing your draft.

~

### And Another Thing ...

DON'T SKIP THIS SECTION. It could make the difference between success and failure.

The Golden Rule can transform your writing. I know because I have seen the Golden Rule has helped countless students and participants in my writing seminars. But there's a hitch. And to avoid a bloody mess, I want to to consider a simple caution.

Here's my simple warming: Don't think about the Golden Rule while writing your first draft. Just write. Spill words on paper. The, after you have something to play with, use the Golden Rule to check, edit, and refine for writing.

When we try too hard to do something—when you think too much about the process—we often become self-conscious. So if we work to make every line a journey, starting and ending strongly, it's easy to lose the flow of ideas. By concentrating on *technique*, you don't concentrate enough on what you are trying to say. That's a problem.

It's kind of like the golf fan who asks the pro: Do you breathe in or out when you start your backswing? Thinking too much about form upsets focus on what's important—in this case, swinging the golf club and whacking the ball. In all creative endeavors, once you've mastered a skill, it's important for gorget about technique and just let 'er rip.

Whether you're trying to hit a ball or craft a sentence, thinking too much cramps your creative process. By concentrating on technique, you lose the point of the whole exercise. You lose sight of *what* you're trying to do because you're thinking too much about *how* you're doing it.

The solution is simple: *Don't think too much about the Golden Rule as you write your first draft.* In fact, don't think about it at all. Just gather and express your ideas, as best you can. Line by line, just write one sentence after another. Don't worry about journeys or starting and ending strongly. *Just get your ideas down on paper, line by line.*

Don't use the Golden Rule until you have out something down on paper. Then use the Golden Rule to check whether you start and and finish strongly in every line, paragraph, section, and whole piece.

The Landscape View's greatest benefit, after all, comes with the editing process. It makes it easy to check the beginnings, endings, and middles *after you have written them.* So when you write, just let the lines flow, one after another. Then, once you've drafted a section, check the lines.

Here's where the magic comes in. Over time, by composing one line at a time, you'll internalize the imperatives of the Golden Rule. When you edit a passage using the Golden Rule, you'll develop the skill to craft sentences with clarity and power. Constructing strong sentences and passages according to the Golden Rule—and checking them—will become almost automatic.

How can you internalize the Golden Rule even faster? I advise students to use the Landscape View when writing emails and social media posts. Most people who read these notes won't notice anything funky about the format. In short order, this practice will pay off. One survey found that students write 10 times as much in emails as in formal assignments. When you use the Golden Rule in all your emails and texts, you will burn it into your brain. You will make it second nature.

Researchers call this process "deliberate practice." When you repeat an action, intently, you rewire you brain. Actions that at first require attention become automatic. By intently practice the Golden Rule, with the Landscape View, you will make a habit of crafting strong sentences and paragraphs.

The Landscape View will improve your writing even if you are a seasoned writer. This approach focuses your attention on what matters—on sentences, lengths, variety, beginnings and endings. It also offers a *process* for editing. By using the Landscape View, you will develop the clarity and vibrancy that readers deserve.

# MODELING THE GOLDEN RULE OF WRITING

Start Strong            Bridges or Brackets            Finish Strong

To write well, make everything a journey—every sentence, paragraph, section, or whole piece.
Start in one distant place and finished in another, different place.
Make sure the journey shows important change.
Make sure the steps along the way lead to the end.

How do you ensure a meaningful journey?
Start strong and finish strong.
Right just one sentence per line; when finished, hit the return key.
Then write a new sentence.
Skip a space to separate paragraphs.

So what does "start strong" mean?
Usually, as your default approach, tell the reader, right away, who does what.
Sometimes, to start strong means to provide an important setup.
Tell the reader, in other words, essential information to make sense of everything that follows.

So what does "finish strong" mean?
It means one of two things.
Whenever possible, complete your thought.
Otherwise, leave the reader with a powerful question or image.
Satisfy or intrigue the reader, line by line, as you move the piece forward

The middle of a passage connects the beginning and the end.
As a bridge, the middle shows the reader the steps needed to get from the beginning to the end.
As a bracket, the middle offers asides with important background information or attributions.

The Landscape View helps to focus on what matters—and to fix problems without too much unnecessary work.
Rather than searching dense blocks of type, you can run your finger down the left and right sides of the page to find the beginnings and endings of sentences.
The Landscape View also displays, at a glance, whether you offer a mix of longer and shorter sentences.
Since a typical word document allows 20 to 24 words per line, you can also see when your sentences might be getting too long.
Above all, the Landscape View teaches us to make writing decisions consciously.

# II

---

# PORTRAYING PEOPLE

In your work as an architect, planner, preservationist, or environmentalist, your No. 1 purpose is to *serve people*.

You might have a private client, like someone looking to build or refurbish a new house or office building. You might work with a "friends of the park" group or the board of a business improvement district. Or you might partner with a grassroots organization that promotes affordable housing, environmental cleanup, or fair tax policies. Or maybe you collaborate with someone in a public agency, like a planning or redevelopment agency or a transportation or parks department.

To succeed, you need to know about those people—their interests, their hopes and dreams, their intellectual and emotional makeup.

Or maybe you see your work in broader terms. You want to serve all the people of a community, not just the ones who hire you. So you need to understand the challenges of living, working, or recreating in that place. To do so, you imagine the needs of a small business person, a mother who takes her children to a park, Millennials who love the nightlife, or sportsmen who hike and canoe in the great outdoors.

Whatever the challenge, you need to understand your work in *personal terms*. How can we best serve the *people* who create and use spaces?

And so we begin our writing process with the profile of a person.

The goal is to get to understand what makes your clients or populations "click." Who are they? Where they come from? What they want? How can we understand their history and psychology? What are their contradictions? What are their desires?

Years ago, I was a city planner in Boston. My job was to go into all of the city's neighborhoods and find out what their people needed and wanted. I went to them all—from Back Bay and Beacon Hill near the downtown, out to Dorchester and Roxbury, and farther out to Roslindale and West Roxbury. In total, my team and I held about 120 meetings in the city's sixteen neighborhoods.

We held meetings at least once every other week in each of these communities. Between the meetings, we met with smaller groups of residents, business people, and advocates. We also ventured out to explore parks, business districts, residential areas, historic sites, transit nodes, and more.

Only when we understood our clients—the *people* of the neighborhoods—we could begin to develop a planning vision for improving their community.

That's what we're doing in this unit of our writing program. We will learn how to create profiles of people: their hopes and dreams, their barriers and struggles. That way, we can understand what we can do for them as a placemaker.

Here's the plan. We start by exploring what kinds of questions to ask about people and their stories:

- Chapter 2: Character
- Chapter 3: Narrative

Then we move to the mechanics of writing:

- Chapter 4: Sentences
- Chapter 5: Words

By starting with characters, we connect with the ultimate purpose of our work.

Ready? Let's go.

2

# CHARACTERS

It begins with a character, usually, and once he stands up on his feet and begins
to move, all I can do is trot along behind him with a paper and pencil trying to
keep up long enough to put down what he says and does.

— WILLIAM FAULKNER

Each morning my characters greet me with misty faces willing, though chilled, to
muster for another day's progress through the dazzling quicksand the marsh of
blank paper.

— JOHN UPDIKE

I n the summer of 1968, after graduating from Macalester College, Tim
O'Brien came home to find a draft notice in his mailbox. As a student
leader, O'Brien had demonstrated against the Vietnam War and worked
for Eugene McCarthy's presidential campaign. He agonized over whether to
report for military service or flee to Canada.

All summer O'Brien worked in a pig factory in Minnesota. He blasted
grapefruit-sized clots of blood from the carcasses that passed on a moving line
overhead.

As the date of his military induction approached, O'Brien got in a car and
drove north, stopping just south of the Canadian border. An old man put him
up in a cottage for six days. One day the two went out on a boat to fish. As
they sat with their lines in the water, O'Brien realized he could leap out and
swim to Canada. But at that moment, he decided to report for military duty.

He started crying—not because of a fear of war, but because he realized that he was too cowardly *not to fight* a war he considered immoral.

As he tells the story in *The Things They Carried*, O'Brien journeys from a state of uncertainty to a state of cowardice and commitment. As O'Brien ponders his lack of nerve at the lake, he remembers his boyhood ideals: "Tim O'Brien: a secret hero. The Lone Ranger."

Tim O'Brien told the story differently to a group of students at Brown University. "All I could tell you," O'Brien said, "was that I played golf and I worried about getting drafted."

The Tim O'Brien who wrote the book not the same Tim O'Brien who was a character in the book. So which one was more real? On one level, he told the "true" story to the students at Brown. But to relate the larger truths of his Vietnam experience—to tell a "truer" story—O'Brien fictionalized his story. He took embellished his story to reveal larger truths about youth and innocence and war.

You will do the same with every character you create, fictional or real. All characters are creations. Whether we take "real life" figures like Napoleon, Gandhi, or Tim O'Brien—or fictional characters like Huck Finn, Holden Caulfield, or Tim O'Brien—characters are creations of the author. The author selectively gathers piles of information about his character, discards most of it, and creates a person to highlight some truth about life.

Could O'Brien have told a more factually accurate tale? Of course. Maybe the real Tim O'Brien was not as colorful as his novel's hero. But when you dig deep, the real O'Brien offers plenty of material for drama. If not, O'Brien could find a story about one of his fellow G.I.s or college friends. Or he might create a portrait of O'Brien's hometown or Army battalion. Any person's life, as the essayist Alain de Botton says, offers a suitable subject just as soon as "they start to rattle the bars of their cages."

Extraordinary events happen in many ordinary lives. Read Studs Terkel's books and you see that even the most ordinary people lead rich, complex lives: ministers and teachers, housewives and factory workers, lawyers and accountants, cooks and janitors, scientists and artists. Or read the rash of memoirs published in recent years. On every conceivable topic—homelessness (Jeannette Walls's *The Glass Castle*), abuse (Margaux Fragoso's *Tiger, Tiger*), rags to riches (Christopher Gardner's *The Pursuit of Happyness*), mental illness (Elizabeth Wurtzel's *Prozac Nation*), dementia (Carol O'Dell's *Mothering Mother*), family life (Frank Gilbreth's *Cheaper by the Dozen*), teaching (Bel Kaufman's *Up the Down Staircase*), faith (Anne Lamott's *Traveling Mercies*)—ordinary people tell their stories to express timeless themes.

Whether your characters are ordinary or larger-than-life, show their complexity and drive. "Character is that which reveals moral purpose," Aristotle writes in *The Poetics*, "showing what kind of things a man chooses or avoids."

Push you characters hard to discover what they choose and avoid. Put your characters in challenging situations; make life hard on them. As soon as they begin to resolve their problems, throw new challenges their way. Kick your characters; as soon as they get up, kick 'em again. Test their capacity to learn and grow.

How do you know when you have a character worth developing? "I have to be able to *defend* this character," says Aaron Sorkin, the screenwriter for *The West Wing* and *The Social Network*. "You want to write the character as if they are making their case to God why they should be allowed in heaven."

~

### Element 4
### Compile Dossiers for Your Characters

To SEND your hero and other characters on their journeys, you need to know who they are and what they're trying to do.

So learn everything possible about your characters' lives. Know the most intimate details of their physical, mental, and spiritual lives. Don't just discover the surface facts of your characters' lives; explore the backstories. Don't just find your characters' names; discover how they got their names and what they mean. Don't just talk about their jobs; find out what work means to them emotionally.

Be complete. Don't dismiss any ideas as unimportant. Each detail, some-how, matters. Just as a P.I. gets his best stuff while tracking down unlikely leads, you will discover telling details when you fill in the information for each of these four categories:

**Personal Background**
Name
Age and birthday
Birthplace
Parents' ethnic and religious background
Parents' upbringing, hopes and fears, and careers
Place in the family's birth order
Relations with siblings and other relatives

**Physical Characteristics**
What others notice first
Body and build
Hair and eye color
Sound of voice
Conversational oddities
Physical peculiarities
Mannerisms while walking, talking, working, and playing

**Growing With Others**
Activities and hobbies as a child ... and as an adult
Sidekicks and mentors
Intellectual and emotional influences
Rivals and foes at different stages of life
Not-so-good influences—skeptics, and tempters
Political leanings—and major political influences
How the character changes over the course of life
Turning points in life

**Psychology**
All-consuming desires
Pathological maneuver
Most admirable qualities
Least admirable qualities
Sexual identity
Philosophy of life
Optimism or pessimism
Energy level
What the character does when alone
What the character thinks about when alone
Greatest fears at different stages of life

Gathering so much information might seem like overkill. But you need to know *everything* about your characters before you can decide what's important.

When you gather these details, you can move from *characterization* to *character*. Characterization offers the simple surface facts of a person's life; character goes deeper to the heart and soul of their life. We find people's character in the choices they make in their most difficult moments.

By defining the character, the dossier helps to tell the story. In fact, it's almost impossible to create a dossier without also beginning to tell the story.

### Case Study
### Tracy Kidder's *House*

What happens when a couple decides to build their dream house? How does the mission get accomplished?

Tracy Kidder's *House* tells such a story. His tale involves three sets of characters. The star of the story is an architect named Bill Rawn, a strapping Renaissance man who lives in the Boston area. The clients are a couple in western Massachusetts, Judith and Jonathan Souweine. The builders are a team led Jim Locke, an old-school craftsman who struggles to make a living.

Kidder shows, in telling detail, all of the elements of the project. We see the excitement and creativity, compromises and adjustments, grinding work and uncertainties and setbacks, and, finally, the depth and soul of a good place made well.

To tell this story, Kidder first does what every architect and every client must do. He takes stock of all of the major characters. He explores their backgrounds, physical characteristics, upbringing and relationships with others, and their psychology.

The Souweines are a classic yuppie couple—educated, sophisticated, and tasteful, but also entitled and hard-driving. Consider some of Kidder's observations about Jonathan:

> Jonathan is polite and very direct. In conversation he tends to curtness, but let him get on a subject that truly engages him, such as a coming election, and he becomes positively garrulous, talking so swiftly that his words slur. ... Jonathan started college on a basketball scholarship. ... He gave up his scholarship, went to Columbia, participated in protests against the Vietnam War and campaigned for a liberal, antiwar candidate for Congress, and went on to Harvard Law School. ... "If I'm confronted, I'll instantly fight." ... Jonathan has always shared the household chores. ... Of the friendships they share, Judith says, "In most cases I'm closer to a friend than Jonathan because Jonathan doesn't talk to people." ... Jonathan, she says, has little aesthetic sense, and he agrees. He is their organizational genius, though. ... They have a fine, sturdy marriage, which is more than a marriage. It is an enterprise. They are a formidable enterprise. ... Jonathan and Judith had imagined in some detail a house that would suit them functionally. Jonathan had already begun making lists. ...

Kidder describes the affluence of both families, their need for lots of room for their family, their stubborn bargaining style, and their summer vacations with the man who would become their architect. Before we reach page 50, we get detailed dossiers on the clients, architects, and builders.

Like architects and planners, storytellers need to understand the characters' background, values, and goals. People's ideals and interests often lead to conflict. What seems reasonable to one person might seem unreasonable to another. To build places that serve people's lives—and to interact with them effectively—we need to know the characters in these stories.

~

### Element 5
### Explore Characters' Lives, Zone by Zone

WHEN YOU FIRST MEET SOMEONE, you begin conversations with superficial questions and answers. *Where do you go to school? What do you do? Where do you live? Where did you grow up? Are you married? Do you have any kids?*

Before we can ask deeper, more personal questions, we need to build a foundation. We need to understand the superficial facts of a person's life before we can probe deeply. We need to earn trust before we can explore someone's most intimate stories and feelings.

Imagine what would happen if you asked intimate questions in your first meeting. *Nice to meet you. Does your family have a history of alcoholism? Abuse? Have you ever been arrested? Do you fantasize about a neighbor or coworker? Have you ever cheated on your taxes?*

Even psychiatrists, priests and rabbis, and other confidantes must start with simple, unthreatening questions. Counselors might learn intimate information right away—"Father, my husband is cheating on me"—but they have to work hard to find the deepest truths. The opening revelation is really just the beginning of a more revealing dialogue.

So start exploring your characters at their outside edges. Get to know the basic information first, then move inward.

Characters live in four zones. Let's look at them, one by one.

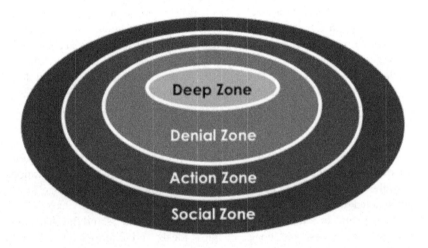

**The Social Zone:** Here, people play roles assigned by society. People and institutions around us—in our families, schools, workplaces, and community —set powerful expectations and incentives. We make decisions, sure; but the world around us determines the range of our possibilities.

"I did not direct my life," said B.F. Skinner, the father of behaviorist theory. "I didn't design it. I never made decisions. Things always came up and made them for me. That's what life is."

To understand how people behave, Skinner focused on what he called "conditioning"—how repeated actions shape people's habits and decisions. Skinner started by studying rats. When a rat performed an action and got a reward (usually food), that rat was more likely to perform the same action again. In time, the rat got conditioned to respond to prompts in specific ways.

Likewise, society establishes a complex set of rewards and punishments for people in every situation. These rewards and punishments define our roles as parents and children, boss and worker, priest and parishioner, coach and player, clerk and customer, and more.

In Skinner's world, roles and rewards rule. People act like lab rats, responding the demands and incentives in order to maximize pleasure and minimize pain.

**The Action Zone:** All of us all have the capacity to act with purpose. When we see the world around us, assess threats and opportunities, and decide on possible courses of action, we can take *action*.

To act, we need to make decisions consciously, rather than just go with the flow. We need to figure out what matters, assess possible courses of action, decide to act, and then *act*.

Too often, we allow our circumstances to constrain our action. We get in a rut. Rather than actively deciding, we take the course of least resistance. But, contrary to what Skinner says, we are always *capable* of making up our own minds and acting. Even in the direst conditions, action is possible. Even under terrible physical constraints, we still have the capacity to decide how we want to respond to those constraints. And then we can act, however limited our choices.

Consider the case of Victor Frankl. A prisoner in Nazi camps in World War II, Frankl did not know whether he would survive. But he noticed that the prison's survivors focused on what they loved, not on the brutality of the conditions. And so Frankl decided, consciously, to focus on the possibilities of the future. He thought about reuniting with his wife, even though he didn't even know if she was still alive.

Action requires responsibility. "Ultimately, man should not ask what the meaning of his life is, but rather must recognize that it is he who is asked," Frankl writes in his classic *Man's Search for Meaning*. "In a word, each man is questioned by life; and he can only answer to life by answering for his own life; to life he can only respond by being responsible."

To act, you must be willing to accept responsibility for your own life. By taking responsibility, you make yourself a complete human.

If Skinner depicts a world that seems determined by outside forces, Frankl depicts a world open to conscious action.

**The Denial Zone:** When confronted with an uncomfortable truth, our first response is denial. All our lives, we carry heavy baggage—insecurities, hurts, and feelings of inadequacy. This baggage can be so harmful that we sometimes even deny our powers to act. People suffer, Albert Ellis said, because they refuse to face the truths of their lives. "You largely constructed your depression," Ellis said. "It wasn't given to you. Therefore, you can deconstruct it."

Facing deep-seated problems is hard. We have lived with most of our problems our whole lives. We have, in fact, constructed a whole way of life around those problems. It's hard to give up a lifetime of attitudes and beliefs, stories and rationalizations, even when they hold us back. Honesty and change require courage. Most of us would rather dwell in denial than take on the hard work of overcoming our dysfunctional ways.

What about your characters? Who in your story denies the truth about their families or own behavior? Who struggles to acknowledge addiction, abuse, moments of meanness or cowardice—or other truths? Who lives with shame or fear? And what do they do to avoid facing these truths?

**The Deep Zone:** Most of our drives and desires are buried deep in our subconscious—so deep, in fact, that we don't know they exist. But by confronting the issues in the outer zones, we can dig into this deep zone.

Sigmund Freud, the father of modern psychoanalysis, believes our deepest struggles occur outside our consciousness. At the center of this struggle is the battle between Eros and Thantos, the individual's love and death instincts. Unconscious struggles bubble underneath the surface, beyond our attention, until a crisis forces us to address it. Therapy, Freud believes, can bring these unconscious drives and desires to the surface. But that requires hard work.

Carl Jung believes that Freud oversimplified man's mind and soul. Every person's psyche, Jung teaches, is connected to mankind's "collective unconscious." Deep down, the human race shares a common heritage of stories and feelings. "This collective unconscious does not develop individually but is inherited," Jung says. "It consists of pre-existent forms, the archetypes, which can only become conscious secondarily and which give definite form to certain psychic contents."

To understand any character, then, we need to understand ideas and emotions that extend back for ages. The Deep Zone includes not only the primal urges of Eros and Thantos, but also the deep, eons-old desires for family and friendship, beauty and creativity, mythos and meaning.

As your characters wrestle with their psyches, how deep will they go? Will they play out the roles that society makes for him? Will they attempt to act consciously? Will they wrestle with their own denial and confront their own warring instincts? Or will they, possibly, go deeper still?

### Case Study
### Planning in Progresso

In early 1996, the architect Christopher Alexander visited a group of small landowners, residents, business people, artists, architects, and others in a neighborhood of Fort Lauderdale called Progresso.

Located just north of the city's booming downtown, Progresso was a motley collection of bungalows, low-rent apartments, and vacant lots. For years the people of Progresso attempted to rescue their neighborhood from crime and blight. Mostly they failed. Many paid princely sums for their property, expecting that downtown's growth would move northward; alas, growth moved in every direction except north.

On the northern end of Progresso was a decrepit old train station, where the industrialist, developer, and railroad tycoon Henry Flagler had set up shop in the city's infancy. To the south of Progresso was a massive tent holding hundreds of homeless people. On the east and west were major thoroughfares that isolated the community from nearby communities.

Alexander came to Progresso at the invitation of Anthony Abbate, a prominent architect who grew up in Fort Lauderdale. Abbate sensed that Progresso was stuck because its people did not understand, deep down, either the neighborhood's potential or the hard decisions they would need to take to realize that potential. Progresso needed a jolt, a fresh vision.

When Alexander arrived in town, he led a walking tour of the area. Afterwards, at community meetings, the community discussed the possibilities for transforming Progresso.

The people of Progresso, Alexander advised, needed to search deep inside themselves to understand their potential. It's not enough, he said, to think about nuts-and-bolts projects, big-bang developments like a university campus, or zoning codes and tax benefits. Somehow, Alexander said, they needed to dream big and envision how Progresso might overcome its stagnation.

Before Alexander's arrival, Progresso had moved through the first three zones of understanding—the social, the action, and the denial zones. With Alexander's help, Progresso would move into the deep zone.

**The social zone**: The people of Progresso were a mixed lot. Absentee landowners included the owner of low-income units and speculators, including the heir of an early TV inventor and manufacturer, a lawyer, and a developer. Residents included oldtimers who had lived, modestly, in classic old-style Florida saltboxes, students, and Haitian immigrants. Some lived cheaply but had substandard units, while others paid too dearly. Many knew each other from community meetings, but only superficially. They lived in the social one, where outward appearances masked deeper realities.

**The action zone**: Progresso experienced many failed efforts to transform Progresso. One developer bought major pieces of property and then promoted a plan to get Florida Atlantic University to locate a campus there. But he failed to rally community and political support; in fact, he aroused widespread suspicion. Other property owners worked to revive the area. An antique dealer bought a building at the old train station, next to a wine store that did a thriving mail-order business. A sculptor and a painter bought studios, hoping to create a new arts district. A young architect bought a multi-unit building and rehabbed it himself.

These efforts lacked cohesion and usually failed. A lot on the northern end of the community, which experienced constant turnover, was symbolic of the start-and-stop efforts to revive the area. One of its many failed businesses was a coin-operated Laundromat called Helpy-Selfy, which featured a topless bar near the washing machines—not an ideal image for a new urban village.

The area's greatest potential lay in a special designation as a "community redevelopment area," eligible to receive tax and infrastructure benefits. But without a plan, the city government would not offer infrastructure and other resources to the area.

**The denial zone**: Over time, Progresso's people got stuck in an endless loop, telling the same stories about missed opportunities. Meetings often turned into gripe sessions. Residents complained that city government invested in other, well-heeled neighborhoods more than Progresso. They complained about decrepit lots, substandard housing that undermined local property values, and the city's decision to house homeless people in the tent.

Many residents developed cynical attitudes. The owner of low-income housing units gave new tenants pepper spray to welcome them to the neighborhood. Many residents distrusted the Haitians, who were packed into tiny homes on 25-foot lots. Kids riding bikes were considered threats. When newcomers came to town, like an antique furniture seller, people gossiped and predicted the worst.

Longtime middle-class residents distrusted new property owners who, they feared, would gentrify the area and drive them out. But no such gentrification took place. Large landowners were unwilling to do anything with their property unless they could realize big returns on their investments; they more they paid for their properties, the less willing they were to embrace modest projects.

The stories and suspicions were a form of denial. "If only" was a common refrain. People got stuck telling their version of the story of Progresso's failure. These stories prevented Progresso from developing a path forward. They could not see what they had in common—and how they would have to change their approach in order to achieve a greater community vision.

**The deep zone**: With the arrival of Chris Alexander, the people of Progresso began a deeper conversation about their values and the neighborhood's potential. Alexander's tour began the process. Tony Abbate recalls: "We experienced the neighborhood directly: every gap in the sidewalk, the smells of trash and trees, chatting on sofas on a front stoop, and children walking barefoot through standing water at a school bus stop." At the community meeting, Alexander called Progresso "a hell of a problem" but also "a tremendous opportunity." At one point Alexander asked people to close their eyes and imagine the community they wanted to live in. The test, Alexander said, was whether "each bit of the neighborhood actually reflects the human soul and the individuals who inhabit the place."

Alexander asked them to consider the area's open spaces and lush trees as the basis of a necklace of parks. He asked them to see the potential for the area's small street grid to give rise to a vibrant, pedestrian-oriented urban village. He asked them to see the patchwork of small lots not as an impediment—which made it difficult to consolidate space for big project—but as an advantage. Rather than surrendering to master plan, they would be better off fixing the neighborhood, one lot and one street at a time.

Through their work with Christopher Alexander, the community developed a deeper understanding of their potential—and the reasons behind past failures. Later planning efforts (including one that I led in the summer of 1996) built on Alexander's ability to "go deep" in Progresso. By the early 2000s, after another study by Tony Abbate and his students at FAU, Progresso had gained some planning tools and resources to promote mixed-use development. A new park opened. Infrastructure got built. The pace of development picked up.

Progresso's journey was halting and required compromises. No one claims to have achieved the deep, soulful place that Alexander envisioned. But by following Alexander's admonition to "go deep," the area overcame years of blight and frustration. The area, Abbate says, is now "a vibrant community that continues to grow piece by piece, property by property, fulfilling a pattern language developed by the residents and property owners."

∾

### Element 6
### Find Your Characters' Throughlines

TO TAKE A GREAT JOURNEY—AND to become a deeper person—your characters need a powerful desire. They must strive to achieve a vision, even if it takes a while to understand that vision. Once they find their vision, they need to be obsessive about it. As Martin Luther told Charles V: "Here I stand; I can do no other."

Stage actors and directors use the term "throughline" to describe a character's deepest ambitions and drives. A character expresses this desire simply:

*I want to ...*

The throughline shapes the character's every decision. Consider Shakespeare's Hamlet. What is his great desire? Is it to ascend to power? Achieve truth? Avenge his father's death? Salvage his mother's integrity? Restore the kingdom? You can make a case for each of these motivations. How you portray a character's actions depends on which throughline you embrace for the character.

The philosopher Nietzsche puts the challenge this way: "Become who you are." All of us have a destiny. Our purpose in life is to realize that destiny. What do you want to be? A great teacher? Entrepreneur? Seller? Parent? Coach? Writer? Friend? Leader? Follower? Whatever it is, be prepared to make whatever sacrifice is necessary to achieve it.

To make the character unique, express that his or her desire in *specific ways*. No one strives or makes sacrifices for general and vague ideals. The ideal of "freedom," for example, may excite some patriots; but they need to personalize their emotions before they are willing to embrace sacrifices and hardships. American rebels hated King George, Confederates hated Yankees, and Allied soldiers in World War II hated Nazis. So give your character something *concrete* to love or hate.

Make the character's desire so intense that he will make great sacrifices to realize it. Give your character not just a powerful *goal*, but also a compelling *approach* to realizing that goal.

A philosopher named Harry Frankfort distinguishes first- and second-order desires. First-order desires represent your primary goals in life; second-order desires include everything you must do to achieve those primary goals. You might call second-order desires willpower—the desire to *do something* about desires rather than just talk or wish for them.

If you won't make the sacrifices necessary to realize your dream, you don't really *want it*. Lots of kids want to be professional athletes, actors, musicians, and astronauts. At least, that's what they say. But to become an athlete, to take one example, you also need to *want* to work out, eat the right foods, get sleep, avoid drugs and alcohol abuse, and train your mind. You have to *want* to grind out practices on tough days, work on fundamentals when your friends are having a pool party, and make long road trips to games.

By looking hard at your character's messy life, you can figure out the answer to the ultimate question: What does the character care about so much that he will sacrifice *anything* to achieve it?

### Case Study
### Throughlines of Prominent Architects

Architects have a rare privilege. They get to translate their life's passions into places that can last for generations. If architects understand the driving forces of their lives—and the lives of their clients and communities—they can create spaces that embody those values.

Consider the throughlines of a handful of prominent architects and builders:

**Le Corbusier**: *I want to make large-scale development, functionality, and simplicity the driving force for all society.* Corbu wanted to rip out the tangles and complexities of historic urban communities. His dream was to build vast developments consisting of tall buildings, parks, and highways. In his 1924 work *Towards a New Architecture*: Corbu writes: "We must create a mass-production state of mind: A state of mind for building mass-production housing. A state of mind for living in mass-production housing. A state of mind for conceiving mass-production housing."

**Frank Lloyd Wright**: *I want to use architecture to blend buildings into nature.* Using modern elements like concrete and glass, Wright sought to embed buildings into the environment. Arguing that "form and function are one," Wright created simple, clean, open designs that enabled people to detach from the messiness of modern, urban life. At the same time, Wright wanted to nest these modern structures into nature. "No house should ever be *on* a hill or on anything," he wrote. "It should be *of* the hill. *Belonging* to it. Hill and house should live together, each the happier for the other."

**William Levitt**: *I want to use the methods of mass production—uniform designs, assembly line, interchangeable parts, specialization—to create cheap single-family homes.* Levitt and his brother Alfred mass-produced homes for the Navy during the war by breaking the production process into 27 distinct steps. Levitt applied these methods to the construction of suburban homes after the war. "We channel labor and materials to a stationary outdoor assembly line," he said, "instead of bringing them together inside a factory." Levitt homes were simple and, at first, monotonous. Critics, like the singer Malvina Reynolds, derided these Levittown homes as "little boxes made of ticky-tacky." But Levitt didn't care. Neither did the Levittowners, who have evolved and thrived over the years.

**Christopher Alexander**: *I want to create buildings and public spaces that foster a sense of "wholeness."* By focusing on the desires of ordinary people living in the community—not outside interests and imperatives—Alexander builds homes, civic buildings, work spaces, and streets and open spaces that fit into the simple "patterns" of people's everyday lives. Great places, Alexander teaches, are organic and evolve to serve people's deepest values and aspirations. Every project, Alexander argues, should not just create a new structure; it should also "repair" whatever ails the larger setting.

**I.M. Pei**: *I want to blend the aesthetics and sensibilities of ancient traditions (like Chinese gardens) with the basic functional needs of the project.* In his public and private projects—from the John F. Kennedy Library and Museum of Fine Arts in Boston to the Louvre in Paris—Pei gives modernism a touch of tradition. "I believe that architecture is a pragmatic art," Pei once said. "To become art it must be built on a foundation of necessity." To meet the needs of the client, Pei embraced technology, within the context of the project. He combined minimalism with the tasteful style of Beaux Arts classicism.

**Frank Gehry**: *I want to make buildings vast works of flamboyant art that blend into existing communities.* Gehry's signature projects, like the Guggenheim Museum in Bilbao, excite people's imaginations. His projects' exuberance taps people's deepest human desires and traditions. "Bilbao is a sanctuary of free association," *New York Times* critic Herbert Muschamp writes. "It's a bird, it's a plane, it's Superman. It's a ship, an artichoke, the miracle of the rose. A first glimpse tells you the second glimpse is going to be different ... [and] the third is going to be different still."

These throughlines drive every aspect of these architects' work. When they took on a project, they knew what values and approaches they would use.

With this clear throughline, they could meet their clients' needs and desires into the mix.

~

### Element 7
### Use the Wheel of Archetypes

STORYTELLERS HAVE USED archetypes for millennia to portray characters. An archetype is an embodiment of a basic human drive. Humans are, of course, complicated. They are heroic and mean-spirited, loyal and unreliable, wise and foolish, brainy and emotional. Archetypes take these basic qualities and express them through characters.

Archetypes provide simple ways make sense of a complicated world. We cannot help but use these kinds of stereotypes to make quick judgments. We not only decide who to approach and who to avoid, but also how. Remember the early scene of *Mean Girls*, when a student explains the different cliques at school:

> You got your freshmen, ROTC guys, preps, JV jocks, Asian nerds, cool Asians, varsity jocks, unfriendly black hotties, girls who eat their feelings, girls who don't eat anything, desperate wannabes, burnouts, sexually active band geeks ...

To be sure, archetypes simplify the world too much. The groups on the *Mean Girls* map are more complex than their labels. But they offer a useful shorthand to understand motivation and behavior.

To understand characters, see how they interact with different types. ROTC guys, for example, might not choose to interact with burnouts. But when they must, the interaction shows them in ways we might not imagine when they do their early-morning drills. The same goes for the ROTC guys' interaction with the Asian nerds, the girls who don't eat, and the band geeks.

Let's chart eight distinct character types. They come in four pairs of opposing values—hero and villain, mentor and tempter, sidekick and skeptic, mind and heart.

**Hero**: The hero's journey provides the story's focus. Often forced into action by a crisis, the hero seeks something big. He might want fame or fortune, admiration or wisdom, family or friends. Whatever the hero wants, the audience wants for him.

Usually likable, the hero pursues ideals we all can admire. No one, of course, can be perfect. We need to see the hero struggle to face his own flaws. What makes the hero admirable is his (eventual) willingness to step out of his "comfort zone"—his normal way of life, which requires little effort or thought —and strive to become a better person.

Virtually every great story has a great hero. Heroes' characters vary as much as the human race—innocent (Huck Finn) or clever (Sherlock Holmes), trapped (Rabbit Angstrom) or adventurous (Odysseus), wise (Jesus) or courageous (Ivan Denisovich), lecherous (Humbert Humbert) or upright (Atticus Finch), lazy (Oblomov) or industrious (Horatio Alger), well rounded (Jane Eyre) or shallow (Babbitt).

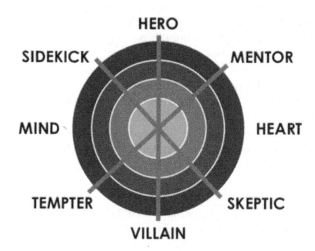

**Villain**: The hero's victory does not come easily. At every turn, the villain and other characters attempt to block his way.

The villain rejects the hero's virtues, which often represent the villain's own repressed or damaged qualities. The villain resents the hero's success and righteousness. So he blocks the hero physically and psychologically. He conspires with others to undermine the hero. He lies and deceives. In the process, he tests the hero's mettle and morality.

Villains do not consider themselves bad, at least not completely; you, as their author, must find a way treat the villain sympathetically. Blake Snyder, a screenwriter and script doctor, suggests giving every villain a "save the cat" moment—that is, a moment when he does something for humane reasons. Rather than denouncing villains, the best stories explore their complexity.

Search for what's admirable; find their struggles, vulnerabilities, wounds, even their hopes and dreams. Search for the moments that forged their character, the choices that put them on the dark side.

Like heroes, villains vary in their makeup and morality. Consider the different drives of great literary villains—political ambition (Lady Macbeth), narrow-minded authority (Javert), jealousy (Mrs. Danvers), revenge (Iago), psychological illness (Norman Bates), sadism (Nurse Ratchett), and pure evil (Satan).

No hero can test and develop his capacities—physical, intellectual, or moral —without a worthy opponent. Make your villain as complex and intriguing, even worthy of some love and understanding, as possible.

**Sidekick**: Most heroes need a sidekick or alter ego, a loyal companion who joins in their adventures. The sidekick supports the hero but also provides a contrast. Loyalty is the sidekick's reason for being.

Think of the sidekick as an extension of the hero. The sidekick cares more about his friend's interests—making him happy—than his own. When a crisis emerges, the sidekick supports him. When someone questions the hero—even when the hero makes mistakes and needs to be challenged—the sidekick defends him.

Literature and film are filled with memorable sidekicks. In The Bible, Moses found his ability to speak through Aaron. In mythology, Enkidu supports Gilgamesh and Patroclus supports Achilles. In Miguel de Cervantes's *Don Quixote*, Sancho acts as the practical counterpoint to Quixote's romanticism. In Daniel Defoe's *Robinson Crusoe*, Friday supports the leader of the isle of cannibals. In Arthur Conan Doyle's Sherlock Holmes stories, Watson helps the brilliant detective.

The sidekick offers an insider's view of the hero. He lives close enough to get an intimate view. But his view is limited. Not a hero himself, he does not understand many events until they're over—just like the readers of the story.

**Skeptic**: Standing outside the hero-sidekick alliance, the skeptic often gets jealous and even angry. Sometimes actively and sometimes passively, he questions the hero and his pal, whatever they say or do. Whatever the hero proposes and the sidekick disposes, the skeptic opposes.

Skeptics doubt what they cannot see. In The Bible, the disciple Thomas resists believing that Jesus had been resurrected. "I have to put my finger where the nails were," Thomas says. "If I can put my hand in his side, then I'll believe you." When Jesus shows his wounds, Thomas believes him. Jesus is disappointed in the doubting Thomas. "There will be many who do not see me and are still willing to believe," Jesus says. "These people are special to me."

Skeptics often dampen the spirits of other characters. When a hero begins a perilous journey, skeptics can be heard muttering that "it just won't work." Skeptics question and quarrel, ridicule and rant, sneer and scold.

But by asking tough questions, skeptics often play a constructive role. They help others to think through their actions: *Is this really the right job for you? Is he the right man for you? Do you think you should take this trip? Should you risk speaking out?*

Detectives offer compelling skeptics. They know that no one tells the whole truth. Raymond Chandler's character Philip Marlowe and Dashiell Hammett's character Sam Spade see past the facade of deluded clients, corrupt cops, corner-cutting prosecutors, jealous spouses, manipulating lawyers, and more. "I don't know which side anybody's on," Marlowe cracks in *Murder, My Sweet*. "I don't even know who's playing today."

**Mentor**: The hero needs wisdom for his journey. The mentor offers the knowledge and judgment that comes from a lifetime of experience.

Usually an older figure, the mentor has succeeded in his life but has also fallen short. He has overcome his youthful flaws—impulsiveness, temper, irresponsibility, and grandiosity—and now offers his hard-won knowledge to his protege. He supports and protects the hero, helping him to gain the wisdom he needs to succeed.

The mentor wants, above all else, for the hero to realize his full potential. And so he freely offers him time, listens to his dreams with empathy, and sets high expectations. The protege knows the mentor will offer his support for the whole journey.

The mentor challenges the protege to take on big challenges. He prods the protege to do the right thing, avoid shortcuts, and act by the highest standards. By doing things the right way, the mentor teaches, you give yourself the best chance to succeed—and, even more important, strengthen your moral core.

The mentor's name comes from Homer's *Odyssey*. Athena, the goddess of war, takes the form of an old man named Mentor to guide the young Telemachus while his father is away. "You should not be clinging to your childhood," Mentor tells Telemachus. Even without his father to guide him, Telemachus must become a man.

Often, mentor's wisdom is captured in simple aphorisms. Consider the wisdom of Father Zosima in Fyodor Dostoevsky's *The Brothers Karamazov*:

> "Love redeems and saves everything."
> "Many times, it is necessary to treat people as if they were
>     children, or as if they were sick."
> "What is Hell? It is the suffering for being no longer able to love."
> "Everything passes, only truth remains."

An elder in the monastery, Father Zosima heals the ill and guides younger priests. He wins the affection of the townspeople by living out his values.

To be a true mentor, it's not enough to give good advice. The mentor also needs to follow his own wisdom. Shakespeare's Polonius offers sound advice. "To thine own self be true," he says in *Hamlet*. "Neither a borrower nor a lender be." But Polonius is pompous and vain; he speaks well but invites ridicule. A true mentor, while never perfect, lives his ideals and does not bloviate like Polonius.

**Tempter**: Opposing the mentor—and, usually, the hero's best interests—is a tempter. As the mentor guides the hero to do the right thing, the tempter tries to lure him with easy answers. His message is as simple as it is dangerous: *Why work hard? Why consider other people's concerns? Take the easy way out!*

The greatest story of temptation comes from the story of Adam and Eve in the Garden of Eden. When a serpent urges her to eat from the Tree of Knowledge, to "be like God," Eve gives into temptation. Eve and Adam are then cast out of the state of innocence and purity, filled with shame. The New Testament shows the glory that comes from resisting temptation. Jesus resists the devil's temptation after he fasts for 40 days and nights. Each time the devil challenges him to show his special powers, Jesus resists.

The tempter sometimes plays a positive role, bringing lightness and laughter to the hero. In Shakespeare's *Henry IV, Part 1*, Falstaff lures Prince Hal into all kinds of merrymaking and pranks. Falstaff makes Hal a more complete man. But the partying cannot last forever. When Hal becomes king, his new responsibilities impel him to cast off Falstaff:

> Presume not that I am the thing I was;
> For God doth know, so shall the world perceive,
> That I have turn'd away my former self ...

By following Falstaff, Hal enlivens his spirit. By later rejecting him, he becomes a man.

**Mind**: The mind character takes a rational, intellectual approach to life. All problems can be reduced to cool calculation of pros and cons. When making a major life decision—whether to take a job, move to a new town, marry, have children—he focuses on the tradeoffs of time, money, and status.

Brainy characters understand that most problems require discipline and thought. Hermione, who plays the role of the intellect in the Harry Potter series, insists on the magic power of brains. "It's logic, a puzzle," she says. "A lot of the greatest wizards haven't got one ounce of logic. They'd be stuck in here forever."

The mind character often plays the key role in detective stories. In Edgar Allan Poe's "The Purloined Letter," Dupin uses logic to find a letter that a thief has used to blackmail a politician. Since he knows the thief is a poet, Dupin reasons that he would find a clever way to hide the letter—in a letterbox, in plain sight, where police would never look.

Lisbeth Salander, the computer hacker in Stieg Larsson's Millennium trilogy, uses her brains to defeat her abusers. She can get inside any computer program, remember the details of everything she reads, and survive on the street. She also plots an ingenious strategy to defeat her sadistic guardian and overcome her evil father.

**Heart**: Rather than reducing problems to rational calculations, the heart character understands the need to honor the deepest part of the soul.

With awareness of the heart, we all draw from our deepest wells of energy and intelligence. We can persevere when the odds are stacked against us. With empathy, we can understand what other people are experiencing—and how they fit into our lives. Connected to other people, we grow and learn and act well ourselves.

People who know what they value, *deep down*, act swiftly; they do not suffer a "paralysis of analysis." When they see someone doing something wrong, they respond instantly. Because they hold their values deeply, they do not hesitate when confronted with a moral challenge. They know what's right and what's wrong, and they act accordingly.

When you create a story—either real or fiction—keep these types in mind. Your story becomes complete only when you develop all these types and show how they interact with each other.

## Case Study
### Robert Moses and Jane Jacobs

Over the years, New York's planning and development wars have become a cottage industry in publishing. Jane Jacobs began the process with *The Death and Life of Great American Cities*, the unsparing 1961 philippic against large-scale planning. Robert Caro's *The Power Broker* focused this critique on Robert Moses, the man who did more to shape New York City and other cities than anyone else in history. Dozens of books and articles, most notably Anthony Flint's *Wrestling With Moses,* have continued the debate.

The Jacobs-Moses story resonates because these battles shaped the world where we now live: the highways, bridges, tunnels, public housing, parks, and beaches. This dialectic—between big and small, technocratic and grassroots—still animates politics and planning in our day.

The story also resonates because the characters are so primal. Moses was the ultimate power broker, the creator of a political empire that stretched across New York City to the region and the state. By controlling revenues of authorities—and thus, contracts and jobs for countless people in city, state, and even federal politics for decades—Moses made himself untouchable. The only modern parallel in modern American history was J. Edgar Hoover, who single-handedly ran the FBI for decades and terrorized anyone who crossed him.

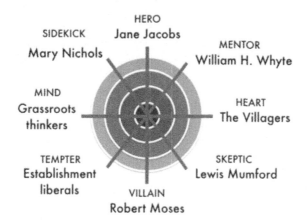

Jacobs, meanwhile, was the classic New York grassroots activist, horrified by the abuses of Moses, his minions, and servile politicians and bureaucrats. With her keen observations of cities, from building stoops to public housing high rises, Jacobs developed a powerful critique of Moses. Then, with the help of likeminded neighbors, she fought the Moses machine.

The Moses-Jacobs battles involved all kinds of other character types as well. Let's just look at the story with Jane Jacobs as the hero and Robert Moses the villain.

Jacobs's mentor, William H. Whyte, was a sociologist who explored the conformity of modern society and explored how cities were being demolished and rebuilt in the image of the "organization man." Jacob's most persistent skeptic, Lewis Mumford, was the day's great urban historian who questioned whether Jacobs understood the massive forces shaping cities. Her sidekick, Mary Perot Nichols, was a journalist who tracked the politics of Greenwich Village.

Two archetypes—the heart and mind—were played by whole communities of people. Residents of the Village, from the small shopkeepers to the mothers to the professionals, provided the heart of Jacobs's world. Jacobs's intellectual influences included the renegade journalists at *The Village Voice*, Jacobs's colleagues in journalism and architecture, and the larger communities of lawyers and zoning experts who taught Jacobs how politics works.

~

### Element 8
### Spin the Wheel of Archetypes

ONE STORY'S hero is another story's villain. Looked at in a different light, or facing a different set of challenges, a hero may begin to look less than heroic and a villain more than villainous. When we look at a character in a new way, in different circumstances, characters reveal a whole different set of qualities.

So develop your characters by casting them in unfamiliar roles. Show them contend with buried fears. Give them courage when they fret. Create a situation where the mentor tempts the hero. Depict the sidekick acting disloyally. Get the villain to behave well and the hero to behave badly.

If the eight basic character types can be seen as points on a wheel, see what happens when you spin the wheel and put the characters in unfamiliar roles.

To understand the power of switching roles, consider the concept of shadows. Carl Jung describes the shadow like this:

The shadow is that hidden, repressed, for the most part inferior and guilt-laden personality whose ultimate ramifications reach back into the realm of our animal ancestors and so comprise the whole historical aspect of the unconscious.

A shadow also hides the positive side of a personality. Sometimes characters are reluctant to admit their positive qualities because they would upset their self-image (as a tough badass, as a realist, or as a cynic) or upset others' expectations of them (this is common in gangs and other peer groups).

All of us deny some of our deepest desires, out of fear or shame. But those desires don't go away. They lurk beneath the surface. *That's the shadow.* Shadows give characters richness and complexity. No one can be heroic without wrestling with internal as well as external demons.

The shadow's greatest power comes from the character's refusal to embrace it. If we would all just acknowledge our deeper desires and fears, we could address them. But we deny them—and the shadow never leaves. Wherever we go, our shadow goes with us.

Our shadow is, above all, insecure. Even if we are accomplished, decent, and good-looking, we think of ourselves as failed, flawed, and frumpy. When we look in the mirror, we see flaws. And we think that everyone else must see the same flaws and judge us harshly.

When you change characters' roles, you find deeper characters. And then, you have a chance to create a compelling story.

### Case Study
### Moses and Jacobs, Redux

Suppose, for the sake of argument, that Robert Moses was the hero of the battle for the soul of New York City? As brutal as he could be, Moses modernized the city. He took a city of small villages, parochial and set in their ways, and transformed them into a dynamic, integrated engine.

Today's New York—a global capital of finance, technology, culture and the arts, education, medicine, and much more—was made possible because Moses was willing to use a "meat ax" to pursue big projects like bridges, highways, parks and beaches, and public housing. Like Baron von Haussmann in Paris and Vienna decades before, Moses saw that New York could only operate on a grand scale if it was willing to forge a massive, connected *system* out of a vast collection of small, insular communities.

With Moses as the hero, Jacobs takes the role of the villain. In this reading, she is a sentimentalist who understands small-scale neighborhood dynamics but not the massive change that cities need to thrive in the modern world.

Other characters fill the other archetypes. The Moses mind, for example, was shaped by the British intellectuals and public servants that Moses studied as a young man; British ideas about civil service and political authorities helped Moses understand the tools needed to make change happen. Moses's emotional touchstone was Governor Al Smith, who guided him as a young man and gave him his first opportunity to build parks, roads, and bridges. Smith's top aide, Belle Moskowitz, served as Moses's mentor early in his career.

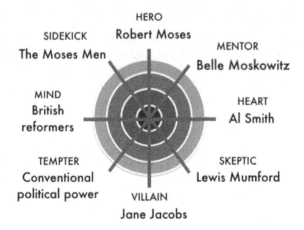

Moses had a whole team of sidekicks. The "Moses Men"—the army of engineers, designers, financiers, lawyers, and managers who carried out Moses's will—were intensely loyal. Moses's skeptic was Lewis Mumford, the historian and critic who doubts about many of Moses's projects.

Two temptations shaped Moses's career. Early in his career, he gave into the temptation for conventional political power and ran for governor in 1934. He lost badly. Had he won, Moses never could have created his massive machine, free of real accountability. The other temptation—the lust for power for its own sake—Moses could not avoid. By the end of his career, he pursued more destructive projects and disdained the democratic process.

~

**And Another Thing . . .**

AN OLD LITERARY DEBATE ASKS: What matters more, character or plot? It's a tired debate. You cannot have characters without a plot, and you can't have a plot without characters. Characters and plot are two sides of the same coin. Still, pressed to say what matters most, I'd say character. Here's why: Nothing interests people more than the idea of people.

We humans love looking at ourselves. In the story of Narcissus, a beautiful boy gets lost looking at his reflection in a pool. He confuses this image with reality. And he spends his days gazing at this image until he dies. Like Narcissus, we humans love to look at things with our own qualities, wherever we go.

This fascination with the human form carries over to inanimate objects. Consider the Old Man of the Mountain, an outcropping of rock on the White Mountains in New Hampshire. Viewed at an angle, the rock resembled the profile of an old man. Well, *sort of*. For years, people fell in love with that jagged piece of rock. Government officials put the Old Man of the Mountain on the state's U.S. quarter.

Tourists traveled hundreds of miles to see it. When the outcropping fell off a few years ago, some New Hampshire residents began a movement to restore it.

Philosophers have a word for this kind of projection—*anthropomorphism*. We project human qualities onto all kinds of nonhuman things—animals, organizations, buildings, machines, and nature.

To win your reader's attention—and keep it—start by telling stories about *people*. Then help the reader to empathize with the characters. Arouse people by getting them to feel the actions of others. When you make the reader feel something, the reader *cares*.

# 3

# NARRATIVE

Tell me a story of deep delight.

— ROBERT PENN WARREN

Rita Charon remembers the moment when she became the doctor she was meant to be.

Early in her career, Charon didn't always take time to understand her patients' lives and problems. Then along came a woman named Luz. When Luz complained about headaches, Dr. Charon prescribed acetaminophen. Later Luz asked Dr. Charen to fill out paperwork for disability benefits. Rushing to an appointment, Dr. Charon signed the forms. But she wondered about Luz's plans. She suspected that Luz might be abusing the system.

Feeling guilty about her brusque treatment of Luz, Dr. Charon asked her to come in for a visit. Luz then explained her real reasons for seeking disability benefits. The oldest of five girls who lived with her father and uncle in Yonkers, Luz had suffered sexual abuse since she was 12 years old. Now that she was 21, she wanted to rent an apartment in Manhattan and take her sisters with her. She wanted to protect them from the abuse she had experienced.

After learning Luz's real story, Dr. Charon enlisted social workers, emergency shelters, and support groups. She helped Luz find an apartment. She also continued to serve as her physician. She even cared for Luz's dying father.

That experience, Rita Charon says, taught her that doctors need to make storytelling a part of their care. It's not enough, she decided, to isolate symptoms and disease for treatment. It's also not enough to analyze patterns of behavior, like diet, exercise, and relationships. To provide care, doctors need to understand their patients' stories. So Dr. Charon has become a. leading figure in "narrative medicine," a movement to get doctors to write and tell stories about their experiences.

Telling stories can transform everything we do in life. Professionals in all fields—medicine, law, business, and education—perform a number of important tasks but do not always understand the people they work with. Administrators, meanwhile, swim in an ocean of statistics and procedures, isolated from the larger dramas of life. When you use stories to engage people— doctors, patients, family members, friends, coworkers—you can understand and transform lives.

Stories offer all of us a way to create richer lives for ourselves. Stories make us human; they make us whole. Stories might not make all things possible. But they give all possible things a chance to come true.

~

## Element 9
### Give Your Story a Narrative Arc

To give your story shape — and to make it a complete and unified experience —move the reader through three distinct phases.

Two and a half millennia ago, Aristotle outlined the basic imperatives of storytelling in his masterpiece *The Poetics*. This brief guide to the elements of drama remains the seminal work. In Aristotle's words:

> A whole is that which has a beginning, a middle, and an end.
>
> A beginning is that which does not itself follow anything by causal necessity, but after which something naturally is or comes to be.
>
> An end, on the contrary, is that which itself naturally follows some other thing, either by necessity, or as a rule, but has nothing following it.
>
> A middle is that which follows something as some other thing follows it.
>
> A well-constructed plot, therefore, must neither begin nor end haphazardly, but conform to these principles.

Dividing all drama into a beginning, middle, and end might seem simplistic. And many authors violate the rule. The French filmmaker Jean-Luc Godard once quipped: "A story should have a beginning, a middle, and an end, but not necessarily in that order." But for most stories—and for other kinds of communication as well—readers need a journey that moves through these stages.

Aristotle's arc makes a story whole. Something important changes over the course of a story. That change produces a new understanding. The hero becomes a different person by the end of the journey. Other characters do as well. As Aristotle explained, drama offers a complete, unified, and internally consistent story "of a certain magnitude" to explore the human condition.

Let's see how it works, step by step.

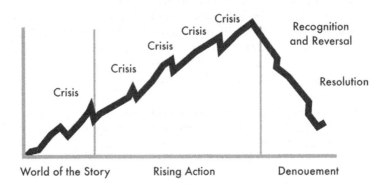

**Act I: Into the World of the Story**. Most stories begin with characters living ordinary lives in a stable environment. This is the world of the status quo, the comfort zone, and *Ho hum, what's for supper?*

In Act I, we meet the main characters and learn about their world. We see them interact with family and friends. We see them express, and pursue, their hopes and values. We learn their "back stories," the events that shaped their identity. We watch them play settled roles and embrace established values. They're "set," at least in their own minds.

Beneath the placid surface we see hints of trouble. A world that appears stable actually teems with contradictions and tensions. A priest hides a secret of abusing children. A ballplayer struggles with a deadly disease. A man has an affair. A student struggles with depression. A business partner embezzles company funds. A mobster struggles with his family.

Then a crisis rocks the world of the story. The hero—and other characters, too—are called to meet daunting challenges. Storytellers sometimes call this the "inciting incident." I call it the "trigger of trouble." This moment must involve conflict—between the hero and other people, his community, and even himself. Conflict is essential. As the spy novelist John le Carre once noted, "The cat sat on a mat," is not the beginning of a story. "The cat sat on the dog's mat" is.

And so the story begins in earnest.

**Act II: Crisis and Conflict**. Most of us, even the most courageous among us, cannot face a crisis directly—not at first, anyway. It's like staring directly at the sun; it's too much to handle. We usually deny that a problem even exists. Even when we acknowledge the problem, we do not really embrace it fully. We try to get rid of it without making any significant changes in our approach to life.

Just think of the examples from your life. Ask yourself: Have you ever known an alcoholic who went to AA as soon as his drinking problem got serious? Or a troubled couple who immediately sought counseling to address their tensions? Or a professional who sensed, right away, that his career was veering off track? How many people face their crises immediately, with an eagerness to learn and change? Maybe some, but not many.

Over time—after denying and then minimizing the crisis—the story's hero realizes that he cannot avoid the problem. So he confronts a piece of the problem. He refuses to acknowledge the whole problem; that would be too painful or difficult. So he picks off a piece, hoping that the rest of the crisis will disappear. But the crisis doesn't go away; in fact, it gets worse. Reluctantly, then, the hero and other characters take on bigger and bigger pieces of the problem.

Tension mounts. The greater the challenge, the greater the stakes. The greater the stakes, the greater the resistance. The greater the resistance, the more profound the experience. By making harder and harder choices—reluctantly—the hero transforms himself. He grows.

Toward, the end of Act II, the hero recognizes a need to transform his life. Halfway measures, he now understands, cannot answer his challenge. To use Aristotle's terms, the hero reaches a moment of "recognition" and "reversal." He understands the problem for the first time. By embracing this problem rather than denying it, he gains the power to confront it.

In retrospect, the hero's true condition seems so obvious. What takes so long for him to face his challenges? It's really quite simple. All of us struggle to face reality. We deny our problems not just to avoid them, but also because we need to break these problems into smaller pieces. The hero is no different. He *cannot* confront his crisis early in the story. He must face it, grudgingly, in stages. Eventually, after a long struggle, he transforms himself.

**Act III: A new world is born**: The story eventually reaches a resolution, which puts characters and issues in a new place.

Theater people call the final part of the story "the slow curtain." Characters settle their accounts—finish off foes, reconcile with friends and loved ones, embrace new roles and expectations. They say, in effect: *Ah, this is how life's going to be from now on.*

As you end the story, make sure you can capture the meaning of this resolution. You should be able to summarize it in a simple phrase. When Brian Piccolo dies at the end of *Brian's Song*, the resolution is not "Hero dies," but "Hero dies with courage, touching all who know him." When Willie Stark gets assassinated at the end of *All the King's Men*, the resolution is not "Politician gets killed," but "Corruption ruins politician and others." When Dorothy returns to Kansas at the end of The Wizard of Oz, the resolution is not "Girl returns home," but "Girl returns home a mature, wiser young woman."

With a strong conclusion, the story comes full circle. The point of the journey and its struggles becomes clear. To the story's hero–and to its reader–all the pieces come together to create something whole.

At every stage of the process, show the emotional undercurrents of the story. For every scene, ask yourself: What are the emotional effects of this moment? A story is not a sequence of events; it's the sequence of *meaningful* events. Make sure your narrative arc vibrates with emotional power.

## Case Study
### Richard Chenoweth's 'The Most Beautiful Room in the World?'

In the early days of the American Republic, leaders like George Washington and Thomas Jefferson sought to create a design for the U.S. Capitol building that would reflect the hopes and values of the new nation.

Washington laid the cornerstone of the capital in 1793. But the early planning faltered. As Richard Chenoweth writes: "The building's progress during the years of Washington and Adams administrations was marked by changes of plan, ill will among principals and city commissioners, difficult logistics in the newly laid out city, and generally shoddy workmanship." It did not help that the man hired for the project lacked experience in architecture and building. When Jefferson became president in 1801, only the Senate side (the North Wing) of the building was complete; the House side (the South Wing) was a foundation with an elliptical brick wall. That wall was nicknamed the "bake oven" because of the way it retained heat.

President Jefferson hired Henry Latrobe, an English architect and engineer, to complete the design and construction of the South Wing, which contained the Hall of House of Representatives. The Hall, Jefferson hoped, would symbolize the light and openness of the nation's most democratic institution.

Jefferson's vision dated back to 1985 when he served as minister to France. Exploring Paris, Jefferson discovered the Paris grain market (*Halle aux Bles*). The building's vast glass roof allowed the sun to flow into the room and create a dazzling dance of light and shadows below. Jefferson described it as "the most superb thing on earth." Jefferson wanted the Capitol to offer the same light-splashed experience as the Paris building.

But Latrobe resisted this vision. A glass roof, he warned, would drip from condensation and leakages. Besides that, the light would overwhelm the area below. "So spangled a ceiling, giving an air of the highest gaiety, will I think destroy the solemnity that is appropriate to the object of this edifice," Latrobe wrote Jefferson. Latrobe wanted to light the hall with a large lantern in the room's center. The two debated the issue. "I cannot express the regret I feel," Jefferson wrote, at the idea of abandoning the massive sky dome. It was "the distinguishing merit" of the structure, he said, and would make it "the handsomest room in the world, without a single exception." Latrobe eventually relented and the project got under way; the Hall of the House of Representatives would have its dazzling glass roof.

Even after agreeing to realize Jefferson's vision, Latrobe tried to persuade Jefferson to change his mind. He painted a watercolor rendering that showed the magnificence of the room with two lanterns instead of the glass dome. He also designed the roof's frame to be strong enough to accommodate the lantern, just in case. Like all good architects, he built a "Plan B" into the project.

Despite all the conflicts, Latrobe completed Jefferson's building. The glass dome held 100 windows, in bands of five, around the periphery of the domed interior. Between the banks of windows, a Philadelphia artist named George Bridport painted images of coffered panels—a touch of *trompe d'oeil* to compensate for the project's budget limitations. Latrobe also began to fill the Hall, with platforms, mahogany desks, and chairs atop carpeted platforms. He even designed a statue of liberty, which the Italian sculptor Giuseppe Franzoni carved.

But the British invaded Washington in 1814 and burned the Capitol to the ground. The building would rise again—work began the next year—but with a different design and style.

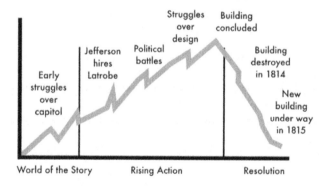

So that's the story of the first U.S. Capitol. We know about Jefferson's vision only because of the work of Richard Chenoweth, a Princeton-based architect and artist. Here's the story behind *that* story.

A graduate of the University of Virginia, Chenoweth was always fascinated by Jefferson's architectural vision. While tracking Jefferson's experiences in Paris, Chenoweth discovered how the *Halle aux Bles* fired Jefferson's imagination. He wondered what the Hall of Representatives, the building inspired by the *Halle*, looked like. After the British burned Washington, no images of the structure survived. So Chenoweth set out on a quest to recreate Jefferson's long-gone vision. It was like an episode of *CSI—The Lost Capitol*.

Chenoweth studied Latrobe's original construction documents, contracts, letters with Jefferson, and other materials about the era's architecture and building materials. Information about the foundation and vaults helped establish a baseline. When he found scattered drawings of elements of the burnt capitol, Chenoweth used his Mac to create images of the building. Using this "forensic" approach, as well as his own expertise as an architect and builder, Chenoweth was able to show how the old building looked, in minute detail.

Since then Chenoweth has also researched what the statue of liberty might have looked like—and even sculpted his own version. Chenoweth's work has been featured on PBS, CBS, and other media outlets.

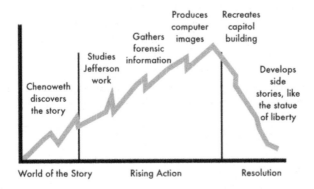

All stories are really many stories, with many arcs. As a storyteller or analyst, you need to know your audience so you can tell the most relevant story. Which of these stories matters more? If you're an architect historian, maybe the Jefferson-Latrobe story resonates more. If you're an investigator and historian, the second story might matter more.

~

### Element 10
### For Complexity, Show More Than One Arc

A GOOD STORY requires the hero to face a crisis and confront barriers, again and again, until he grows and becomes a better person.

A *great* story, however, requires at least two or three compelling characters to confront separate sets of barriers—and for the arcs of their stories to overlap at times. Each of the character's journeys helps us to understand the others' journeys.

If every character's life is a separate narrative, then several overlapping stories add richness and complexity to the tale. Sometimes the characters support each other; at other times, they battle each other. At the intersections of these arcs, we see how characters both pursue their own goals and deal with other people seeking different goals. This creates another dimension of conflict. How do they handle these conflicts? Do they grow or get stuck? How do the winners and losers respond to the outcomes? How do they change?

One person's rise often comes with another's fall. One person's struggle leads to another's opportunity. One person's tragedy transforms the landscape for all. The lives of different people come together and then separate, again and again, throughout the story. These overlapping arcs give the story complexity.

A love story, then, would not only follow the arc of the couple who meet and fall in love, overcoming many barriers along the way; it would also track the stories of the families, social circles, and careers. A political tale would not only follow the career of the president or union leader, but also his family's saga, his opponents' careers and projects, the community or ideology he represents.

Think of some common sets of arcs in stories:

- As one character succeeds in the world by cutting corners and making compromises, another struggles to do things the right way.
- As one character discovers and pursues important desires, another rises by conforming to community ideals.
- As one character pursues a secret mission, her colleagues pursue their own goals without understanding their comrade.

Often one arc spins off another. The major arc gives rise to a character who goes her own way, only to cross paths with the main characters later on. A political leader, for example, helps a protege get started—only to confront that character later as a competitor.

To write storylines for arcs, create "before and after" statements. Consider, for example the before-and-after summaries of the classic *Wizard of Oz*:

- Dorothy moves from innocence and helplessness to self-knowledge and strength.
- Dorothy's friends move from helpless, broken spirits to trustworthy and self-aware allies.
- The Wicked Witch moves from heartbreak and rage to a tragic fall.

The many arcs of a story—two or three or more—move forward independently. When the arcs intersect, they offer special insight.

## Case Study
## The Suburbanization of America

In little more than a generation, America became a nation of suburbs.

The early "streetcar suburbs," of course, sprouted in the late 1800s outside Boston, Philadelphia, Chicago, and Los Angeles. Often, those suburbs got absorbed into the city as outer neighborhoods, folded into the rest of the city with its transportation system, utilities, and public services. Postwar suburbanization changed all that. Now, people settled in communities that were neither urban nor rural, often far from the city and isolated from its ways.

Suburbanization involved three overlapping narratives, which reinforced each other.

**Technology**: The car transformed America, allowing people to commute long distances. Meanwhile, production and distribution went "horizontal," requiring vast single-story structures that required lots of (suburban and exurban) land and easy access to highways. The electric grid spread far from city centers, allowing suburban and rural development. Appliances and TV brought people indoors, reinforcing suburban lifestyles. The air conditioner made the Sunbelt's sprawling growth possible. Computers made "remote" working possible; the Internet then drew shopping away from urban centers.

**Policy**: Zoning separated activities, abetting suburban-style living. Zoning often included racist restrictions, trapping blacks in the city while encouraging whites to flee. The national highway system expanded the distances that people could travel. Housing policies subsidized new construction and home ownership. Banking policies encouraged racial discrimination and segregation. Urban renewal demolished urban neighborhoods. Consolidation of schools and other functions led to regional services. Vast military spending benefitted mostly exurban areas.

**Culture**: The rise of radio and then TV drew people out of the public realm and into the home. Consumerism refocused Americans toward individual appetites. Malls became the American way to shop; by 1987 malls accounted for half of all consumer spending. Uprooted, Americans loosened their ties to community, moving an average of once every five years—usually away from city centers.

Fear not this graphic. And don't not take the separation of arcs too seriously. I only mean to illustrate how different stories unfold alongside each other. Each narrative is, by itself, compelling, with vivid tales, characters, emotions, and stakes.

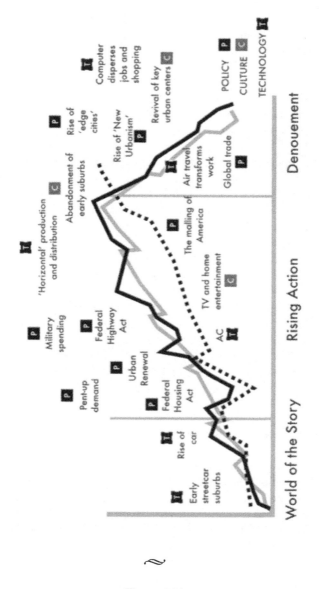

**Element 11**
**Show Characters Hitting Brick Walls**

In 2008, a computer scientist at Carnegie-Mellon University named Randy Pausch attracted national acclaim with his "last lecture." Dying of pancreatic cancer, Pausch spoke with joy about life and learning, family and friends. As his journey ended, he celebrated life.

Pausch talked about "brick walls," the barriers that we all face in our everyday lives. Those brick walls could be trivial (a traffic jam) or profound (a cancer diagnosis). Rather than lamenting them, Pausch called them essential parts of our growth and development:

> Brick walls are there for a reason. The brick walls are not there to keep us out. The brick walls are there to show how badly we want something. Because the brick walls are there to stop the people who don't want something badly enough. They are there to keep out the other people.

What happens when characters hit brick walls? How do they deal with barriers? Do they get angry or accept the reality of the situation? Do they embrace responsibility or cast blame? Do they show a team spirit or angle for personal benefit? Do they adjust to changing circumstances or stubbornly cling to their first approach? Do they devise a strategy to climb over the wall? Do they seek help from others?

By facing a series of crises—brick walls—heroes and other characters stretch themselves to accomplish extraordinary feats.

All of literature's great characters— Oedipus and Odysseus, Hamlet and Macbeth, Don Juan and Tom Jones, Jane Eyre and Carrie Meeber, Santiago and Tomas, Holden Caulfield and Rabbit Angstrom, to name a handful—battle both external and internal foes to realize their potentials. Each faces daunting problems with limited powers.

"We only think," John Dewey reminds us, "when we are confronted with a problem." *That's the story.*

## Case Study
## Robert Caro's *The Power Broker*

When the master builder Robert Moses began exploring Long Island, he found the world of F. Scott Fitzgerald's *The Great Gatsby*—a lush habitat of the rich that excluded ordinary working class folks from its beaches and parks.

The island was a natural wonderland, which extended 108 miles from New York Harbor to Montauk Point. With more than 100 miles of beaches, the island offered ideal places for ordinary New Yorkers to find recreation. Packed together in the city's tenements and cramped factories, city people needed recreational places to enjoy their few days of leisure. But as Moses discovered, the island's elites—the robber barons and other rich families, the paid-off politicians and their enforcers—blocked their quest.

Here's how Robert Caro describes the frustrations of city folk as they sought escape on Long Island';s beaches:

> When the families of New York City reached Long Island, they found the milk and honey sour indeed.
>
> If they were headed for the North Shore on Northern Boulevard, 60 feet of

smooth macadam shrank to 18 at the city line. The cars heading east had to fit into a single file. As they crept along, the paving of the boulevard deteriorated, so that each family had to watch the cars ahead jounce, one after another, into gaping potholes, and then wait for the jolts themselves. More and more frequently, if the earth was dry, thick clouds of dust hung over the unpaved stretches turning dirty the gay dress Mother had worn for the excursion.

As the families drove, they could see on either side of them, through gates set in stone walls or through the openings in wooden fences, the beautiful meadows they had come for, stretching endlessly and emptily to the cool trees beyond. But the meadows and trees were not for them. The gates will be locked and men carrying shotguns and holding fierce dogs on straining leashes would point eastward, telling the families that were parks open to them "farther along." There was no shade on Northern Boulevard and the children became cranky early. In desperation, ignoring the NO TRESPASSING— PRIVATE PROPERTY signs that lined the road, fathers would turn onto the narrow strip of grass between the Boulevard and the wall paralleling it and, despite the dust and the fumes from the passing cars, would try to picnic there. But the guards were vigilant and it was never long until the fathers had to tell the kids to get back into the car. Later, in Oyster Bay Town and Huntington, they would come to parks, tiny but nonetheless parks, but as they approached them they would see policemen at their entrances and the policeman would waive them on, explaining that they were reserved for township residents. There were, the placement shouted, parks open "farther along."

New Yorkers' efforts to enjoy a day at the beach were frustrated, time and time again. When the narrow, bumpy roads didn't deter them, the barriers and guards at the beaches did. Efforts to get a simple day at the beach usually failed.

As Robert Caro describes in great detail, Robert Moses took on these frustrations as his own great struggle. He used any and all means necessary to dislodge the rich so that he could create recreational beaches all over the island. And, of course, he built the roads to get there. When Moses confronted ancient laws, secret agreements, political corruption, and a power structure dedicated protecting the privileged, he fought back.

When Moses encountered brick walls—both literal and figurative—he smashed them.

～

### Element 12
### Nest Journeys Inside Journeys

INSIDE EVERY GREAT journey are a number of smaller journeys. Each mini-journey is a complete in itself; each mini-journey also moves the larger story forward.

Think of a family vacation to the Grand Canyon from (let's just say) your home in Ohio. The first leg of the journey takes you to Indianapolis, where you go to the Indy 500 or visit the state capitol. Then you get to St. Louis, where you see the Cardinals or visit Forest Park. Then you go to Tulsa, Amarillo, and Albuquerque—at each stop, seeing historic and recreation spots—before arriving at the canyon in northern Arizona.

That's how writing works. The whole piece takes the reader on a complete journey, which starts and finishes strongly. Each section takes the reader on a smaller adventure, which also starts and finishes strongly.

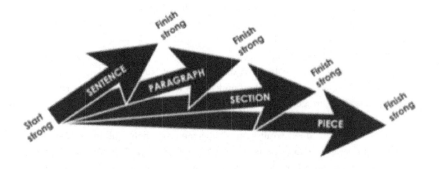

Part by part, journey by journey, the larger narrative takes form. Each part contains its own drama. The dramas of the parts contributes to the larger dramas.

The effect is powerful. The reader gets a whole experience. Each part offers its own value, with its own drama, but also contributes to a larger drama.

### Case Study
### Ian Frazier's 'The Bag Bill'

What is the ideal structure of a piece of writing? It is, I submit, a narrative, which contains a series of smaller narratives, which in turn contain even smaller narratives.

Consider a *New Yorker* piece by Ian Frazier, which describes a political movement to reduce the use of plastic bags. Frazier tracks the campaign for a piece of legislation in New York City that would assess a 5-cent fee for the use of plastic bags in stores. That overall theme of Frazier's piece is simple: *Do-gooder environmentalists are working to rid the city of an unnecessary scourge but struggle against the public's lack of awareness and the well-funded campaign of the plastic lobby.*

Each of the article's eight sections support the overall theme of the article. Consider the controlling ideas of these eight parts:

1. **The activist**: The story's protagonist, Jennie Romer, who has advised efforts to ban or charge for bags in California and is now lobbying New York's City Council to charge fees.
2. **The author**: His efforts to combat the widespread litter of bags in public spaces.
3. **The activist, then and now**: Romer's upbringing, which included regular family trips to recycling centers. Also: her rebuttals to bag-ban critics and her frustration at the slow pace of progress.
4. **Opposition**: Small shop owners and others who claim that a bag tax would drive away customers.
5. **Grassroots efforts**: Volunteers who clean up bag litter in parks and other public places.
6. **Pros and cons**: The arguments for—and against—recycling.
7. **Going deep**: A visit to Staten Island, where Hurricane Sandy "inundated the park's woodland to a depth of perhaps 20 feet and left behind a vastness of shredded plastic in the trees, like the pennants of a cast-of-thousands demon army."
8. **Lobbying**: The ongoing effort to persuade reluctant City Council members—and the news of Mayor Bill de Blasio's support.

Frazier's whole piece offers a compelling journey, showing how an activist promotes her cause, encounters opposition, and devises strategies to address every challenge she faces. Inside the whole piece, each section also creates a its own journey. Inside each sections, the paragraphs also offer clear journeys. Inside each paragraph, the sentences also offer clear journeys.

Let's go deeper, examining a couple of specific examples.

**The level of the paragraph**: The first paragraph sets the tone for the whole piece. The paragraph begins: "Jennie Romer moved from California to New York about four years ago to save the city from plastic bags." The paragraph ends: "She learned how better to advise Los Angeles, which passed its own anti-bag ordinance, in 2012."

That paragraph offers a clear journey, which starts and ends strongly. We begin with today's challenge; we end with the skills Romer needs to meet that challenge, which she learned in L.A.

**The levels of the section**: The whole first section also offers a clear journey that starts and finishes strongly. The section moves from meeting the activist ("Jennie Romer moved from California to New York ...") to an anti-reform group's distribution of misleading flyers: "A representative of the APBA, when told of this occurrence, said that it would never do such an underhanded move." Welcome to the big city, Jennie!

**The level of the whole piece**: The overall piece also traces a clear journey, starting and ending strongly.

Recall that the article opened by introducing Jennie Romer. Here's how it ends: "If the bill passes, perhaps in may, as she now believes it will, she plans to get a small plastic bag tattooed on her side, where it generally will not be seen."

The article, then, takes us from the beginning to the end of Romer's New York campaign—from getting to know her to seeing her celebrate, in her own way.

Nesting narratives requires a strategic breakdown of a piece into smaller, whole sections. Each section should follow the Golden Rule and, at the same time, contribute to a larger work piece that also follows the Golden Rule.

∼

### And Another Thing . . .

THE ULTIMATE GOAL of storytelling is unity and wholeness.

A great story is not just, as the historian Arnold Toynbee once quipped, "one damn thing after another." You need more than characters, events, and backstories. You need to give it all *shape*.

The characters and events of a story, ultimately, force us to grapple with a great question. As a storyteller, your challenge is to force your character to face this question. So ask yourself: Where is your hero going? Is it toward home? Innocence? Redemption? Truth? Honor?

Emotions and values drive characters. Think of the great characters of literature. Would Beowulf matter as just another warrior recruited to kill a monster? Would Macbeth matter as just another rising figure in a royal administration? Would Huck Finn matter as just another young rebel looking for adventure? Would Don Corleone matter as just another mob boss who decides to stay out of the drug business? Without passion and complication, would we care about these characters?

# 4

# SENTENCES

A lot of critics think I'm stupid because my sentences are so simple and my method is so direct: they think these are defects. No. The point is to write as much as you know as quickly as possible

— KURT VONNEGUT

I n *A Movable Feast*, Ernest Hemingway describes the power of the sentence. He muses about how he conquers writer's block:

I would sit in front of the fire and squeeze the peel of the little oranges into the edge of the flame and watch the sputter of blue that they made. I would stand and look out over the roofs of Paris and think, "Do not worry. You have always written before and you will write now. All you have to do is write one true sentence. Write the truest sentence you know." So finally I would write one true sentence, and then go on from there. It was easy then because there was always one true sentence that I knew or had seen or had heard someone say.

If you can write "one true sentence," you can write anything. If you can't, you're doomed.

The sentence is, then, the most important unit of writing. If we did nothing else but study the sentence, we would all write better.

So what is a sentence, anyway? My online dictionary offers this definition:

A set of words that is complete in itself, typically containing a subject and predicate, conveying a statement, question, exclamation, or command, and consisting of a main clause and sometimes one or more subordinate clauses.

This definition, alas, begs the question. A "set of words that is complete in itself" could include everything from a line of haiku to *War and Peace*. I like this definition offered by a legendary advertising copywriter named Eugene Schwartz:

> As much of your thought as you can effectively give the other person at one time.

This definition suggests a relationship between the writer and reader. It also suggests the importance of brevity. Too often, writers forget about the reader; they ramble on and on, using abstract and imprecise language that alienates the reader. Still, Schwartz's definition fails to break sentences into their essential parts. So try this definition:

> A complete statement that shows action or relationships, almost always using a subject and verb.

This definition, like Schwartz's, stresses the importance of keeping things simple. The ultimate goal of the sentence, really, is to say something without confusing matters.

Now what forms do sentences take?

Think of sentences as different kinds of paths. Imagine, first, a short path that moves quickly from one point to another. In this path, not much happens. You just take your subject (and reader) to a different place. Longer paths not only go from one place to another; they also explore sights along the way. These longer paths might form a straight line or bend in different directions. Longer paths might also include detours. Detours, once in a while, add value to the journey; they show how one idea relates to another. Too often, though, detours do not return to the main path.

You get the idea. Like any journey, a sentence-path can be as simple or complex as you want or need it to be. The key words are *want or need*. You need to make conscious decisions to write a short or long, straight or curving, direct or meandering sentence. Our biggest challenge, as writers, occurs when we cease to take control of our work. We write one sentence and then another, without deciding what we want to say or how.

To write well, you need to take charge of your sentences.

~

### Element 13
### Follow the Golden Rule for Sentences

WE HEAR a lot these days about the power of storytelling. Political pundits debate whether candidates offer a "strong narrative." Consultants earn small fortunes by schooling executives on the hero's journey. Advertisers build compelling dramas into 30-second commercials. Narrative, narrative everywhere.

I would like to take it a step further. Every challenge of writing—creating great sentences and paragraphs, selecting the right words and images, getting the grammar right, editing with a sharp scalpel—should take a narrative form. Everything you write, in fact, should offer a complete drama.

*Only when sentences move with all the elements of a great story—vivid characters, compelling goals, strong arcs, rising tensions, revealing twists and turns, and surprises—can they do their job.*

To simplify the task, let me remind you of the Golden Rule of Writing:

- Make everything a journey.
- Start strong, finish strong.

Let's consider two imperatives in turn.

*First, the journey*: Every sentence should take the reader from one state of understanding to another. If a sentence does not give the reader some new insight, you might not need it. Introduce every line with a compelling character, event, or issue. Set out a clear destination, which gives the reader a complete new idea. In the march from the beginning to the end, show the reader one or more surprising ideas or images. And take only the steps you need to get to the destination.

*Second, the start and finish*: To write with power, we need to start with a bang and end with a bang. Tell the reader, right away, who does what. Conclude the sentence with some kind of closure—completing the thought or action or offering a telling image or question.

Without clear starting and finish lines, we wander aimlessly. We can get lazy and write whatever comes to mind. Then the reader gets lost.

When my students began using the Golden Rule to write sentences, they first thought it was too demanding. *Make every sentence a journey? Start strong, finish strong, in every sentence? Really?* But the process actually comes easily. The Golden Rule offers a simple approach, which helps you check your work without much effort.

The key is to focus on the structure of sentences, line by line.

## Case Study
### Michael Pollan, 'Town-Building Is No Mickey Mouse Operation'

In the early 1990s, the Walt Disney Company made a billion-dollar bet that it could create a community that offered the best of small-town and big-city life. The town of Celebration, Florida uses the principles of the New Urbanism movement—compact street grids, wide and continuous sidewalks, accessible parks, homes on small lots close to the street, porches, parking hidden behind homes. The result was is a place that enchanted some and disturbed others.

In 1997, Michael Pollan visited Celebration to assess the experiment. His findings are summarized in this paragraph, which I have broken into pieces:

> If the typical suburb represents a kind of monoculture, street after street of architecturally and socioeconomically identical houses, Celebration has already achieved a striking degree of diversity.
>
> During my walk, I strolled down a street of million-dollar homes facing the golf course, and then turned to find a lane of modest cottages that sell for a fifth as much; walking another block or two, I came to a broad crescent of town-house apartments that rent for as little as $600 a month.
>
> This sort of diversity, while limited—there are no poor in Celebration, and the town is extremely white—is nevertheless rare today in the suburbs, where it is an article of the real-estate faith that people will live next door only to neighbors of the same class.
>
> In Celebration, houses of roughly the same price do face each other across a street, but the service alleys behind those houses deliberately mix high and low, forcing the surgeon and the firefighter to mingle while taking out the trash or getting into their cars.
>
> Stern spoke of deliberately setting up such encounters as one of the many ways that "design can help to orchestrate community."

Pollan's sentences sometimes meander. He wants to take readers on a tour in every sentence. This 139-word paragraph contains five sentences with an average of 39 words.

But Pollan never allows readers to get lost. Each sentence starts with a clear noun and verb. When he wants to explore complicated ideas, he "branches right"—that is, he states his point clearly, right away, and then adds a series of details. Because he starts strongly, he never gets lost as he moves to the right side of the page.

After starting strongly, Pollan always completes his thoughts decisively, usually with an image that brings a point home. Let's rephrase these sentences to show how they start and end strongly:

> If the typical suburb represents a kind of monoculture, ... Celebration has already achieved a striking degree of diversity.
>
> I strolled down a street of million-dollar homes ... but also saw apartments that rent for as little as $600 a month.
>
> This sort of diversity ... is nevertheless rare today in the suburbs, where people will live next door only to neighbors of the same class.
>
> In Celebration, houses of roughly the same price do face each other ... but the surgeon and the firefighter also encounter each other.
>
> Stern spoke of deliberately setting up such encounters ... "to orchestrate community."

In my work with writers—journalists, book authors, teachers and students, business professionals—I suggest building shorter sentences before allowing yourself to write Pollan-length sentences. Master the basics and the you can add complexity and flourishes. But length does not matter if you offer a clear journey that starts and ends clearly and strongly.

∼

### Element 14
### Give Every Sentence Clear Blasts

ALL WRITING explores action and change. The most important tool for that exploration is the verb.

The verb makes sentences move. The verb activates the sentence. It generates the energy needed to drive the other parts of the sentence. The subject can't do anything without the verb. So give the verb special attention when constructing a sentence. Make sure the reader can visualize what happens. Most simply, state:

*Who does what to whom?*

Start with the subject: *Who*. Then say what happens: *Verb*. Finally, say what gets acted upon: *Object*.

Grammatically speaking, the Subject-Verb-Object blast uses *transitive* verbs. That means that the subject acts *on something or someone else*. Of course, subjects and objects can be anything—a person, animal, object, and even a concept or a feeling. So you might think of the blast like this:

*Who/what does what to whom/what?*

Not every blast shows someone acting on something or someone. Sometimes, you care less about the *object* than the *context*. You want to know the context—*when, where, why* or *how* the action takes place.

Grammatically speaking, this blast uses *intransitive* verbs. That means that the subject does not act on *something or someone else*.

If you give your reader a clear blast, whatever the topic, like this—

*Who/what does what to whom/what/when/where/why/how?*

—you'll never fail.

Try to put at least one blast in every sentence. Use active verbs to charge it full of energy. As a general rule, give the reader a blast right away—at the beginning of the sentence. If you don't put your blast at the beginning, make easy to find. Don't meander too long before delivering the blast.

**Case Study**
**Ted Steinberg's Gotham Unbound**

In a history of natural New York, Ted Steinberg describes how New York destroyed the marshlands of Queens to accommodate new development.

Steinberg's sentences are long. This 163-word paragraph contains seven sentences, averaging 23 words.

> In 1916, as New York City *began* to tackle the Jamaica Bay marshlands, the Rockaway Peninsula Association *began ditching* 4,200 acres of meadow abutting the bay in Nassau County. From there over 140 islands *dotted* the landscape east along the shore, many still wild and not even named. Islands *varied* in size from less than an acre to as much as a few hundred, and their importance to animal life is hard to overstate. In these nurturing lands, marine species from shrimp to seahorses to sea bass *got* their start. Egrets and herons *flocked* there in search of food. On the sand bars and in mud flats in the middle of the complex of bays, clammers from the villages of Freeport and Baldwin *dug* for steamers and *took* them away by the boatload. Into this rich environment—a hunters' paradise of shorebirds and waterfowl—*came* the mosquito exterminators determined to carry out trench warfare, and, like twentieth-century conquistadors, they *helped* themselves to naming rights.

Some of these sentences are complicated. The last two sentences, numbering 34 and 30 words, demand the reader's attention. But Steinberg never fails to make clear who does what. Every sentence uses a clear blast. Every sentence uses an action verb. In these seven sentences, the action verbs are *began, began ditching, dotted, varied, got, flocked, dug, took, came,* and *helped*.

Even in complicated sentences, Steinberg makes his point clearly. In the last sentence, he took 11 words before he got to the verb *came*. But Steinberg cues us to wait for the verb with his cliffhanger opening, "Into this rich environment," and its modifier marked with em-dashes.

~

**Element 15**
**Create Revolver Sentences**

THE BEST WRITING MOVES FORWARD, with energy, from one blast of action to the next. With each blast comes new information, new sensations, new twists. Each burst changes something.

Sentences contain as few as one blast, as many as a half-dozen. Like a Colt .45 revolver, the blasts come in rapid succession. So think of your sentences as six-shooters. Be ready to fire as many blasts as necessary to convey the point of your sentence.

When composing a sentence, we often get lost in a thicket of nouns, pronouns, adjectives and adverbs, passive verbs, and prepositional phrases. If we simply focus on verbs—the whole series of blasts in our writing—we could easily fix our problems.

To test whether your sentences contain enough blasts, take on the persona of Charles Kingsfield from *The Paper Chase*. Kingsfield is the professor at Harvard Law School who demands maximum effort and brooks no mental sloppiness. On the first day of class he challenges his students: "You teach *yourselves* the law. *I* train your *minds*. You come in *here* with a *skull* full of *mush*, and if you sur*vive*, leave *thinking* like a *lawyer*." Kingsfield emphasizes every three or four words, to force his audience to listen.

Use the Professor Kingsfield Test for verbs. When you *read* your writing aloud, *emphasize* the verbs in each of your sentences. When it *sounds* right— clear, energetic, informative—you *have succeeded*. When it *sounds* clunky or vague, you need *to rewrite* your passage around the bursts of action.

## Case Studies
### James Carse's *Breakfast at the Victory* and Alice Goffman's 'On the Run'

Real energy comes from action. When you offer readers a series of specific actions, they can visualize and hear and feel what happens, moment by moment. Each action—each verb—pushes the scene forward. Each moment changes the story or analysis.

Consider James Carse's profile of Ernie, the owner and proprietor of the Victory Luncheonette in Greenwich Village in the 1960s and 1970s. The diner provided a place for strangers to come together and feel at home, among friends, even if their time was short and fleeting. See how Carse describes Ernie:

> Unaware that he was one-legged, I was momentarily caught by Ernie's odd but graceful movements as he worked the narrow space between grill and counter. Like a Sufi dervish, he was bobbing and sweeping in long, slow circles, cutting a bagel here, popping the toaster there, opening the coffee spigots on two cups at once, buttering a bagel with a single sweep, scrambling an egg in what looked like a dented aluminum helmet, brushing litter from the counter, cutting another bagel, flicking back the coffee spigots at the last possible moment—all the while contributing abbreviated comments to conversations with half a dozen customers. ...

Ernie shows that a single person can "make" a place. At the same time, the place sets the opportunities and limits for the people who inhabit it. The design of the Victory's small kitchen area determines Ernie's movements:

> The cooking equipment of the luncheonette had been so arranged that Ernie

could reach every part of it by pivoting on a single foot. Two huge coffeemakers were against the wall; the sinks, cutting board, and toaster were tucked under the counter. Although he could get to either end of the counter with a single giant step, he delivered most of the food by speeding it along the counter, dangerously skirting open stacks of jelly donuts and corn muffins.

The scene—the man and his work—is captured in Carse's simple prose. Look at Carse's revolver of verbs: *caught, worked, bobbing, sweeping, cutting, popping, opening, buttering, scrambling, brushing, cutting, flicking,* and *contributing*. The verbs alone tell the story.

Alice Goffman, meanwhile, presents a tragic story in her work on the culture of poverty in inner-city Philadelphia. In this passage she shows the environment's profound impact on children's behavior.

Children learn at an early age to watch out for the police and to prepare to run. The first week I spent on Sixth Street, I saw two boys, five and seven years old, play a game of chase in which one assumed the role of the cop who must run after the other. When the "cop" caught up to the other child, he pushed him down and cuffed him with imaginary handcuffs. He patted the other child down and felt in his pockets, asking if he had warrants or was carrying a gun or any drugs. The child then took a quarter out of the other child's pocket, laughing and yelling, "I'm seizing that!" In the following months I saw children give up running and simply stick their hands behind their backs as if in handcuffs, or push their bodies against the car, or lie flat on the ground and put their hands over their head.

Look at Goffman's action verbs: *learn, watch, prepare, spent, saw, play, assumed, caught, pushed, cuffed, patted, felt, asking, carrying, took, laughing, yelling, seizing, saw, give up, stick, push, lie,* and *put*.

In one paragraph, she uses 30 action verbs and one passive verb (*had*).

~

### Element 16
### Make Some Sentences More Complicated

SO FAR WE have sung the praises of the simple sentence—and for good reason. Simple sentences take the reader on a direct journey, without any confusing side trips. These sentences show who (or what) does what. And they show the object of that action, or when, where, why or how it takes place.

But sometimes we need to pack more information into a sentence. We want a strong blast, but we also want context or background information. For example:

Even though leading scientists say global warming poses a threat requiring an international strategy, the Trump Administration pressured the Environmental Protection Agency to halt action on climate change policies.

The blast of this sentence is "Trump Administration pressured the Environmental Protection Agency." But the other ideas—that "global warming poses a real threat" and it "requires an international strategy" and "to halt action on climate change policies"—give us important information. These ideas complete the thought.

These three formats offer room to provide just the right amount of context and nuance.

- **Simple sentence**: The architects examined the building.
- **Compound sentence**: The architects examined the building and their partners lined up financing.
- **Complex sentence**: With a complete renovation in mind, the architects examined the building from top to bottom.

Of course, you can go much further. Let's make the complex sentence even more complex:

With a modern design in mind, the architects examined the building—from the old, decaying roof to the rotting windows to the troubled foundation

As you add new material, make sure you can read the words easily. Don't allow the extra information to take you off track. Keep the journey clear and the images vivid.

The best writers use all of these sentence structures. Sometimes you need to make simple, direct statements, both for pacing and meaning. Other times, you need to show relationships, twists and turns in thinking.

## Case Study
### Richard Sennett's *Conscience of the Eye*

Richard Sennett has been one of the most creative and influential social theorists of the last generation. He writes about urbanism, class, planning, the public realm, participation, anarchism, capitalism, work, discipline, religion, theater, music, alienation, and citizenship—to name just a few of his interests.

It should come as no surprise, then, that Sennett's writing style can get complex. In his quest to create a detailed tapestry, Sennett explores a wide range of ideas and cases. In his sentences, he starts, veers off the subject, veers back, and then marches in a new direction.

In his discussion of street grids, Sennett acknowledges that grids make economic development simpler. Their stardardized lines and land parcels "rationalize" land development. At the same time, grids obliterate both the environment and the community's history.

> The grid can be understood as a weapon to be used against environmental character—beginning with the character of geography. In cities like Chicago the grids were laid over irregular terrain; the rectangular blocks obliterated the natural environment, spreading out relentlessly no matter that hills, rivers, or forest knolls stood in the way. The natural features that could be leveled or drained, were; the insurmountable obstacles that nature put against the grid, the regular course of rivers or lakes, were ignored by these frontier city planners, as if what could not be harnessed to this mechanical, tyrannical geometry did not exist.

This paragraph contains three sentences, which can be simplified like this:

> The grid is a weapon.
> Rectangular blocks obliterated the natural environment.
> The grid obliterated natural features—or just ignored them.

At the core level, these sentence structures are simple. But Sennett complicates them with dense collections of examples and ideas. Rather than offering details, one by one, he packs them into longer and longer sentences (20, 33, 48 words).

Now consider this passage, in which Sennett explores people's need for relief from urban life. To meet these needs, they build great outdoor spaces, like New York's Central Park.

> Whenever Americans of the era of high capitalism thought of an alternative to the grid, they thought of bucolic release, such as a leafy park or a promenade, rather than a more arousing street, square, or center in which to experience the complex life of the city. The nineteenth-century construction of Central Park in New York is perhaps the most bitter example of this alternative, an artfully designed natural void plan for the city's center in the expectation that the cultivated, charming territory already established around—as bucolic and refreshing scene as any city could wish for within a few minutes drive from his house—would be razed to the ground by the encroachments of the grid.

Here are the cores of these two sentences:

> When seeking relief, we chose bucolic relief, not nature-friendly neighborhoods.
> Central Park allowed untrammeled development outside the park.

Again, Sennett's basic structures are simple. But he packs lots of examples and ideas into two long sentences (47 and 70 words).

Sennett wants to fill the reader's platter. He wants the reader to dig deep. I would have used shorter sentences—smaller platters, if you will. Readers need a chance to absorb one plateful of thoughts before taking in a new one. Still, I appreciate Sennett's desire to avoid fragmenting his argument.

Let me, then, suggest a middle way. Let's try to preserve Sennett's complex thinking while allowing the reader to absorb his ideas more easily. Let's rewrite the second passage like this:

> Whenever Americans leaders sought escape from the urban grid, they thought of bucolic release. They chose a leafy park or a promenade, rather than bringing nature into streets and squares. The construction of Central Park offers a case in point. The park was an artfully designed Eden for the city's center; outside the park, at the time, were places as natural as could be found anywhere. But over time, development obliterated the nature that once thrived in the neighborhoods. Because Central Park provided "nature," few people resisted the development that drove nature out of the rest of the city.

My passage uses both short and long sentences; the lengths of these sentences are 14, 16, 10, 26, 13, and 20 words. Longer sentences allow for more complex ideas; shorter sentences give the reader a chance to breathe and absorb ideas.

~

### Element 17
### Alternate Short and Long Sentences

GOOD WRITING REQUIRES a mix of short and long sentences. Too many short sentences, without a break, feel like water torture: *Drip, drip, drip.* Too many long sentences feel like a difficult hike through a dense forest.

Alternating short and long sentences gives writing a pleasant tempo. The reader stays alert, ready to take in everything that comes along. Sometimes it's easy; sometimes it takes work.

Physiologically, we need variety. Any time we do something—including reading—we trigger a complex chain of chemical reactions. When we hear the booming opening of a song on the radio, we are aroused. We cannot help but take notice. But if that booming style continues for much longer, we get exhausted. So in the subsequent passage, the composer moves softly and sweetly. After developing those softer themes, she returns to harder themes.

That same process works in all forms of human expression and activity. Football games present a series of high-velocity, violent plays; between those plays, the players and fans get a respite as the quarterback huddles and the defense gets into position. Action movies likewise shift back and forth from action to respite. Even still art—painting and sculpture—shifts back and forth from action to repose.

Varying sentence lengths also helps to convey different moods. Short sentences usually indicate rapid action; longer sentences indicate a more complex idea. Great writers like Ernest Hemingway use both short and long sentences to capture the mood.

What counts as "short" and "long" has evolved over the years. In the last century, the average length of sentences has shrunk, as reading has become universal and the pace of life has quickened. The more people who read, the more writers have to appeal to the attention spans of those readers. Take a look at the average length of sentences of notable authors two or more centuries ago:

- Philip Sidney, *Arcadia* (1590): 75
- Thomas Hobbes, *The Leviathan* (1651): 39.26
- John Bunyan, *The Pilgrim's Progress* (1678-1684): 31.61
- John Locke, *An Essay on Human Understanding* (1690): 49.8
- Jonathan Swift, *The Battle of the Books* (1698): 39.8
- David Hume, *History of England* (1754): 39.8
- Sir Walter Scott, *Ivanhoe* (1820): 32.1

Now look at the average sentence lengths of authors from the last century:

- Ernest Hemingway, *The Old Man and the Sea* (1952): 14.4
- Richard Feynman, *Six Easy Pieces* (1961-63): 21.2
- Martin Luther King, *Why We Can't Wait* (1964): 12.4
- Truman Capote, *In Cold Blood* (1966): 14.5
- Stephen Hawking, *A Brief History of Time* (1988): 15.2
- Ken Follett, *The Pillars of the Earth* (1989): 12.4
- Jon Krakauer, *Into the Wild* (1996): 18.9
- William F. Buckley, *Nearer My God* (1997): 20.5

Research shows that today's readers best comprehend sentences that average 17 or 18 words. Feel free to write long sentences when you need to connect a wide range of ideas. Also feel free to be brief. Mix those long and short sentences around the average of 17 to 18 words and you will never lose your readers.

**Case Studies**
**Edward Robb Ellis's *The Epic of New York City* and Stewart Brand's *How Buildings Learn***

In 1887, a silk merchant named John Stearns bought a small parcel of land at 50 Broadway, in Lower Manhattan. Rather than build a standard stone masonry structure with thick walls, he decided to build a one of the first skyscrapers in New York. Stearns created a steel skeleton, supported by a cement foundation, which bore the weight of a 13-story structure.

Scientific calculations suggested that the building would survive the lashes of a major storm. But no one knew for sure. When a hurricane swept through the area, with winds up to 80 miles an hour, a crowd gathered to watch the spectacle. But Gilbert wanted to get close. Edward Rob Ellis describes the scene in these two paragraphs, formatted here with one sentence per line:

> Gilbert grabbed a plumb line and began climbing a ladder left in place by workmen when they had quit work the evening before.
> Stearns followed at his heels.
> From the crowd arose screams:
> "You fool!
> You'll be killed!"
> The architect and businessman could barely hear them above the shriek of the hurricane.
> Stearns's courage gave out when they reached the tenth floor.
> There he sprawled full length on a scaffold and held on for dear life.
> Gilbert, who felt the risk of his reputation was worth the risk of his life, continued to climb the ladder, rung by painful rung, his knuckles whitening with strain and gusts of wind battering him unmercifully.
> When he reached the 13th and top floor, he crawled on hands and knees along a scaffold.
> At a corner of the building he tugged the plumb line from a pocket, got a firm grip on one end of the cord, and dropped its leaden weight toward the Broadway sidewalk.
> He later reported, "There was not the slightest vibration.
> The building stood as steady as a rock in the sea."
>
> In that moment of triumph Gilbert rashly jumped to his feet on the scaffold.
> His hat had been tightly crushed on his head.
> Now he snatched it off and waved it exultantly.
> The wind knocked him down.
> It scudded him toward one end of the scaffold.
> He gulped.
> He prayed.
> Wildly he grabbed about him.
> Just as he was about to be swept off the end of the board and

down to certain death, he caught a rope lashing about in the
wind from an upright beam of the tower.

His grip held.

The rope held.

He steadied himself, eased down onto his knees, and carefully
picked his way back to the ladder.

Climbing down the ladder, he was joined by Stearns at the tenth
floor, and the two men then made their way slowly back to
street level.

Spectators cheered the heroes of the hour and gave way to let
them pass.

Locking arms, their chins upthrust, the architect and the
businessman marched up Broadway, dumbfounding Trinity
Church members just leaving the morning service by singing
in unison:

"Praise God from whom all blessings flow . . ."

Action scenes move briskly with a mix of short and long sentences. Short
sentences convey the series of actions. Longer sentences provide an opportunity to explain complex ideas, without interrupting the flow.

Yo-yoing short and long sentences also works for descriptive writing. Take
a look at this passage from Stewart Brand's *How Buildings Learn*:

Most building adaptation is, like most building evolution,
vernacular.

You don't have to look far to see it.

The majority of people live in homes they own.

The majority of workers work in offices.

Apart from high turnover retail spaces, where do you find the
highest rates of change within contemporary buildings?

In owner-occupied houses and in office buildings.

Whereas the remodeling of shops and restaurants is often the
work of professional designers, the constant change in homes
and offices is usually done by the occupants in a manner
classically vernacular—informal, pragmatic, alive with
offhand ingenuity, officially invisible.

Direct, amateur change is the norm.

In this passage, Brand writes sentences of 9, 9, 9, 7, 18, 7, 40, and 6 words.
After six short sentences, Brand gives us one Big Gulp sentence, and concludes
with another short sentence. He uses the short sentences to bring us to a more
complex topic—how buildings get renovated over time. At this point, he can
use lots of words without exhausting the reader.

~

### And Another Thing . . .

SOME WRITERS REBEL against the imperative of simple sentences. They say it robs them of the chance to develop their own style: *If William Faulkner can make long sentences work, why can't I?* Sure, Faulkner used meandering sentences to suggest the complexity of relationships and history and to evoke a Southern Gothic mood.

But wait. Before he broke away to create his own longform style, Faulkner mastered the fundamentals of simple sentence construction. Like Picasso, who mastered representational work before inventing cubism, Faulkner knew how to do all the basics. Look at this passage from *Light in August*:

> They enter the kitchen together, though Mrs. Armstid is in front. She goes straight to the stove. Lena stands just within the door. Her head is uncovered now, her hair combed smooth. Even the blue garment looks freshened and rested. She looks on while Mrs. Armstid at the stove clashes the metal lids and handles the sticks of wood with the abrupt savageness of a man. "I would like to help," Lena says.
>
> Mrs. Armstid does not look around. She clashes the stove savagely. "You stay where you are. You keep off your feet now, and you'll keep off your back awhile longer maybe."
>
> The young woman does not answer at once. Mrs. Armstid does not rattle the stove now, though her back is still toward the younger woman. Then she turns. They look at one another, suddenly naked, watching one another: the young woman in the chair, with her neat hair and her inert hands upon her lap, and the older one beside the stove, turning, motionless too, with a savage screw of gray hair at the base of her skull and a face that might have been carved in sandstone. Then the younger one speaks.

Faulkner's 16 sentences total 196 words, an average of 12 and a half words per sentence. The passage uses 145 single-syllable words, 44 two-syllable words, and seven three-syllable words. Simplicity itself.

Even when he wrote longer sentences, Faulkner delivered a series of clear blasts. You never get confused about who's doing or saying what to whom.

Faulkner mastered complexity. But before that, he mastered simplicity.

# 5

# WORDS

The difference between the right word and the almost right word is the difference between lightning and the lightning bug.

— MARK TWAIN

Open a book or magazine to a random page and find a word you don't know much about. You might be amazed by the journey of discovery that follows.

I did that once and found *adumbrate*. Merriam-Webster's online dictionary says *adumbrate*, a verb, means "to foreshadow vaguely" or "to suggest, disclose, or outline partially." A 1932 *New York Times* headline declares: "Events Adumbrate Happier Times." The word originates in the Latin *adumbrates*, a simple combination of *ad* ("to the") and *umbra* ("shadow").

As we consider adumbrate, look at its sister word *umbrage*. That word, meaning "vague suggestion" or "feeling of pique," also comes from the idea of a shadow. *Penumbra*, meaning the area of a shadow, offers another useful derivation. Americans learned this word when, in the 1974 *Roe* v. *Wade* decision, the Supreme Court ruled a woman's right to an abortion existed under the *penumbra* of the right to privacy.

Defining words is like going to a progressive dinner. You track down the meaning of one word, chew on it awhile, and then move on. You devour the next word, with all its flavors, and then move on again. At the end of the process, you understand a whole bunch of related words.

How many words do we actually need to communicate well? The average working vocabulary is 20,000 active words. For 95 percent of common texts—like newspapers, blogs, and memos—we use just 3,000 words.

Still, the greater your vocabulary, the more nuanced your understanding of the world. Every word offers distinctive ideas. Even when words are close in meaning—like *spoon* and *scoop*—knowing both allows you to describe things with greater precision.

Just because you have a large vocabulary doesn't mean you need to flaunt it. Think of words like utensils in a well-stocked kitchen. Your cabinets and drawers hold not just the basic pots and pans, spoons and knives, but also colanders, sifters, turners, whisks, tenderizers, and dozens of other tools. You would never use a sifter or a grater just because you owned it; you would use it only when it enabled you to do specific tasks better. Likewise with vocabulary. Build a rich supply, but use words only when they add value to your work.

Not many people spend time flipping through dictionaries and thesauruses. But it's not a bad idea to go on quests for just the right word, to look up the word you don't know—or don't know precisely—to build a bigger vocabulary. You might not see any need for a word like adumbrate right away, but just knowing it stretches your mind.

~

### Element 18
### Use Simple Words, Almost Always

GIVEN a choice of a simple or complex word, use the simple one. Given a choice of a short or long word, use the short one.

Simple words are democratic. Simple words invite more people to join the conversation. John Maeda, a designer at the MIT Media Lab, puts the matter, well, simply: "Complexity implies the feeling of being lost; simplicity implies the feeling of being found." When people feel "found," they can join the conversation.

When you use simple words well, you can bring more exotic, unfamiliar words into the mix without losing the audience. That was Shakespeare's approach. The Bard used twice as many words as other playwrights in Elizabethan England; he also invented whole new locutions, without bothering to define them. But he never confused his audience. He surrounded arcane references with common language and familiar situations. So even if a playgoer did not know a particular word, he could still follow the action.

Linguists talk about "density" to describe the simplicity or complexity of language. Dense writing uses more "content" words, that is, specific, specialized terms. In their study *Writing Science*, M.A.K. Halliday and J.R. Martin detail the density of five sentences. Look at these sentences below, which show content words in italics and density scores in parentheses:

- But we never did anything very much in *science* in our *school*. (2)

- My *father* used to *tell* me about a *singer* in his *village*. (4)
- A *parallelogram* is a *four-sided figure* with its *opposite sides parallel*. (6)
- The *atomic nucleus absorbs* and *emits energy* in *quanta*, or *discrete units*. (8)
- *Griffith's energy balance approach* to *strength* and *fracture* also *suggested* the *importance* of *surface chemistry* in the *mechanical behavior* of *brittle materials*. (13)

We read the first few sentences easily. But the later sentences come hard. If we know only six of the eight content words in the fourth sentence, we might not understand the point. Even when we know all eight terms, we might still struggle. It's just too much to process.

Distracted by bunches of complex words, readers struggle to process passages. So always look for the simplest word. When you need to use a technical word, define it. If you define it well, it *becomes* simple for your reader. Take the term *atomic nucleus*. Until we reached high school chemistry or physics, that was a complex, abstract term for most of us; afterwards, it became simple.

What about using a variety of words? Variety, of course, can keep your writing sprightly. But variety for variety's sake just causes distraction. Use the simplest word possible for the occasion.

Consider one of the most useful verbs you'll ever see: *To say*. Novices often use different words to say *said*, especially when writing dialogue. So they say that a president *argues, declares*, and *cajoles*. A ballplayer *stutters, barks*, and *mumbles*. A philosopher *cogitates, elucidates, complains*, and *demurs*. These synonyms disrupt the flow of ideas. Avoid that distraction; just say *said*. If someone says something interesting, you don't need to dress it up with synonyms.

The same standard applies to foreign words. Given a choice between a foreign and an English word, use the English one. Expressions like *rendezvous* (meeting), *bete noire* (something dreaded), *faux pas* (mistake), *gauche* (clumsy), *raison d'etre* (purpose for being), *wunderkind* (prodigy) do not, by themselves, damage a sentence. You can use them once in a while. But take care. They can annoy and distract the reader.

### Case Studies
### John McPhee's *In Suspect Terrain* and Adam Goodheart's '9.11.01'

John McPhee, the master of long-form journalism, explains complex subjects by using a layman's vocabulary. Open any McPhee work and pick a random paragraph.

Here, McPhee's *In Suspect Terrain* explains the geologic foundations of New York's skyscrapers:

The towers of midtown, as one might imagine, were emplaced in substantial rock, … that once had been heated near the point of melting, had recrystallized, had been heated again, had recrystallized, and, while not particularly competent, was more than adequate to hold up those buildings. Most important, it was right at the surface. You could see it, in all its micaceous glitter, shining like silver in the outcrops of Central Park. Four hundred and 50 million years in age, it was called Manhattan schist. All through midtown, it was at or near the surface, but in the region south of Thirtieth Street it began to fall away, and at Washington Square it descended abruptly. The whole saddle between midtown and Wall Street would be underwater, were it not filled with many tens of fathoms of glacial till.

McPhee sprinkles technical terms in this passage, but not so many that you need to scramble to a dictionary. By creating vivid, accessible scenes, McPhee helps the reader understand even difficult ideas by understanding the larger context.

McPhee uses contrast to show New York's luck in its deep hard geologic foundation:

New York grew high on the advantage of its hard rock, and, New York being what it is, cities all over the world have attempted to resemble it. The skyline of nuclear Houston, for example, is a simulacrum of Manhattan's. Houston rests on 12,000 feet of montmorillonitic clay, a substance that, when moist, turns into mobile jelly. After taking so much money out of the ground, the oil companies of Houston have put hundreds of millions back in. Houston is the world's foremost city in fat basements. Its tall buildings are magnified duckpins, bobbing in their own mire.

Because his words are mostly simple, McPhee can offer unfamiliar terms (like *montmorillonitic*) when he wants to offer precision. Like all great writers, McPhee offers value to both specialists and lay readers. Commonplace reference points, offered one by one, help us to understand less familiar ideas.

Above all else, McPhee shows patience, so he can introduce complex ideas without overwhelming the reader. McPhee is happy to take as long as he needs to expand our vocabulary so that we can follow his story.

Now look at Adam Goodheart's description of the technologies that made skyscrapers like the World Trade Center possible:

If architects had only steel to work with, the interiors of their skyscrapers would have just been little more than dark and dreary warrens. Office towers of ten and 20 stories required, for their basic functioning, a whole list of innovations that are now taken for granted, but that were still brand new in the second half of the nineteenth century: electric lights and central heating, passenger elevators and fire escapes, telephones and flush toilets. As fate had it, all these appeared on the American scene at approximately the same time, and all of them, moreover, required a wholly new type of city to support them: one with reliable, centrally managed electric and gas companies, sewer systems, water mains, fire departments, elevator inspectors, telephone operators, trash collectors. Did the modern city give birth to the skyscraper, or vice versa? The answer, probably, is a bit of both.

Of this passage's 147 words, 91 are only one syllable, 31 are two, 19 are three, five are four, and one is five. The shortness of the words—83 percent are just one or two syllables—keeps the pace brisk. Of course, length does not correspond perfectly with simplicity. Some short words express complex ideas and some long words express simple ideas. But in this case, simplicity rules.

～

### Element 19
### Use Longer Words as Precision Instruments

"EVERYTHING IS vague to a degree you do not realize," Bertrand Russell once said, "till you have tried to make it precise."

When you cannot express an idea precisely with short words, use longer ones. Don't worry about length or origin. Use the word that best states the concept you want to explore.

To describe a smooth, sweet flow of sounds, use *mellifluous*. To describe dominance of certain ideas in society, use the term *hegemony*. To refer to Gandhi's system of nonviolent direct action, use *Satyagraha*. To describe religious beliefs about the end of time, use *eschatological*.

These may not be common dime-store words. But they give us precision that other words lack. Most readers can handle esoteric words if you provide a simple definition or create the right context. Don't show off, but use big or exotic words when they do the work that small words cannot.

To explain a technical issue, you often need to deploy specialized vocabulary. An architect, for example, needs to use concepts like *articulation, massing,* and *fenestration* to explore design. None of the concepts is difficult when explained. But with too many arcane, unfamiliar concepts, the reader can get overwhelmed. As long as you define your technical vocabulary—simply, at the moment of use—you won't overwhelm your readers.

Check each word's precise meaning. Start with the dictionary. You might be amazed what you discover. Because we usually learn vocabulary by hearing others use words, in print or in speech, we often miss the full meaning of those words. And so we use words imprecisely in our own writing.

Let me give an example. For years, I used the word *fulsome* to mean abundant or copious. And I was right. But fulsome also means, according to Merriam-Webster, "aesthetically, morally, or generally offensive." When I looked up the word, my understanding shifted. "Fulsome praise" refers not only to enthusiastic plaudits, but also to treacly or manipulative praise. I now remember both the positive and negative connotations.

While we're on the subject of *treacly*, which means sickly sweet or sentimental, let me relate another dictionary discovery. Treacly derives from treacle, which refers to a medicine used to treat poisonous bites. Treacle also refers to a blend of molasses, invert sugar, and corn syrup. Now that I know more than one dimension of treacly, I might deploy that word in new contexts.

A writer named Ammon Shea once spent a year reading the 20-volume *Oxford English Dictionary*. He discovered hundreds of words that work more precisely than common words. *Petrichor* refers to the loamy scent that comes after a spring rain, *prend* to a mended crack, a *vicambulist* to someone who wanders around cities, and a *kankedort* to an awkward situation. If any of these words can express a thought most precisely—and you do not string out a long sequence of words that only a sesquipedalian reader could digest—then go ahead and use it. There is nothing wrong with prompting someone to use a dictionary once in a while.

When you choose words, don't just consider the precise definition. Consider the sounds they make and the feelings and ideas they evoke. I like *kankedort* and *prend*, in part, because they sound like what they describe. *Kankedort* sounds clumsy, unsmooth: an awkward situation. *Prend* rhymes with *mend*.

To discover the most precise vocabulary, explore the language of experts. If you write about health, plunge into the details of cellular biology, nutrition, and energy. If you write about politics, go deep into all the areas of policy and rhetoric and debate. If you write about sports, make a list of every move on the field, court, or rink. Every realm has a long list of precision verbs. Find them and use the ones most suitable to your audience.

## Case Study
### Kevin Lynch's *The Image of the City*

Years ago, I coordinated a planning project for the City of Boston. Most evenings, I held open meetings in the city's 16 major neighborhoods. My job was to ask people what worked, what didn't work, and what they would like to change in their neighborhoods. Citizen complaints centered on fragmented streetscapes, badly designed parks, underutilized buildings, ugly architecture, scary transit stations, polluted rivers and streams, noise and visual pollution, to name just a few.

Occasionally, in meetings and documents, we used terms that baffled the neighborhood folks. We talked about *streetscapes, transit-oriented development, legibility, continuity,* and *focal points.* At first I considered these terms simple and ordinary. What idea could be more obvious than, say, *transit-oriented development*? TOD, to use the shorthand, is a form of development (like housing, retail and offices) that is organized around transit (like subway stations and bus stops). The idea seemed as simple as it was sensible. Why not build more homes and businesses close to subway stops? That way, people could get to work without a car—and fewer cars might crowd the streets.

Since we were spending all our working hours with planners, architects, preservationists, and developers, those terms *seemed* simple to me and my planning colleagues. But some neighborhood folks thought we were using unnecessary lingo, putting on airs and trying to confuse them with our fancy-pants planning lingo. A simple idea to me was foreign to others. Any time you work in a specialized field, you have to be careful about using terminology that is not obvious to your audience.

Open any classic work on planning and you will find a number of these geeky/technical terms. Here's a partial glossary from Kevin Lynch's classic *The Image of the City*:

- *Legibility*: How easy it is to recognize the elements of a place, like major buildings, paths, landmarks, borders, and forbidden areas.
- *Imageability*: The qualities of an object that make it easy to visualize and understand.
- *Cues*: The signs, usually visual, that help guide and orient people in a place.
- *Wayfinding*: The ability to know where you are—and to spot important landmarks—while on a journey.
- *Emotional security*: The feeling of ease that people feel while using a place.
- *Orientation*: How well an area helps people to know where they are and move around.
- *Focal point*: An object, often a building or monument, that attracts people's attention.
- *Apparency*: The clarity with which something—a building, path, ornamentation, design, messages—presents itself in a community.
- *Perceptual learning*: The process of understanding the physical object, which occurs by comparing that object with previous experience and the larger context.
- *Visual hierarchy*: The arrangement of things in space, from one extreme to another (usually along the lines of importance).
- *Line of motion*: The direction and speed of travel, which is affected by the straightness of the path and
- *Nodes*: An intersection of paths, which provide opportunities for moving in a different direction.

- *Decision points*: The place, on a path or other part of a space, where a person needs to figure out how to proceed.
- *Singularity:* The extent to which an object—like a statue or building or window—stands out against all others.
- *Gradients*: How different scales of objects or spaces are arranged. For example, most homes move from public spaces (foyer, living room, dining room) to less public spaces (kitchen, bedrooms, bathrooms, study, playroom).

None of these concepts is especially difficult. All, in fact, refer to common experiences and ideas. But when using any specialized lingo, take care. When introducing an idea, define it right away—as simply as possible, with an example or two. And never overwhelm readers by packing these terms close together.

∼

### Element 20
### Use Active Verbs, Even to Describe Passivity

VERBS POWER WRITING. Verbs show people doing things—cooking meals, throwing balls, shopping for clothes, singing songs, talking with neighbors ... everything that makes the world work.

Active verbs engage the parts of the brain involved in performing actions. When you use phrases like "She threw the ball" or "He sang the song," you activate the parts of the brain involved in kicking and singing. The mere use of the words arouses those physical sensations.

To make writing a physical experience, use active verbs. Stimulate the reader's brain by showing someone *dance, shuffle, skip,* and *amble; buy, sell, spend,* and *invest; sleep, dream,* and *wake; sit, lie,* and *lay; add, subtract, multiply,* and *divide; drink, sip, eat,* and *chew; love, hate, tolerate, ignore,* and *scrutinize; know, notice,* and *show; break, rip, fix, patch,* and *repair; sing, hum, twist* and *shout; teach, learn, listen, hear, accept,* and *ask; play* and *pray, run, gun* and *whisper; work, clean, put, organize, cut, hurt, heal, count,* and *draw; mess, straighten,* and *sort; travel, drive, park, speed, slow down, merge,* and *cut off.*

You get the idea. I listed all those verbs to suggest the wide range of actions in this world. Read those words again. Note when the words produce a *physical reaction.* Interesting, isn't it, just how physically it can be to decipher squiggles on a page?

Make a habit of searching for verbs in your reading. Read modern authors like Tom Wolfe, John Irving, Elizabeth Gilbert, Frank McCourt, Philip Roth, Dave Eggers, Jonathan Safran Foer, and Anne Lamott. See how they use verbs to create a motion picture.

Pick up a dictionary and a thesaurus. Look for lists of verbs. I know, that sounds mechanical, contrived, and nerdy, but it isn't. It's just a way of acquiring more tools for your toolbox. A pulp novelist named Deanna Carlyle published *1,000 Verbs To Write By*, a collection organized by kinds of action— variations on the verbs *walk, run, jump, touch, took, pull, push, had, held, put, hit, was, react, sit, stand, smell, taste, think, say, hear, lie, enter, feel, seem, leave,* and *turn.* Trolling such lists strengthens your word power.

Our world is one giant field of energy. Wherever we go, energy either bursts out or gets suppressed. The reader needs to see, feel, hear—*the reader needs to experience*—that energy.

## Case Study
### Pete Hamill's *Downtown*

Using active and telling verbs requires hard work. Using *to be* and *to have* —which essentially asserts that one side relates somehow to another thing —comes easily. *To be* and *to have* work fine for simple statements, to offer a pause in the action. But to drive our prose forward, we need action words.

In this passage, Pete Hamill remembers his early years as a reporter for the *New York Post*, exploring the streets of New York:

> On mornings when I had little money, or worked past the deadlines on other stories, I would leave the Post through the Washington Street exit and head for Broadway. The great street at that hour was usually thick with frantic people, bumping one another, dodging 'round one another, grumbling their apologies, then dashing across the paths of careening taxicabs. I loved plunging into the tumult, knowing that I was on my own while almost everyone else was going to work. My treks took me past Trinity and the Equitable Building, where I had lounged away so many lunch hours, then into the rushing infantry rising from the subways at Fulton Street. In a coffee shop with a street counter, I'd buy a cardboard cup of coffee and a cheese Danish. I had the morning papers with me, but usually I also had a book. On days of decent weather, I'd head for City Hall Park. There I'd bow my head in reverence to the Woolworth Building (often humming some lines from the tune "Million Dollar Baby"), find a bench, sip the coffee, and gaze at the vanished majesties of Park Row.

Look at the verbs in this paragraph: *had, worked, leave, head, was, bumping, dodging, grumbling, dashing, loved, knowing, plunging, was, going, took, lounged, rising, buy, had, had, head, bow, humming, find, sip,* and *gaze.*

Out of 26 verbs, only five were forms of *to be* or *to have*. The rest, action verbs, show Hamill living life to the fullest.

∾

## Element 21
## Avoid the Verbs 'To Be' and 'To Have'

OVERUSING the verbs *to be* and *to have* ruins more writing than any other habit. *To be* and *to have* do not show people actively doing things; they just indicate some state of existence. I call them couch-potato words. They just lie around, passively, while the rest of the world acts with purpose.

Most writers cannot resist using these verbs. In fact, seven forms of the verbs *to be* and *to have* rank among the 35 most-used words in the English language, according to the *American Heritage Word Frequency Book*. That's *one in five* words. No other verbs appear on that list.

Let's look at some passages from business memos and college papers. Start with this passage from an insurance analyst:

> 2010 showed the major risks we *have* to cope with. There *were* a number of severe earthquakes. The hurricane season *was* also eventful—it *was* just fortunate that the tracks of most of the storms remained over the open sea. ... The severe earthquakes and the hurricane season with so many storms demonstrate once again that there must *be* no slackening of our efforts to analyze these risks in detail and provide the necessary insurance covers at adequate prices.

This clunky passage contains only five instance of *to be* and *to have*. But those passive verbs pull the passage away from simple, clear thinking. So the passage wanders on, for 79 words. These 22 words convey the ideas much more clearly:

> The earthquakes and hurricanes of 2010 reveal the costly risks of severe weather —and the need to analyze risks to insure property.

Simple and clear. Two verbs—show and analyze—enliven the shorter passage. The verbs act like magnets, giving shape to the filings of the other words.

Consider the following pairs of sentences. The first set shows sentences using *to be* and *to have*; the second set shows sentences with strong action verbs. Which sentences work better?

### Sentences Using Passive Voice
The Episcopal Church is caught between rival factions of the gay marriage controversy.

Immigration officials have a hard time patrolling the Mexican border.

Mitt Romney's choice of a running mate is expected a month before the convention.

**Sentences Using Active Voice**

Conservative and liberal factions of the Episcopal Church
    disagree about the ordination of gay priests.
Coyotes and drug smugglers overwhelm immigration officials at
    the Mexican border
Mitt Romney will pick his running mate a month before the
    convention.

The sentences in the second set, with active verbs, convey more precise information. They also force us to look for more details, which bring a scene to life. You know who's doing what to whom.

In my years as a college teacher, I struggled to get my students to use action verbs. Despite my preaching the power of action verbs, my students continued to use *to be* and *to have* without much thought. Habits die hard, right? Without a concerted effort to stop, most of us maintain bad habits. We do what's easiest. We take the course of least resistance.

What to do? One day, at wit's end, I banned the verbs *to be* and *to have* from the next paper assignment. I knew it was a radical step. It's unnatural to remove the two most common verbs from your vocabulary. But I wanted to force my students to look for active verbs that conveyed exactly what they wanted to say.

When I first issued the ban, students grumbled and complained. "All kinds of great writers use *to be* and *to have*!" they cried. "This makes writing even a simple sentence hard!"

True, true. But sometimes you need an artificial constraint to develop a skill. Musicians, athletes, surgeons, actors, standup comics—everyone who wants to do something well—achieve mastery by isolating skills for deliberate, concerted practice. They focus, intently, on changing their behavior, converting lazy actions into purposeful actions. Coaches call it "deep practice." Such work helps to transform bad habits into good habits.

The ban worked. The students wrote the strongest sentences I had ever seen in college papers. The previous week's batch of papers contained dozens of unclear sentences. This new batch contained not one. And so we continued the ban all semester. Under the ban, no student gave me a single paper with an unclear sentence. Amazing.

The ban, I must admit, produced some silly passages. Instead of saying "She *had* an impressive library," you'd get "She *possessed* an impressive library." Does "possessed" really work better than "had"? In this case, no. I'd like to see something like this: "She owns hundreds of books in a number of disciplines—psychology, philosophy, history, and fiction." Or: "She accumulated an impressive library."

So what happened to the ban? After a few weeks, amended it. I allowed students to use *to be* and *to have*—but only when they explained, in a footnote, why it worked better than other possibilities.

Once you kick the *to be*-and-*to have* habit, you can go back to using these verbs when they work best. But stay on guard. Do not let passivity creep back into your work. Every time you write a draft, search your document for all forms of these verbs—*am, is, are, was, are, were, been, has, have, had*. If possible, replace them with verbs that convey action.

## Case Studies
### Edward R. Ford's *The Details of Modern Architecture* and Janette Sadik-Khan's *Street Fight*

Despite the imprecision and passivity of *to be* and *to have*, these two work-horses often serve useful functions. They offer clear statements of the *conditions of life*. True, they fail to capture movement and action; but they do provide worthwhile snapshots. Consider this passage from Edward Ford's *The Details of Modern Architecture:*

> Construction *is* not mathematics; architectural construction *is* just as subjective a process as is architectural design. Construction *involves* a more complex set of concerns, the application of scientific laws, and a tradition (or perhaps a conventional wisdom) as to how things *ought to be* built, but that tradition and that wisdom *are* no more or less valid then they tradition or conventional wisdom as to how buildings should appear.

Or look at this passage from Janette Sadik-Khan's *Street Fight,* her memoir of her years as transportation commissioner in New York City:

> There *were* likely practical reasons why Broadway took the path it did; it may *have been* the shortest distance between precolonial settlements in Manhattan, avoiding hills, rivers, and swamps. Any sense, Broadway *was* New York City's earliest desire line. Desire lines *are* naturally occurring travel patterns that reflect where people naturally want to travel. In modern urban planning, desire lines *are* the natural, spontaneous way that people use public spaces, often contradicting the way the space was designed. These signatures *are* usually direct, practical, and leave physical evidence, like a footpath worn into a park lawn where pedestrians cut a corner to get from one sidewalk to another. They may also *become* visible over time and reveal themselves deductively, such as when people ride bikes through a park for one block to reach a bridge entrance instead of taking a three-block route along one-way streets.

Now let me pose a challenge to you. Rewrite these passages to eliminate all uses of *to be* and *to have*. When do these verbs offer *the best possible way* to express a thought? And when do they muddle the discussion and suck the energy out of the passages?

~

### Element 22
### Avoid Bureaucratese and Empty-Calorie Words

A GLUT of gross and pretentious words is the curse of our bureaucratic age.

Bureaucrats avoid simple speech for three reasons—to provide shorthand for insiders, to obscure and avoid difficult questions, and to avoid the hard work of simple expression.

**Shorthand**: To write for broad audiences, professionals use general categories (e.g., "people," "low-income," "test scores") and acronyms (e.g., SES, ROI, FAR, at-risk). Shorthand, of course, can be useful. But when we pack passages with too much jargon, we lose all sense of the subject. We make matters abstract.

Professionals also put -ize at the end of nouns to make them into verbs. "Let's prioritize our goals," a government planner says. "Parents need to regularize their routines," a child psychologist says. What's wrong with that? Simple: It prevents us from thinking through what we want to say. Avoid -ize by saying that "Let's decide what's most important" or "Parents need to set routines."

The -ism ending, common among academics, is almost as bad. It oversimplifies everything. Look at this collection of -isms: liberalism, conservatism, fascism, communism, socialism, capitalism, Marxism, Maoism, feminism, pacifism, Bushisms, and a hundred more. As catch-all terms, -isms indicate a general idea. Too often, though, these broad terms avoid the details that matter.

**Avoidance**: To avoid controversy, bureaucrats and professionals steer clear of language that might, in some way or other, offend one group or another.

We dance around words about race, sex, religion, handicap, age, class, and even beauty. We don't want to insult anyone with bluntness or crudeness, but as a result we avoid speaking the truth.

Consider how we address people we once called crippled. Because the word started to sound awkward or mean, we replaced it with *handicapped*, then *disabled*, then *physically challenged*, and finally *differently able*. But a writer named Nancy Mairs, who happens to be handicapped, insists on calling herself crippled. "I refuse to pretend that the only differences between you and me are the various ordinary ones that distinguish any one person from another," she writes. The euphemisms, she says, amount to avoidance at best and a patronizing and superior attitude at worst.

In his classic *1984*, George Orwell coined the term "Newspeak" to indicate language that deliberately mislead. Politicians and bureaucrats use Newspeak to deny unpleasant truths. So *taxes* become *revenue enhancements*, terrorists become *freedom fighters*, deaths of civilians becomes *collateral damage*, and an invasion becomes an *incursion*.

**Laziness**: There is one last reason bureaucrats and specialists use gross and pretentious language. They get lazy. Consider the following pairs of words.

Help—Facilitate
Set priorities—Prioritize
Near—In proximity to
About—Approximately
Give—Distribute
Use—Utilize
If—In the event that
Size—Magnitude
About—Approximately

The first words in these pairs are simple, clear, and sprightly. The second words are long, clumsy, overblown. Too often we use the second of these expressions. The question is why.

This language is common in big organizations, where officious officials try to puff up their own importance. When you work with such people, it's easier to use the ugly words than simple, sprightly words. We get lazy and our language suffers.

How we speak, George Orwell argues in "Politics and the English Language," determines whether we think clearly enough to maintain our freedom. "If you simplify your English, you are freed from the worst follies of orthodoxy," he said. "[W]hen you make a stupid remark its stupidity will be obvious, even to yourself."

To understand anything well, we need to strip it down to its essentials. To do that, avoid bureaucratese and words that lie.

## Case Study
### Rory Stott's '150 Weird Words Only Architects Use'

Like all specialists, architects and planners have a language all their own. The *enfilade* of their words present a *facade* or *skin* of *materiality* that *negotiates* and *deconstructs* the *motifs* of their *esoteric* work.

Got it?

The words in italics come from Rory Stott's enlightening, sometimes scary, survey of architectural lingo. Some other examples:

Pastiche ... vault ... Sustainability ... arcade ... ergonomy ... fenestration ... genus loci ... truncated ... charrette ... parti ... regionalism ... phenomenology ... threshold ... Brutalism ... massing ... cantilever ... postindustrial ... curvilinear ... Corbusian ... diagrammatic ... rectilinear ... vernacular ... modular ... permaculture ... blobitecture ... exurbia ... modular ... deconstruction ...

typology ... parametric ... walkability ... program ... verticality ... skin ... mullion ... building envelope ... gentrification ...

These words offer value to discussions of architecture and planning. They describe specific concepts, often with telling metaphors. The challenge is to make sure to define and illustrate each concept before applying it to a description or analysis.

As Stott points, out, architects often convert simple, sprightly words into obscure, technical lingo. Some examples include *concept, space, fabric, negotiate, dynamic, language, gesture, proud, grain,* and *device.* With this *repurposing*—another of my favorites!—architects sometimes confuse people. Ordinary people use fabric to refer to the materials of clothes, curtains, drapes, and the like; architects use it to refer to the material qualities of buildings and townscapes. Fair enough. Just make sure to place the word into context, so readers understand whether you refer to the term's ordinary or technical meaning.

Architects also love obscure words like *organic, sequence, iteration, juxtapose, liminal, ephemeral, hybrid, generative, paradigm,* and *morphology.* Many of these terms perform useful work: They refer to specific things or processes for which other words would be inadequate. The challenge is to define and illustrate the words before using them.

~

### Element 23
### Avoid Aggressive Adjectives and Adverbs

Do you want to write smart, clever, witty, creative, insightful, brainy, surprising, fresh, analytic, engaging, scintillating, and even thrilling prose?

Then avoid using adjectives like those in the previous paragraph. Use adjectives only to express something specific, to set up a description, or to surprise the reader.

The French philosopher Voltaire once called adjectives the "enemies of nouns." Rather than coming up with just the right nouns, we fall back on blah nouns and dress them up with adjectives.

Adjectives fail us for two reasons: They are vague and exhausting.

**1. Vague**: Too often, adjectives just wave at meaning. Consider the following adjectives: *big, strong, smart, unique, tall, tired, quick, fat.* Each of these words raises the question: Compared to what?

Take a look at these sentences that rely on adjectives:

> They live in a huge house.
> The company agreed to a complicated settlement.
> Vanderbilt has a rigorous liberal arts curriculum.
> Molly is an accomplished girl.

Now look at sentences that use specific information.

> The 6,000-square-foot house sits in five acres of woods.
> The company agreed to a 329-page settlement, which details 16 separate provisions and defines 46 terms.
> Vanderbilt students must take at least two courses in seven out of eight "core" subject areas.
> In addition to winning a National Merit Scholarship, Molly plays soccer, edits the student newspaper, and performs in a local theater.

Which provides the best view of the subject? It depends on your goal. To make a general point and move on, use the sentences in the first group. To give a clear picture, use those in the second group.

**2. Exhausting.** Adjectives do the most damage in clusters. When we use bunches of adjectives, we risk dizzying the reader. Consider Thomas Wolfe's *Look Homeward, Angel*:

> The nostalgic thrill of dew-wet mornings in Spring, the cherry scent, the cool clarion earth, the wet loaminess of the garden, the pungent breakfast smells and the floating snow of blossoms ... inchoate sharp excitement of hot dandelions in young earth ... good male smell of his father's sitting-room ... smooth worn leather sofa, with the gaping horse-hair rent ... blistered varnished wood upon the hearth ... the brown tired autumn earth ... fat limp underdone bacon ... large deep-hued string beans smoking-hot ...

Exhausted? Me too.

Of course, we need adjectives. Consider the passages "He wore a red hat" and "Young jockeys prefer experienced horses." These adjectives all perform useful work. Why? "Red" refers to something specific; "young" and "experienced" make clear comparisons. As summary statements, these work fine.

So when do adjectives work well? Adjective work best when they orient the reader, usually by setting up a more detailed description. They also may work when they elicit surprise—when they jolt the reader. Let's get a little deeper.

**1. Precise:** Adjectives work best when they refer to a one-and-only thing. The adjectives *unique, first, blue, stationary,* and *transitory* say something precise. *Unique* means one of a kind. *Blue* is a specific color (*royal blue* or *baby blue* or *periwinkle* might work better). *First* refers to a singular position. *Stationary* contrasts with something in movement. *Transitory* means something that does not last.

**2. Setup:** Adjectives often perform a useful service introducing a complex idea. Consider the following passage: "Vanderbilt has a rigorous liberal arts program. Students must take at least two classes in seven "distribution" areas.

The adjective "rigorous" gives you a general idea; "two classes in seven areas" explains that idea.

**3. Sensations**: Sometimes adjectives evoke useful sensations. Wolfe's phrase "wet loaminess of the garden" works. But for this phrase to resonate, the reader needs a moment to soak up the sensation. When the adjectives come fast, one after another, we cannot process all the sensations. If you use an adjective, make it specific.

**4. Surprise**: Adjectives work best when they surprise the reader. I smiled when I read Thomas Lynch's description of a vacation on the beach at Santa Barbara, California: "The Pacific was pacific." The Book of Jeremiah talks about a "basket of naughty figs." That suggests a way to find surprising adjectives: use adjectives in unfamiliar contexts. So we might talk about an "impatient smile" or an "ambitious fear." In these examples, the adjective serves as a metaphor.

Mark Twain once had good advice for editing: "Substitute 'damn' every time you're inclined to write 'very'; your editor will delete it and the writing will be just as it should be." Try the same trick for adjectives.

Now, about those adverbs . . .

Years ago, Gabriel Garcia Marquez started going to AA—Adverbs Anonymous. Admitting that adverbs held a power over his writing that he could not control, he stopped using adverbs altogether.

Adverbs—modifiers of verbs, usually ending in -ly—damage writing even more than adjectives. If you use an adverb, it means you're probably not using an action verb.

Consider the following passages:

> She walked briskly down the street.
> He eyed her knowingly across the bar.
> He hungrily ate the Chinese food.
> She eagerly plunged into the consulting project.

Words like "briskly," "knowingly," "hungrily," and "eagerly" do not tell us anything specific. When we say that someone ate hungrily, for example, we have an idea that he attacked the plate with zeal. But what does that mean? Did he eat a whole meal in ten minutes? Did he eat food he normally refuses? Did he eat so quickly that he got indigestion? Did he eat faster than everyone else? Did he eat off others' plates?

Even when adverbs *seem* to describe something, they often just repeat ideas; presumably, a person would not eat food unless he was hungry. If he eats for other reasons—boredom, frustration, nervousness—paint the whole picture so the reader can figure it out.

When you find an adverb in your drafts, cut it and see if the sentence loses meaning. The verb probably does enough work on its own. If not, consider using a different verb, which conveys action. "He ran to get to the meeting" beats "He moved quickly to get to the meeting." One more example: "The crowd greeted the speaker with boos and catcalls" beats "The crowd treated the speaker rudely."

Search your drafts for these common adverbs: *again, also, always, constantly, down, even, ever, frequently, generally, hardly, here, how, however, in general, increasingly, just, more, most, mostly, never, no longer, normally, now, occasionally, off, often, on, once, only, out, over, rarely, really, regularly, so, sometimes, still, then, there, too, twice, up, usually, very,* and *well.*

Occasionally adverbs offer brevity, a virtue. "The bicyclist deftly avoided the runner," then, might work better than "The bicyclist moved off the sidewalk to avoid the runner." Whatever you do, do so *consciously.*

### Case Study
### Justin Davidson's 'The Master' and Herbert Muschamp's 'The Miracle in Bilbao'

Critics love hyperbole. Their job description is to judge others, usually on deadline. They often assess things—buildings, movies, books, music—on the basis of first impressions. In their judgments, critics often do not have the time to observe closely or second-guess their early assessments. Rather than going deep, they resort to adjectives and adverbs.

Consider this brief passage from a magazine profile of I.M. Pei, the architect whose masterpieces include the addition to the Museum of Fine Arts in Boston, the east wing of the National Gallery in Washington, the Bank of China Tower in Hong Kong, the Mesa Laboratory of the National Center for Atmospheric Research in Colorado, and Kips Bay Plaza in New York City.

> Pei was working as Zeckendorf's in-house architect in the '50s, when he designed the affordable-housing complex at Kips Bay Plaza. The immense grids of precast concrete can feel gloomy and even anti-urban in their brooding, repetitive length, but at the time, their muscular minimalism seemed boldly idiosyncratic, a world away from the generic brick boxes of public housing. The project was a triumph of stinginess and practicality, the kind of accomplishment that might have led to a life of frictionless corporate servitude. ...
>
> Eventually, he visited the Anasazi village carved into the earth at Mesa Verde National Park and came away determined to fashion something similarly powerful, perpetual, and enigmatic. He produced a cluster of reddish concrete columns, as heavy and pensive as a stand of spruces or Rodin's *Burghers of Calais.* With thick walls, sparse windows, and narrow balconies hooded by slablike roofs, the complex's stony beauty suggests both the mysteries of science and the ruggedness necessary to study the pitiless weather.

Behold the cascade of adjectives and adverbs in this short passage: *in-house, affordable, immense, precast, gloomy, anti-urban, brooding, repetitive, muscular, boldly, generic, brick, public, frictionless, powerful, perpetual, enigmatic, reddish, concrete, heavy, pensive, thick, sparse, narrow slablike, stony, ruggedness,* and *pitiless.* Many of these 28 descriptors add value. But not all. Which ones fail to evoke images? Which ones are too vague and therefore add much to the passage? For those weaklings, how might we do better?

In "The Miracle in Bilbao," Herbert Muschamp compares Marilyn Monroe's performance in *The Misfits* with Frank Gehry's Guggenheim Museum, a structure of vast titanium curves that sits on the banks of the Nervion River:

> What twins the actress and the building in my memory is that both of them stand for an American style of freedom. That style is voluptuous, emotional, intuitive and exhibitionist. It is mobile, fluid, material, mercurial, fearless, radiant and as fragile as a newborn child. It can't resist doing a dance with all the voices that say "No." It wants to take up a lot of space. And when the impulse strikes, it likes to let its dress fly up in the air.

Muschamp uses his adjectives the way a meat-and-potatoes man puts sour cream on his potato. He tosses it in big dollops: first "voluptuous, emotional, intuitive and exhibitionist," then "mobile, fluid, material, mercurial, fearless, radiant and fragile." Since the reader probably comes to the piece with images of Bilbao and Monroe, these adjectives speak to something specific. Still, Muschamp's liberality with adjectives gets overwhelming. Avoid the temptation to use such linguistic globs.

### And Another Thing . . .

Picture a child curled up on a window bench reading a book. Or a commuter as she grabs a strap on a subway while reading a newspaper. Or a college student peering into a computer screen to read a blog or document.

Reading looks passive, but really it's physical. Our job, as writers, is to provide enough energy—and enough emotion—to keep the reader physically engaged.

Specific, precise words help us to get the reader physically involved. Abstract words create a distance between the subject and the reader. If I read about the "collateral damage" of war, I will approach the subject with detachment; if I read about guerrillas or drones killing innocent people, I get a sense of the violence and feel empathy for the victims. If I hear abstract arguments about global warming, I feel detached; if I see the human tragedies of Hurricane Katrina, I respond emotionally.

But emotions don't just prompt us to care. They also prompt us to *think.*

Consider debates about diet. When we think of "meat" or "poultry" abstractly—as just another commodity in the grocer's refrigerator—we think shallowly. But when we think about how chicken farms operate—when we see the animals confined in small spaces without light, pumped with hormones, made so fat they cannot even stand—we develop a deeper understanding of the issue.

When possible, then avoid abstractions. Use words that touch people *physically and emotionally*. Use words that connect the reader with the subject, vividly and intimately. Then you'll be able to combine the best of both heart and mind.

# III

---

# DESCRIBING A PLACE

A well-designed and well-functioning place improves the lives of everyone in the community. A great place can make people more efficient and creative, happy and connected, energetic and centered. A great place makes people more complete and whole.

In *The Timeless Way of Building*, the architect Christopher Alexander called the sum total of these attributes the "Quality Without a Name." I call it QWAN, for short.

QWAN speaks not just to a place's physical makeup but also its values and aspirations. It reflects the *soul* of a place.

Great places do not just provide the opportunity for people to *do things*. Homes don't just provide containers for us to rest, eat, sleep, and get ready for life outside. Parks don't just provide containers for play. Schools don't just offer containers for learning.

Great places also create *meaning*. They help people to nurture relationships with others. They help us to explore how the world works—and how it might work better. In great places, we discover who we are and what we might become.

Describing a place could be the most important work you do as a placemaker.

Placemakers need to understand places at two moments in time—how they look and operate *now* … and how they might look and operate *later*.

Before we can develop a vision for a place, we need to understand its current conditions. What is this place and what is it for? How big is it? Where is it located? How are the elements of place—the centers, boundaries, pathways, furniture, and lookouts—located? What are its shapes and colors? How does the light work? How do people move around? How do the places *serve people*?

To understand a place, observe it from every angle, at all times of day and night, in all four seasons. Observe it when it's full of activity and when it's quiet and empty.

Most people notice only the obvious aspects of places. When we focus on one aspect of a place (like a path overlooking a pond or a garden in a city park) we don't focus on other aspects (the hidden nooks, service buildings, unused passageways, hidden infrastructure). So we have to train ourselves to see like a movie camera, spanning the space, zooming in and out, looking high and low. We have to seek out the hidden places, or else they will stay hidden.

That's the challenge of this unit of our writing program. We want to learn how to describe a place so that we can serve the people who use it.

Here's the plan. We start with two content topics:

- Chapter 6: The World of the Story
- Chapter 7: The Senses

Then we move to explore an essential writing skill:

- Chapter 8: Paragraphs

Earlier, I said that the sentence is the most important unit of writing. But mastering the paragraph might improve your writing more than anything else. Why? Each paragraph is a mini-essay—a whole treatment of one aspect of your topic. Even a long piece (like a major article in *The New Yorker*) uses only a couple dozen paragraphs. If you write great paragraphs, it's relatively easy to organize them into a compelling piece.

Ready? Let's go.

6

---

# THE WORLD OF THE STORY

The center of reality is wherever one happens to be, and its circumference is whatever one's imagination can make sense of.

— MARGARET ATWOOD

Picture a gray stone mansion on a hill. A rusted iron gate, chained and padlocked, surrounds the property. Inside, a long driveway leads to the massive structure. The house stands lifeless; no smoke comes from the chimney and the windows look shabby and neglected. Grass and moss have overtaken the driveway. Woods crowd the mansion's edges.

With every detail, you experience tragedy and loss. That mansion was once full of love and life. Windows glowed with light and curtains danced in the soft breeze. Inside people ate great meals and sang into the night. A beloved matron ran the house while her husband tended to the affairs of business. As the seasons came and went, people played tennis and swam, picnicked and tended gardens, received visitors and embarked on trips.

The whole history of the people—their spirit, their identity—is captured by this place. So is the tragedy that befell the household with the death of the matron and the vengeful anger of the housekeeper.

You might recognize this scenario from Daphne du Maurier's novel *Rebecca*. From the book's very first line—"Last night I dreamt I went to Manderlay again"—we experience the mysterious power of this place.

Great stories focus on people, their passions and struggles. But to know people, you need to know the places of their lives. Places not only contain the characters and action, but also the boundaries and basic rules for action. In a sense, the setting is the "extra" character of your story, creating possibilities and barriers, just like the flesh-and-blood characters.

Alfred Hitchcock, cinema's master of suspense, sometimes plotted his films by first describing places. Once he identified the locales, he developed characters and storylines to fit those places. Hitch explains:

> Of course, this is quite the wrong thing to do. But here's an idea: select the background first, then the action. It might be a race or might be anything at all. Sometimes I select a dozen different events and shape them into a plot. Finally— and this is just the opposite of what is usually done—select your character to motivate the whole of the above.

Hitchcock built *The Man Who Knew Too Much* this way:

> I would like to do a film that starts in the winter sporting season. I would like to come to the East End of London. I would like to go to a chapel and to a symphony concert at the Albert Hall in London.

Once he had a setting, Hitchcock figured out which characters belonged and what they would do in that setting.

Whether or not you use Hitchcock's approach, survey all the possible scenes as you develop your story. If you write about sports, consider the stadium, practice fields, locker rooms, bars, and after-hours nightclubs. If you write about the civil rights movement, start with the streets, lunch counters, churches, schools, and jails. If you write the life of a high school, think about classrooms, corridors and stairwells, pizza joints and Saturday night party spots.

Place matters. So create the settings that reveal the values of the people and periods of the story.

~

### Element 24
### Create Small, Knowable Places

RECALL a time you went to a big city, like New York, Chicago, or Los Angeles, for the first time. How did you cope? Probably by finding a place apart from the hubbub—a coffee shop, a library, a friend's apartment—to collect yourself and make plans.

Likewise, the characters in your story need small, knowable places. Small settings provide predictable containers for action. The less distracting the settings, the more readers can pay attention to characters and action.

TV dramas and sitcoms shows succeed, in part, because they depict the action in small spaces. People come and go in living rooms, bars, offices, and other limited spaces. The audience focuses on the characters and story. Predictable places never disorient the viewer.

The setting reflects the characters' values and status. The working-class Bunkers of *All in the Family* live in a drab row house in Queens, their living room focused on a TV. The upper-crust Huxtables of *The Cosby Show* live in an elegant brownstone in Brooklyn Heights, their living room a showcase for antiques and art. In *Friends*, the characters meet in hip singles' apartments and a coffee bar. In *The Office*, the characters work together in the drab regional branch office of Dunder-Mifflin.

Even when story extends far and wide, small spaces still contain the action. In Homer's *Odyssey*, as the hero sails all over the Mediterranean, he and his crew regularly repair to their ship. In Jack Kerouac's *On the Road*, Sal rides his motorcycle to New York, San Francisco, Los Angeles, Denver, Chicago, and Mexico City. In *Blue Highways*, William Least Heat Moon drives an RV across America. The vehicles not only contain the stories, but also offer symbols of the characters' values.

Within a small space, objects play a critical role. Every prop reveals something about the characters, their community and culture. Props provide something for the characters to use; they give us an excuse for action. Look at this passage from "Fun With a Stranger," a short story by Richard Yates:

> Miss Snell kept a big, shapeless old eraser on her desk, and she seemed very proud of it. "This is my eraser," she would say, shaking it at the class. "I've had this eraser for five years. Five years." (And this was not hard to believe, for the eraser looked as old and gray and worn-down as the hand that brandished it.) "I've never played with it because it's not a toy. I've never chewed it because it's not good to eat. And I've never lost it because I'm not foolish and I'm not careless. I need this eraser for my work and I've taken good care of it.

A simple object—a key prop in a classroom, a small knowable place—offers instant insight into a stern, dreaded primary school teacher.

I realized the full power of the prop when listening to a radio interview with the economist Barry Bluestone. Talking to Tom Ashbrook of NPR's "On Point," Bluestone described working at a Ford plant in during his college summers in the 1960s. Bluestone brought an object for show-and-tell. "This is a two-barrel carburetor from 1964," Bluestone announced, as if the audience could see. "It went into a Mustang and there's a good chance that I built that thing." Bluestone then recounted watching a worker at a McDonald's restaurant a few days before. "I'm looking at a guy operating a fryolator and he's going through the exactly same motions that I went through but he's making one-fourth what I made."

When I heard this, I was amazed. Simply bringing an object into the conversation, acting as if we listeners could see it, Bluestone activated the visual parts of our brains and our memories. He put us on that assembly line in Roseville, Michigan, and in that fast-food restaurant in Boston, Massachusetts. The power of props to enliven a scene—*even when you can't see them*—is profound.

Wherever you set your story—at home or work, out in the larger world or on the road—create a container for the characters and action. Show the characters develop themselves there. Put objects around them; better yet, put objects in their hands.

Once your characters have established themselves in small, knowable places, they can venture into the big, unruly world outside.

## Case Study
### Gary Alan Fine's *Kitchens*

Gary Alan Fine's study of the restaurant industry—and the work of chefs, cooks, waiters, cutters, potmen, and dishwashers—is limited (mostly) to the kitchen. The kitchen's confined space shapes the restaurant's hierarchy and power relations, efficiencies and creativity, and relationships and rhythms. Fine explains:

> Restaurant kitchens are known for being small, nasty, cramped places in which a wrong move spells disaster. Because of the tight spaces, cooks need considerable discipline: "You move in one direction and time your moves to avoid physical conflict with those who work around and beside you. You anticipate such moves reflexively, and a timing, co-ordination, and precision are achieved equal to that of a fine Swiss watch movement.." ... Close quarters provoke interpersonal tensions, just as the luxury of space permits easy impression management. Zones of comfort between co-workers are sacrificed in cramped spaces.

The best restaurants achieve "flow"; everyone in the kitchen anticipates and meets everyone else's needs effortlessly. That requires the right equipment. Substandard equipment can cramp everyone's work. The deployment of that equipment determines whether a kitchen succeeds or fails. Fine explains how a wheel in the center of the kitchen organizes the work of the chef, cook, cutters, and waiters:

> The wheel is a metal turntable with clips on which servers place their tickets when customers have ordered. Cooks examine the orders on the wheel and assume 20 minutes until the dish is to be served. When it is about seven or eight minutes from when the customers will want their food, the server places the ticket on the counter (generally when the customer is half finished with the soup or appetizer). When the ticket is placed on the counter, cooks "go full blast." Some dishes such as lamb en *croûte* are started immediately when the ticket is placed on the wheel, because it takes 20 minutes to prepare. This structure means

that no dish can be served by this restaurant that cooks for longer than 20 minutes.

The kitchen offers a useful model for other small spaces. The best settings have clear boundaries. They stock all the necessary things. They structure people's relationships.

When we focus on a "small, knowable space," we can understand the larger dynamics of the story. In a small space, you can zoom in and capture the essential people, tools, actions, and codes of behavior.

∾

### Element 25
### Map the Character's 'Circles of Life'

NOTHING REVEALS THE CHARACTERS, their ideals, and the possibilities of their lives more than the places where they spend time.

The Zen saying that "you are what you pay attention to" applies to place. The places in your life cause you to focus on some things and not others. To plot a story, then, get an overview of the places where the characters live.

We live in four basic kinds of places:

**Home**: Home is not only where you eat, sleep, and build a life. It's also where you create your intimate relationships and the values that guide the rest of your life. "Home is the place to go that, when you have to go there, they have to take you in," Robert Frost famously said. Home is the place of intimacy, a place where everyone knows your flaws and still loves you.

So what does the home look like? What does the home reveal about your values, your dreams and aspirations? How do you decorate your home? How clean or dirty is it? Are you a neat freak or a hoarder, or something in between? Is your home on a gritty city street or in a leafy suburb?

**Work**: We spend most waking hours at work. Whether or not we like our jobs or coworkers, we accommodate ourselves to them. Is the workplace a rigid place that reflects the company's hierarchy or a loose collection of work groups? Do people work alone in offices, buzz in cubicle hives, or gather for group sessions in open spaces? Or maybe your characters work in a factory or warehouse or showroom or boutique. What makes that space distinctive from other workplaces?

**The Third Place**: Sociologists use this label for the places that attract people in their "off" hours—bars and bookstores, churches and fraternal organizations, gyms and cinemas, coffee houses and retreats, to name just a handful. When you think of a "third place," think of the bar in the TV show *Cheers*, where "everybody knows your name" and where relationships range from the superficial to the intimate.

**Out There**: When not in these three core places, we move around in our cars, on trains and planes, in parks and hiking trails, on sidewalks, in public buildings. We interact with—or avoid—strangers. So what's "out there" like? Is it open and free or constrained? Safe or dangerous? A place of play or commerce? Diverse or homogenous?

Generations ago, children spent most of their free time outside, playing and exploring the world with friends and siblings. Now we plan "play dates" and sign kids up for camps and enrichment programs. Or we leave 'em alone to sit in front of a TV or computer screen. So "out there" is a different place now.

Asked how to construct a story, the journalist and author Gay Talese responded: "Scene, scene, scene." Use circles of different sizes to show how much time your characters spend in what places.

As an example, map out the circles of a hypothetical factory worker's life:

The character in this story, I would say, leads a balanced life. All of us, of course, have different ideas about what makes for the "best" balance. Our values evolve over the course of our lives. Our circles revolve around school and home as in our growing years, college and adventures in college, work and third places in our twenties, and back to home and work as adults.

The circles of our lives shape the way we act. Often, we spend too much time in some circles and not enough in others—by choice or by necessity. We avoid some circles because we feel uncomfortable there. We gravitate to others because they offer "comfort zones," where we do not have to test ourselves.

To develop ourselves fully, we need to choose our circles well. We need many and varied activities—and we need to surround ourselves with people who make us better. We need to avoid circles where people manipulate and undermine us and go to circles where people support and challenge each other.

Take a minute to draw the circles of your life. Show how much time you spend in different places. Now ask yourself: How do I use my time in these circles? How much do these circles give what I need and want in life? How much do they undermine my goals? How is the balance among the circles? Do I spend too much time in some circles and not enough in others?

When you see the circles and their sizes, you get an idea not just where people spend time—and with whom—but also what values they embrace.

**Case Study**
**Robin Nagle's *Picking Up***

Robin Nagle, an anthropologist by training, has always been fascinated with garbage. No city could survive without reliable garbage pickup. Cities are the densest centers of production and consumption. Someone has to remove the trash.

Every day, the New York Sanitation Department covers 6,000 miles of streets, removing 11,000 tons of household trash and 2,000 tons of household recycling. Sanitation workers, known as "sans," also sweep those streets. In the winter, they help to plow and remove snow.

After years of effort—phoning, emailing, visiting, networking—Nagel got permission to accompany sanitation workers on their daily rounds. Then she decided to become a san herself. Her exploration of the sanitation workers takes us to a number of distinct circles of life.

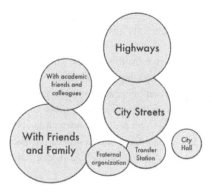

To start, Nagle spends lots of times on the highways that connect the city's major neighborhoods:

I am heading south during the evening rush hour on the Major Deegan Expressway in New York City, carrying a load of densely packed garbage to the dump (more properly called a transfer station). As I thread the truck's 35-ton bulk through thick traffic, well aware that no one is glad to see me, the engine's steady keening aligns with my own sense of caution. Though I own the road—few motorists will play chicken with a garbage truck—50 miles an hour is plenty fast enough for me.

From the city's highways and streets, she drives into the transfer station to dump her load for the day:

> Piercing backup beeps and roaring hydraulics are accompanied by shrieks of metal against metal, and the acoustic onslaught reverberates off the walls like a physical force, so intense that it takes on a kind of aural purity. Workers who spend their shifts inside the facility wear fat red headphones, but those of us only passing through must suffer the cacophony. The best way to communicate is with hand signals.

To become a san herself, Nagle takes courses and passes a series of tests:

> "Good morning," yelled a loose-limbed man in a sanitation worker's uniform. Mo Ragusa could be a tall Mickey Rooney. He was standing before us in a long cinder-block classroom, its yellow walls made yellower by the usual wash of fluorescence. When we muttered an anemic reply, he looked at us with contempt. It was just past 6 on a hot Monday in early summer. Our class of 77 men and two women sat alphabetically in rows of nine tables, simultaneously sleepy and tense.

Every day, she explores the city's neighborhoods:

> Bart's collection truck moved steadily up the street, its many backlights and reflectors bright against the dark evening. I was directly behind him in my own truck, the doors folded open for the warm breeze. We were on the Grand Concourse, one of the city's celebrated thoroughfares and a defining landmark of the Bronx. ... Pedestrians crowded the sidewalks, their arms heavy with shopping bags or schoolbooks. Thick traffic slowed our pace. Bart signaled a left turn and I did the same; a short block later, he signaled another left, heading us back the way we'd just come. Again.

Nagle discovers that sans are really a community, with their own fraternal organizations:

> They gather on the last Thursday of the month at a social hall in Maspeth, Queens, greeting one another with hearty embraces. The loudest welcomes are given to the most recently retired, not yet so far from the daily life of the job; their smiles are wide and their cheeks flush as they endure huzzahs and backslaps. Almost all are men. Their sartorial choices run from T-shirts and jeans to sport coats and dress pants, though a few wear tailored suits.

Wherever she goes, Nagle discovers that she is invisible. Sans are, in the words of one sociologist, an "unmarked" element of city life.

You are picking up garbage in a residential neighborhood when a man walks up to you and tells you he thinks sanitation workers have no right to be in unions because if they did their jobs right they wouldn't need to organize in order to be treated fairly. He then adds a bag to his pile of trash and goes back into his house. You are a union supporter. What should you do?

Robin Nagel answers her own question. As a student of cities, she decides to study this most vital and invisible band of public servants. And we are the richer for it.

∾

### Element 26
### Use Place to Explain Character and Ideas

"FIRST WE MAKE THE PLACE," Winston Churchill once remarked. "Then the place makes us."

To portray people and their journeys, we need to show both sides of that equation. The places where we live not only contain the stories of our lives; they also shape them. Characters understand the world from these places—and then turn around and shape these spaces.

As you write your stories, consider place as one of your characters. Make your places "act" on the characters—enabling them to do this, preventing them from doing that, and shaping their hopes and fears. Consider how the place influences characters in their everyday lives—and in their fateful decisions. Does the place foster energy? Connections? Imagination? Hope? Morality? Or does it foster dread? Lassitude? Fear? Confusion? Conflict?

Consider a few possibilities. New York offers infinite variety and frenzied activity; smaller communities like Missoula, Montana, offer 360-degree access to the splendors of nature. Yale offers the grandeur of an Ivy League school; community colleges offer bunker-like settings but also a leg up for immigrants and left-behinds. A McMansion offers all the trappings and isolation of modern affluence; a saltbox house in a New England town offers a warm hearth and access to town squares.

William H. Whyte, the great city planner, showed how different urban designs affect behavior. Using time-lapse photography, Whyte observed that people congregate at intersections, avoid open plazas, enjoy water fountains, wander toward pushcarts, move chairs and other objects, and seek out sitting ledges and corners. People feel alienated near big buildings and avoid places that expose them to the elements. People in offices congregate near water coolers. Shoppers gravitate toward things they can hold and touch. Families gather in kitchens and TV rooms and seek escape in bedrooms and studies.

Can you imagine Mario Puzo's *The Godfather* without Don Corleone's home or the streets of New York? Can you picture David Schearl, the lead character in Henry Roth's *Call It Sleep*, outside the rough ghettos of Brooklyn and lower east side of Manhattan? Or Holden Caulfield, the hero of J.D. Salinger's *The Catcher in the Rye*, outside Pency Prep or New York? These places offer important information about the characters and their struggles.

When you know a place, you can get to know the people who live and work there. So give your story a vivid, meaningful place.

## Case Study
## Robert Caro's *The Path To Power*

When the Pulitzer Prize-winning biographer Robert Caro first saw the hill country in central Texas, he knew he had found the key to the character of Lyndon Johnson.

On an unforgiving swath of empty space he saw a "huddle of houses," where the 36th president was born and raised. It was a lonely, desolate spot. People sat by the side of the road, waiting for a single car to drive by. It was as isolated as any place in America. The question arises: Why did Johnson's forebears move to such a vast, isolated place?

See how Caro answers the riddle:

> The Hill Country was a trap—a trap baited with grass.
>
> To men who lived in the damp, windless forests of Alabama or east Texas and then had trudged across 250 miles of featureless Texas plains—walking for hours alongside their wagons across the flat land toward a low rise, and then, when they reached the top of the rise, seeing before them just more flatness, until at the top of one rise they saw, in the distance, something different: a low line that, as they toiled toward it, gradually became hills, hills stretching across an entire horizon—to these men the hills were beautiful. ...
>
> The air of the highland was drier and clearer than the air on the plains below; it felt clean and cool on the skin. The sky, in the clear air, was a blue so brilliant that one of the early settlers called it a "sapphire sky." Beneath that sky the leaves of Spanish oaks, ancient and huge, and of elms and cedars sparkled in the sun; the leaves of the trees in the hills looked different from the leaves of the scattered trees on the plains below, where the settlers' wagons still stood—a darker, lush green, a green with depths and cool shadows.

The grass promised settlers a lush and fertile land for farmers—but it was a false promise. The grass had grown long and thick before people settled there. But the topsoil offered just a thin blanket over a foundation of limestone. So when people settled and trod on that turf, the lush grass gave way to a dusty, bare expanse.

The desolate hill country, in turn, yielded poverty, hopelessness, and isolation. It also gave rise to Lyndon Johnson's ambition and impatience, his burning desire to transform the area, bring it technology and education and money—and it gave him the drive to escape Texas for the prospects of power in Washington, D.C.

~

### Element 27
### Use Place to Explore Identity

THE PLACES WHERE PEOPLE LIVE, work, and play leave hints about their characters—how they present themselves to the world, what they do to motivate themselves, and what gets lost in the shuffle.

Consider three questions that a place answers:

**Who am I?** We decorate our homes, offices, and even our cars to advertise our values and aspirations. When we hang art, arrange books, drape curtains, display knickknacks, tack snapshots, or post affirmations, we tell people, "This makes me *me*."

Some places allow little opportunity to advertise our identity. College dorms, army barracks, high-rise apartments, and tract housing limit how you can express yourself. Many housing developments restrict how homeowners may decorate their own homes. Offices constrain expression even more. Still, most people try to give their places a distinctive flavor. When they settle into their homes, people paint this and remodel that, landscape here and plant there. People advertise their identity, wherever they go.

When I was in college, a guy named Dave lived down the hall in my dorm. He had an unusual dorm room. Rather than accepting the dorm's bland furnishings, he brought his own desk, chairs, shelves, and curtains. He installed a big fish tank. He put down a plush rug. When you entered his room, the sounds of Miles Davis and Charlie Parker caressed you. With this setup, Dave told everyone, in a sense: "This makes me *me*."

Whatever you describe, look for the things that characters use to express themselves.

**What do I aspire to?** Sometimes we arrange our space to put ourselves in the mood to work, relax, play, or interact with others. We surround ourselves with furniture, art, music, and mementos that help us to focus on what matters in our daily lives.

People arrange their homes and offices to evoke just the right aspirations. Photos and vacation souvenirs provide reminders of carefree days. A "conversation corner" with comfy chairs guides us to read or chat. A recreation area with a TV or stereo calls us to chill and get social. A work nook inspires us to focus.

Aspirations mark our public spaces too. Civic art, parks, architecture, even bus shelters and signage, tell the world about the community's aspirations. Can you imagine Paris without the Eiffel Tower, St. Louis without the arch, Seattle without the space needle?

Even fakery advertises our aspirations. Back in the 1980s, New York City Mayor Edward Koch covered the exteriors of abandoned buildings with pictures of lively brownstones. Critics said Koch glossed over the area's socioeconomic problems with this architectural wrapping paper. Exactly! By changing people's images of this bombed-out area, Koch encouraged people to imagine something better.

**What do I neglect?** With the first two questions, people consciously shape the worlds where they live, work, and play. But people also behave less consciously, leaving behind hints about their character.

The things we leave behind without thinking—socks, potato chip bags, beer cans, books, and more—offer clues about what we take for granted, how organized we are, and what we do in our day-to-day lives.

Sloppy people cannot be bothered to manage their space. They put a priority on work or play instead of placemaking. (Or they're just lazy.) Neat freaks' spaces, likewise, reflect the order of their minds. They pay attention to one thing at a time. They can be more efficient, but may also be also less creative. Their places help to tell the story.

Hoarders make up a whole different class. Often lost in the past, they refuse to part with old objects—even worthless old newspapers and bags, broken or outdated equipment, tattered clothing, old keepsakes and tchotchkes, outdated records and papers, and more. When asked to toss or give away objects, hoarders experience anxiety and fear.

Let every piece of furniture, every belonging, every arrangement tell something about your characters.

### Case Study
### Joseph Mitchell's 'The Old House at Home'

For real New Yorkers, the most authentic landmarks are not the Empire State Building or the High Line. Far more important are the local institutions that give neighborhoods character—like McSorley's Old Ale House on Manhattan's Lower East Side.

In one of the most famous essays in the history of *The New Yorker*, Joseph Mitchell describes the tavern to explore the identity of the pub's owners and clientele. See how Mitchell brings us into the bar:

> [T]he bar is stubbornly illuminated with a pair of gas lamps, which flicker fitfully and throw shadows on the low, cobwebby ceiling each time someone opens the street door. There is no cash register. Coins are dropped in soup bowls—one for nickels, one for dimes, one for quarters, and one for halves—and bills are kept in a rosewood cashbox. ...

Then Mitchell shows the bar's backstory:

He patterned his saloon after a public house he had known in Ireland and originally called it the Old House at Home; around 1908 the signboard blew down, and when he ordered a new one he changed the name to McSorley's Old Ale House. ... For many years a sign was nailed on the street door, saying, "Notice. No Back Room in Here for Ladies." ...

Mitchell understands the power of props. When you depict objects with some symbolic meaning, you get a real glimpse into the inhabitant's character, as we see here:

Old John had a remarkable passion for memorabilia. For years he saved the wishbones of Thanksgiving and Christmas turkeys and strung them on a rod connecting the pair of gas lamps over the bar; the dusty bones are invariably the first thing a new customer gets inquisitive about. ... Old John decorated the partition between barroom and back room with banquet menus, autographs, starfish shells, theatre programs, political posters, and worn-down shoes taken off the hoofs of various race and brewery horses. Above the entrance to the back room he hung a shillelagh and a sign: "be good or begone." On one wall of the barroom he placed portraits of horses, steamboats, Tammany bosses, jockeys, actors, singers, and assassinated statesmen; there are many excellent portraits of Lincoln, Garfield, and McKinley. On the same wall he hung framed front pages of old newspapers ...

Drinkers—who now include women and a steady stream of tourists—continue to visit McSorley's to consume not just beer but also the ambiance of a tavern that time has passed by. This small world, and its old pictures and knick-knacks, capture an ideal of the local pub that is all but dead.

Which raises a question. McSorely's has become a museum of its past. So is it really authentic any more? Or is it as artificial, in its own way, as Main Street in Disney World? The line between authenticity and artifice can get thin. The next time you visit Manhattan, go to McSorley's, look around, and decide for yourself.

∾

### Element 28
### Place Stories in a Larger World

SUPPOSE YOU'RE A CITY PLANNER. You're designing a park in a residential neighborhood. What do you put in the park? Benches? Gardens? Fountains? Play equipment? Athletic fields? A stage for plays? Picnic tables and grills? Kiosks? Bathrooms?

It depends, doesn't it? You cannot design a park—or anything else—unless you understand the broader setting. You need to know something about the people who live nearby, the daily flows of traffic, business and criminal activity, schools and other parks. To design the park, you need to understand the larger territory.

The same goes for describing settings in stories. To understand any place, you need to understand how people move in and out of the story, from intimate spaces to social spaces, from confined urban spaces to the open expanses of nature. However important the main setting—the "small, knowable place"—we also need to see the story's larger landscape. That landscape supplies the complete cast of characters that moves in and out of the story.

So if you write a story about a school, show the neighborhood surrounding the school, the students' homes, the places they work and volunteer, the sports fields and theaters, the malls and pizza parlors where they hang out, and more. If you write about a business, show the workplace but also outside meeting places, factories, sales stops, tax offices, homes, and more. If you write about sports, show the players and their fans on the field but also in the locker room, homes, player hangouts, fan events, and more.

You get the idea. Moving back and forth, from the inside to the outside of the place, helps us to glimpse the characters' psychology. The home shows the characters' intimate life. Workplaces and "third places"—bars, clubs, and other places where people meet friends—show characters playing their social roles.

People usually behave more intimately inside—but not always. Children from abusive or deprived families, for example, often hide in fear at home and find their real opportunity for expression in schools, playing fields, and other places outside the home. "Third places"—the places between home and work, like bars, union halls, churches, theaters, and sports clubs—sometimes offer more warmth and security than home. Friends often confide in each other more than intimates.

Wherever you take your characters, use those places to reveal the states of their hearts and minds. Let those places reveal their psychology and understanding.

## Case Study
### Rebecca Mead's 'The Garmento King'

New York City's Garment District, not far from Pennsylvania Station, might be the perfect metaphor for the decline of manufacturing in the United States. In the early 1960s, the district produced more than 90 percent of all clothing worn by Americans. The area was clogged with pushcarts filled with clothing, bolts of fabric, and trucks making drop-offs and pickups. A half-century later, the district accounts for about 2 percent of all clothing worn by Americans. Cheap imports and mechanization of production have devastated the district. By 2017, Mayor Bill de Blasio sought to entice the remaining garment companies to get out of the historic district and move to Brooklyn.

Rebecca Mead describes the industry's challenges by zooming into the district. She starts with an overview, which feels like the establishing shot of a movie:

> The stretch of 38th Street between 7th and 8th Avenues, in the garment district, is not one of Manhattan's lovelier blocks. The loft buildings are coated in decades of grime, their large windows stuffed with rattling air-conditioners that drip onto the pedestrians below. Trucks, in various stages of unloading, clot the streets, and the sidewalks are overrun with men pushing handcarts. The gray streetscape has changed little in the 80-odd years since the area was developed for industry, though a Citibike docking station has added an incongruous splash of royal blue. The city recently planted two skinny trees on Eighth Avenue; supported by splints, they shiver at the onrushing traffic, as ill matched to their environs as the girls in stilettos who teeter across the cobblestones of the meatpacking district.

After establishing the context, Mead zooms in to examine the district's buildings:

> Amid the shabbiness, the storefronts of the garment district offer wholesale goods and services of appealing specificity: Jonathan Embroidery Plus sells buttonholes and grommets; Trim Art, Inc., offers rhinestone portraits of Che and Biggie that can be applied to T-shirts. The garment district is one of the few Manhattan neighborhoods that remain largely dedicated to the trade with which they are historically identified. The meatpacking district now reeks of Diptyque candles; at the Fulton Fish Market, the gutters no longer slosh with pungent, scaly ice. But the garment district, which is bordered roughly by 34th and 40th Streets, between Ninth and Fifth Avenues, is still home to more than three hundred factories.

Finally, to introduce the hero of her tale, Mead moves inside one of those buildings. There she finds Andrew Rosen, a second-generation designer and producer who is trying to save the district by modernizing it:

> The Lebros Building, at 270 West 38th Street, houses two dozen garment-related companies. Built in the twenties, the building has a grudging elevator, and the marble floor of the lobby does not appear to have been polished for some time. One day in July, Andrew Rosen, the CEO of Theory, a fashion company, visited Great Look Fashion, on the 11th floor. Inside, on an open factory floor, 70-odd employees were bent over green tabletops, sewing machines whirring. Black pants, in various stages of completion, hung on railings—enough to outfit an army of executive assistants.

Step by step, Mead zooms in on her subject. First she creates the context, then she focuses on her subject.

∾

### And Another Thing . . .

PLACE MATTERS. But how much?

In the 1950s, the psychologists Abraham Maslow and Norbett Mintz designed an experiment to find out. The researchers set up three rooms—one beautiful (with large windows, comfortable furniture, and soulful art), one ugly (set up like a janitor's closet, with drab walls and clutter), and one "average" (clean and functional but not especially pretty). Maslow and Mintz then asked experiment subjects questions about the energy and well-being of the people in pictures.

Participants in the beautiful room judged the people in the pictures to be vibrant and full of life; participants in the ugly room judged the same people to be tired and unhappy. The researchers assisting Maslow and Mintz had similar experiences. The researchers who worked in the ugly room experienced "monotony, fatigue, headache, sleepiness, discontent, irritability, hostility, and avoidance." They also made poor decisions in the ugly rooms.

The world of the story shapes how people feel and behave—and are perceived by others. Well-designed places make it easier for people to do what they want to do. They boost people's energy and focus. Poorly designed places disorient people, sap their energy, and alienate them from others.

Put your characters in different places. Note how they change as they go from home to school to work to mall to ball field to theater to pizzeria to pub. Place determines possibilities. Create settings that make the characters who they are.

# 7

# THE SENSES

Good writing is supposed to evoke sensation in the reader. Not the fact that it is raining, but the feeling of being rained upon.

— E.L. DOCTOROW

Imagine walking home one day and pausing at a gourmet candy shop to buy a piece of dark chocolate.

You first spy the chocolate behind the curved glass shield running along the counter. You see deep brown chunks, darker than the darkest dirt, lying next to light chunks of milk chocolate. The saleswoman wraps the chocolate in white tissue paper, puts it in a cream-colored bag, and hands it to you. Later, you sit in your quiet dining room and open the bag. You hear a dog barking in the distance, but all else is silent. You take the chocolate out, feeling its hardness and rough shape beneath the tissue. You see three smooth edges and one jagged edge. You see a pale dust on the candy's surface.

Then you bring the chocolate to your mouth. You bite a corner. You feel the chocolate's density and resistance. The break sounds like pieces of a plastic toy snapping apart. Before the chocolate breaks, you taste its bitterness with the tip of your tongue. As you move that piece around your mouth, the taste moves with your tongue. The chocolate begins to melt. As the ooze spreads, you savor the chocolate's bitterness, saltiness, sweetness, oiliness.

In that one small act of tasting chocolate, you experience all of the senses. You feel the chocolate, its texture and size. You see its shapes and colors. You feel its density. You hear it snapping and then melting and moving around your mouth.

To describe any scene, describe all the senses. Show what something looks, sounds, and feels like.

Pay attention to how people express themselves. Visual people use expressions like, "Oh, yes, I see what you mean" and "Watch what he does," and use visual cues like maps and charts. Auditory people say, "Oh, yes, I hear what you're saying" and "Listen, that's just not right." Kinesthetic people say, "I know how you feel" and "Let's crunch the numbers," and ask for a demonstration or a chance to try something out.

Tap into all the senses to connect with all readers. Think of yourself as a method actor. Close your eyes and remember how you felt at similar moments. *What did it feel like? What did you see? What were the colors and the lighting like? What did you hear? How warm or cold was the air?* When you feel those emotions, then you can write about them.

The senses affect us so powerfully that we often use one sense to describe another. We use physical words—for heaviness and lightness, hardness and softness—to describe colors. We use visual words—for brightness and darkness, focus and blurriness—to talk about sounds. So we use metaphors to describe metaphors.

Bring all of the senses into your writing. Help the reader see, hear, and feel the action.

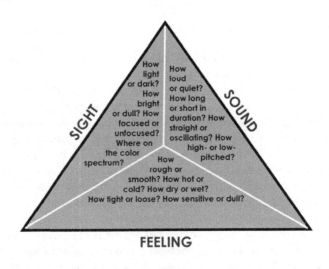

FEELING

~

**Element 29**
**Help the Reader to Feel**

The next time you see people—at work or school, in streets and parks, at the theater or ballpark—pay attention to how they experience the sense of feeling.

When people want to see something, they focus their attention on the object. They concentrate, lean forward, turn their head, and *think*. When people want to hear something, they also focus on the source of the sound, turn their heads, and work to separate the sound they want to hear from those that want to screen out.

Feeling is different. The philosopher Walter Benjamin notices something unusual about the sense of feeling. "Tactile reception," he says, "comes about not so much by way of attention as by way of habit." Feeling is an everyday thing that we usually don't notice. We don't consciously focus on tactile sensations, the way we do visual and audial sensations. And we often miss the implications of feeling things. So we as writers, we need to work hard to bring feeling into our writing.

Consider an experiment devised by a psychologist named Elizabeth Loftus. She showed two groups a videotape of a car accident. She asked one group how fast the cars traveled when they *smashed*; she asked another how fast the cars went when they *contacted* each other. The *smashed* group said 41 miles per hour; the *contacted* group said 32 miles per hour. Then Loftus asked whether the video showed broken glass. Three times as many people from the *smashed* group remember broken glass, though the video showed no broken glass.

To connect with your reader, pay attention to the physical dimensions of your subject. How? Start by remembering a moment of physical pleasure or excitement, pain or anger, loneliness or togetherness. Then describe it, moment by moment.

Think of a breeze drifting across your face. Recall burning a finger on a hot skillet or plunging a hand into a bucket of ice. Remember smashing a softball, falling from a bicycle onto gravel, or swinging an ax against a hard tree. Remember the feeling of embracing a loved one, mixing fingers with dirt as you pull weeds, or sitting on a park bench on a hot summer day. Then connect those feelings with emotions.

Now, when telling stories, tap into these kinds of memories. Describe, moment by moment, the feelings you imagine.

Before the Battle of Bull Run, during the Civil War, a Union soldier named Sullivan Ballou sent a love letter to his wife Sarah. A century and a half after the war, the letter still moves us. Why? See how Ballou evokes emotions by tapping into physical sensations

But, O Sarah! If the dead can come back to this earth and flit unseen around those they loved, I shall always be near you; in the garish day and in the darkest night —amidst your happiest scenes and gloomiest hours—always, always; and if there be a soft breeze upon your cheek, it shall be my breath; or the cool air fans your throbbing temple, it shall be my spirit passing by.

Ballou does not pack his prose with physical words. But he uses them to effect: *If the dead flit ... if there be a soft breeze upon your cheek ... if the cool air fans your throbbing temple.* Ballou evokes common experiences and sensations; the reader can put herself in Sarah's position. We can imagine being with Sarah, years later, when a breeze cools catches her on a warm day—and when that breeze causes her to remember her late husband.

Use sounds that describe texture. Hard consonants sound rough and sharp, while soft consonants sound smooth. The word *crackling* sounds rough, while *luminescent* and *slither* sound smooth.

Read this passage from Charles Dickens's *A Tale of Two Cities*, which describes the storming of the Bastille:

> Flashing weapons, blazing torches, smoking wagon—loads of wet straw, hard work at neighboring barricades in all directions, shrieks, volleys, execrations, bravery without stint, boom, smash and rattle, and the furious sounding of the living sea; but, still the deep ditch, and the single drawbridge, and the massive stone walls, and the eight great towers . . .

This passage helps you feel the sensations of the battle scene. It's not just the sights or sounds. It's also the heaviness of the weapons and the heat of the firing and the penetration of the volleys.

Don't just describe a person, place, or event. Use the words that give the reader a physical experience.

### Case Study
### Malcolm Gladwell's 'The Science of Shopping'

Imagine walking into your favorite store. It could be a gourmet food shop, a sporting goods store, a bookstore, a furniture outlet, or a clothier. What is your experience like?

You probably think first about what you see. You enter to see a display table. You scan the area, considering which way to go. If you know the store well, you might move there automatically. The arrangement of tables and counters directs you to walk along a certain path. You might hear music. You might smell the aroma of pastries or coffee.

But what do you *feel*, physically? What do you *touch*? How does interaction in a space—the tactile sensations involved in touching doors, railings, walls and ledges, furniture, and more—orient us? Physical feeling often gets overlooked in assessments of buildings and public places.

With that in mind, let's see how Malcolm Gladwell describes Paco Underhill, an expert on the sensual experience of shopping. His most important finding, perhaps, is that people are more likely to buy something—like a scarf or tie or sweater or socks—when they can pick it up and touch it.

Paco is considered the originator, for example, of what is known in the trade as the butt-brush theory—or, as Paco calls it, more delicately, le *facteur bousculade*— which holds that the likelihood of a woman's being converted from a browser to a buyer is inversely proportional to the likelihood of her being brushed on her behind while she's examining merchandise. Touch—or brush or bump or jostle— a woman on the behind when she has stopped to look at an item, and she will bolt. ... Paco has transformed [this observation] into a retailing commandment: a women's product that requires extensive examination should never be placed in a narrow aisle.

To succeed, stores need to make sure customers experience pleasant touches and avoid unpleasant touches.

Think about the important places in your life—your home and its various rooms and nooks and pieces of furniture, your office and its workspaces, your community and its streets and parks and meeting places. Now think of the way you physically feel those places.

Finally, think about how those tactile experiences affect the way to see and hear a space.

∼

### Element 30
### Help the Reader to See

WHEN YOU GIVE the reader something visual, you strike up the orchestra in the reader's mind. And just as a symphony offers many different kinds of stimulation—and potential for clashing values—so does vision.

The brain is a network of dense connections. Vision alone contains 30 separate networks that process visual information. Visual cues travel along two primary paths. One interprets the qualities of things (e.g., shape, size, color, texture). The other assesses the location of things (e.g., close or far, high or low).

No visual details reveal as much as the face, which offers telling glimpses into our minds and emotions, whether we're truthful or deceitful, relaxed or nervous, alert or dazed, creative or one-dimensional.

So practice observing faces. Look at people you know or love. Or just find a photograph or painting. Search for clues. Do facial muscles hang on the skull tightly or loosely? What can we tell from the shape of the face, the chin and lips, the forehead and eyebrows? How do the eyes reveal about character? What can we tell from an involuntary twitch or a look away?

Scholars have identified hundreds of specific movements and expressions. These "microexpressions" appear for just fractions of seconds. To do their jobs well, cops, teachers, counselors, supervisors, and investigators all study body language. In an emergency situation—a standoff during a robbery, a hostage taking, or a gang member's threat—interpreting micro expressions can be a matter of life and death.

Decipher body language. How we carry ourselves—not only our faces, but also our arms, hands, legs, and trunks—reveals our moods. When we lower our center of gravity and clench our fists, we subconsciously prepare for attack. When we draw in our chin, close arms and legs, we prepare to defend ourselves. When we open ourselves, we invite others into our world. Consider these basic indicators from body language:

- **Eyes looking up**: A sign that someone is thinking. Often the sign of a visual thinker.
- **Arms crossed**: Defensiveness, creating as barrier with other people.
- **Looking**: Director: confidence, with nothing to hide. Indirectly: Submission or lack of confidence. Sideways: Distraction or auditory style.
- **Glancing and grazing**: A desire to size up the other person, perhaps as a partner.
- **Squinting**: Focusing, intensely, on how well ideas and feelings fit together.
- **Body shift**: Disagreement with the speaker. Often indicates a desire to get out of the "space" that the speaker creates with his remarks.

Color sends signals about mood. Take the color red. What does that show? "Not only am I angry at you," Mark Changizi notes in *The Vision Revolution*, "but do you see all this red in my face? It means that I am in good physiological condition, well-oxygenated, not winded, and ready to *fight*." No wonder red signals alarm. Let's see how all of the major colors symbolize emotions:

- **Red**: Power, aggression, and sexuality.
- **Yellow**: Cowardice, but also joy.
- **Blue**: Tranquility and patience, but also coldness and depression.
- **Orange**: Courage and confidence.
- **Purple**: Extreme anger, sadness, and mourning.
- **Green**: Money and nature, but also sickness, fear, and jealousy.

Rather than appealing only to the mind, the best writers also appeal to the heart. Color gives you one powerful way to do so.

Nothing helps the readers to see as much as action. When we watch or read about actions, we activate the same parts of the brain activated in performing those actions. When I see people hold hands, hit a softball, or scream in traffic, my brain responds as if performing the action. So if you're a writer, describe action carefully, in detail, to evoke the same sensations in the reader.

If you use enough visual detail to excite the reader's imagination, you will enlist that reader in completing the picture.

**Case Study**
**Ann Whiston Spirn's *The Eye is a Door***

How do you read a community space? What do you look for? What phys-ical conditions explain the history of the community? What conditions *mislead* you about that space? How do you identify the physical conditions that *matter*? What conditions *seem* to matter but, in the end, don't?

Anne Whiston Spirn, a community-based planner at the University of Pennsylvania, has spent decades in struggling urban neighborhoods to assess how the obvious clues are not always the telling ones. In her book on seeing, she shows how even the best observers can miss important details in plain sight:

> Boston's Dudley Street neighborhood, once fully occupied by homes and stores, by 1985 was one of the city's poorest neighborhoods, with 40 percent of the land abandoned. Plans to rebuild were underway, but the diagnosis was mistaken, and the plans for treatment flawed. Planners and residents alike believed that the large tracts of vacant land stemmed solely from disinvestment and arson.

The explanation makes sense. In cities across America, from New York to Los Angeles, old vibrant neighborhoods were abandoned and burned to the ground for decades. Urban blight left plenty of clues about its causes. But sometimes those clues miss the point. To understand any scene, we need to look at a bigger picture. Spirn explains:

> They missed the pattern of abandonment—many square blocks of vacant land in the valley bottom and few vacancies on hillsides and hilltops. They failed to recognize the root cause, groundwater movement in a buried floodplain. The clues were there to be read: building foundations cracked by shifting ground, depressions where water collected after rain, a street named Brook Avenue. Historical maps confirmed a connection between vacant land and a former stream, buried in a sewer a century before. Absentee owners had built rental apartments on the buried floodplain in the 1890s, and within 20 years vacant lots began to appear there, the result of high groundwater, soggy soil, and poor maintenance.

The consequences of seeing the wrong things—or *projecting* the wrong things—can be severe. It could mean blaming the wrong people and making the wrong kinds of investments in the wrong places at the wrong time. Worst of all, it could mean fueling another generation of defeatism and cynicism.

> Failing to read those stories and thus to distinguish cause and effect, the planners proposed to build houses for first-time homeowners in the valley bottom, where they would suffer flooded basements and worse. Visual illiteracy can be

dangerous, the costs measured in ill health and the loss of life and livelihood, and it can conceal potential solutions.

Reviving broken communities requires, above all else, close observation. Wherever you go, as an architect or planner or writer, look with fresh eyes. Understand that what we see depends on what we expect to see. So look in places that might not seem important. Look for surprises.

∾

### Element 31
### Help the Reader to Hear

NO ONE KNOWS EXACTLY how language evolved, but one theory holds that people started naming objects with the sounds those objects evoked. Sharp or rough objects, therefore, got names that sounded sharp or rough—*clash, clang bang, rough, jagged, zip.* Soft or curved objects got names that sounded soft or rounded—*bulbous, smooth, spray, sprinkle, whisper.*

Even when we read silently, we hear the textures and tones of the author's voice. If we cannot hear something—or if the word's meaning does not fit its sound—we struggle to make sense of it.

Some linguists say that the meanings of words come from their smallest sounds. The long-e sound of *here, near,* and *teeny,* for example, suggests something diminutive. Low-pitched vowels (like a and o) sound wide and describe bigger things, like *large, far,* and *storm.*

When sounds and meaning match, readers process the ideas faster and better. Take a look at Edward Daily's account of the tense atmosphere of prisoner of war camps during the Korean War:

> Just prior to my falling asleep, a low flying single-engine airplane flew overhead. Could it be an American fighter plane lost and seeking a place to land? Not too far in the distance I heard several explosions and shortly the airplane flew overhead again. Then the sound of the airplane disappeared into the night darkness. ... I dozed off to sleep. I was awakened in the early morning of August 29 by large sounds of shouting coming from the South Korea cell. The door was rapidly opened as the enemy soldiers equipped with burp guns moved inside the cell to single out certain South Koreans.

Listen to all the sounds in this passage—the quiet of dozing off ... the drone of the low-flying plane ... the explosions ... the plane's drone again ... shouting ... the door opening ... the movement of soldiers into cells ... the calls that identified POWs for execution.

Now listen to this description of an atonal Soviet-era composer's work: "An affair of shrieking cluster chords, sputtering streams of pizzicato, siren-like glissandos, and other Xenakis-like sounds." If ever writing should sound discordant, it's in a passage describing discordant music.

When sounds invite speculation, the reader gets involved. With his emotions aroused, the reader tries to figure out what's happening. Each sound turns the story in a new direction. Each sound brings a new level of tension and suspense. Will the Americans rescue the POWs? Or will the Koreans kill them? Just how much abuse can they endure?

Go someplace and let the sounds wash over you. Go to a ballgame and hear the murmur of the crowd, the crack of the bat and the thwap of the ball hitting the glove. Go to a library and listen for the creaking of furniture or the sounds of the heating register rattling or the windows vibrating. Go someplace noisy, like a cafe or school, and listen for the layers of sounds near and far. Walk down the street, ride a bike path, or venture into the woods. Just listen. You might be amazed what you hear.

Speech often provides the most important sounds in a story. Speech offers a kind of voiceover. Whatever your characters say, they offer a unique interpretation of events.

The best quotations and dialogues come in bursts, with pauses that allow readers to absorb the emotions and ideas. To give your writing pep, only quote the words that add fresh meaning to the scene. To indicate gaps in the quotations, use ellipses … like that.

Speech reveals the characters' physical and social makeup. How people interact with others—their levels of confidence, clarity, their smoothness, certainty, and self-awareness—offers insight into their minds and hearts.

Consider, for example, this passage of President Richard Nixon discussing the Watergate burglary with H.R. Haldeman, one of his top aides. Speaking of another aide, Charles Colson, Haldeman tells Nixon "there was more to his [Colson's] involvement in some of this stuff than I realized."

"Which part?" Nixon asked.
"Watergate."
"Colson? Does he know?"
"I think he knows."
"Does he know you know?"
"I don't think he knows I know." …
"Does [John] Mitchell know that Colson was involved, and does Colson know that Mitchell was involved?" Nixon asked.
"I think the answer is yes to both of those."

When Nixon's recordings were first made public, many Americans were surprised by how halting and pedestrian his conversations were. He sounded not like a president, but like an ordinary thug. Those who grew up during the Nixon years, I am sure, hear his low, rumbling voice, almost as jowly as his face. Nixon is often depicted as an all-knowing conniver; here he comes across as a confused conniver.

A little prompting helps readers to hear your characters' accents and rhythm. Tell me that the speaker uses an Irishman's brogue, an Arkansan's twang, a New Yorker's Brooklynese, or a French woman's singsong, and I can imagine the rest.

On rare occasions—and in limited doses—consider using dialect. Dialect captures language just the way people use it. Dialect shows how people elongate or clip their words, how they make words rounder or sharper, spread out or rushed. When you show how people really sound, you put the reader right in the middle of the scene. The best dialect I know comes from Henry Roth. In *Call It Sleep*, Roth shows a boy talking in a Jewish ghetto of New York in the early twentieth century:

> Naa. Dey's two goils in my class, an' anudder kid—a goy. So dey all bought lollipops, an' de goy too. So I follered dem aroun' an' aroun' and den w'en dey finished, dey trowed away de sticks. So I picked 'em up. Goys is dumb.

Roth deploys this rough speech to show characters on the street. He portrays a smoother, more mellifluous language to show the boy and his mother speaking Yiddish at home.

Done poorly, dialect makes characters look like cartoon figures. Dialect may also reinforce stereotypes without giving the reader a vivid experience or fresh insight. How, then, can you offer a sense of the character's accent without getting cartoonish? Try isolating a few expressions. In *Nobody Turn Me Around*, my book about the 1963 March on Washington, I wanted to capture Martin Luther King's accent. But I knew that excessive use of dialect would create a distraction. So I offered short phrases from King's speech:

> King's Southern accent, softened by time spent in his family's bourgeois circles and tempered by years in the North, put a special emphasis on his words: "in the *his-tor-eh* of *ow-a* nation "a *gret* American" ... "symbolic *shadda*" ... "*gret beckon light*."

By citing just a handful of words for emphasis, we get a taste of the speaker's accent. That's enough. Anything more could be a distraction.

## Case Study
### Experiencing the Elbphilharmonie

On the edge of the Elbe River, which snakes through the old German shipping city of Hamburg, sits the world's most innovative new concert hall. The Elbphilharmonie pays homage to both tradition and modernity. Built on an old brick warehouse on a pier, the concert hall resembles a ship casting out to sea.

THE SENSES | 123

Inside, the Elbphilharmonie uses the latest technology to create almost too-perfect sounds.

Over history, music and space evolved together. As the size of churches grew and seating allowed for different musicians to be located around the nave, orchestras could produce vast and complex sounds. The greatest symphonic hall, for decades, was Vienna's 1870 Musikveren, which used a shoebox and bowl formation to disperse the strains of string, the bleats of horns, the thrums and hums of winds, and the booms of drums.

In January 2017, the Elbphilharmonie debuted with performances of Beethoven, Wagner, and modern masters. So how does it sound? Start with Beethoven's "Ode to Joy." The concert's opening piece, began "with the slender, pliable tone of a single oboe—the instrument to which other players tune in halls around the world," as Corinna da Fonseca-Wollheim of *The New York Times* reports. And then:

> Depending on where you sat in the tiered, in-the-round auditorium, you had to crane your neck to see where the first sounds were coming from when the oboist Kalev Kuljus['s] penetrating and clear tone helped to concentrate your ear on the sonic roller coaster that followed, beginning with the metallic aureole of Dutilleux's "Mystère de l'Instant."
>
> The dark, growling rumbles of Bernd Alois Zimmermann's "Photoptosis," in turn, gave way to ... Praetorius's "Quam Pulchra Es." That work was answered by the searing intensity of Rolf Liebermann's "Furioso," with its lightning-fast string scales and luscious, broad melodies. Another Baroque aria, "Amarilli mia bella," by Giulio Caccini, offered quiet reflection before the jaunty finale from Messiaen's "Turangalîla-Sinfonie," its crisp rhythms and fluorescent tone colors vivid and clean. ...
>
> If you were seated in different sections of the hall for the two performances, the sound's warmth varied. The Wagner could have been helped by a greater sense of mysticism: the acoustics cast a clinical light on occasional imperfections. (It was just as unforgiving of a visitor's ill-timed sneeze.) But on the whole, the NDR Elbphilharmonie Orchestra revealed itself as a first-rate group, possessing a radiantly confident brass section and strings capable of producing a toffee-rich tone.

Describing sounds requires onomatopoeia (words that sound like what they describe) and metaphor (words that say they are what they are not). To remember that, think of the classic mantra of meditation: *OM*. Now, look at the words that Fonseca-Wollheim uses to describe the sounds in the Elbphilharmonie—*sonic roller coaster ... growling rumbles ... searing intensity ... lightening-fast ... luscious, broad ... jaunty ... crisp ... fluorescent ... vivid and clean ... warmth ... clinical light ... radiantly confident ... toffee-rich.* Pay attention to each of these descriptors. Visualize the images, then hear the sounds.

What makes the Elbphilharmonie's sounds—even the flaws—so rich? It's the architecture of the place. In the auditorium, 10,000 custom-made acoustic panels line the walls, balustrades, and ceiling. These panels hold a total of 1 million cells, indentations from four to 16 millimeters across. During the design process, algorithms determined the panels' design—how much sound would be emitted and absorbed, depending on the panels' location in the hall. The acoustician Yasuhisa Toyota developed a "sound map" for the hall to determine the physical requirements for optimal sound. That map determined the design and placement of the panels.

Music resounds from the orchestra pit to the furthest reaches of these million cells and then into the audience. If you can capture that experience, you will give your reader an essential part of the experience of place.

~

### And Another Thing . . .

To experience the world, we need to use all our senses. Our lives are as rich as our sensory experiences.

Sensory experience is essential to life. Children given a rich sensual environment—and the opportunity to explore that environment—learn better than children who are cut off from sensual experiences. Infants and toddlers need to crawl, bump and feel, smell and taste, listen and laugh. Children who grow up in barren environments do not develop the neural connections in their brains to learn well and act creatively.

By tapping our physical experiences, sensory language helps us understand even the most complex ideas.

Concrete words (such as "spoon" or "water") take less time to process than abstract words (like "justice" or "moral"). Concrete words activate more parts of our brain, tapping into the rich networks of experiences that we all have.

Using physical words is like watching a movie in hi-definition, full-color, 3-D, surroundsound. Using abstract words is like watching a black-and-white movie with poor lighting and cone camera.

# 8

# PARAGRAPHS

The paragraph [is] a mini-essay; it is also a maxi-sentence.

— DONALD HALL

Here is the first thing you need to know about the paragraph: It evolved as a convenience.

Until the invention of the printing press, writers did not use paragraphs, at least as we know them now. Ordinary people got their stories orally. The storyteller paused at critical moments, giving the reader a chance to absorb and anticipate ideas. Readers, who were rare, concentrated intently as they read page after page of dense text.

A break in text was first indicated by the use of a horizontal line called a *paragraphos*, then by placement of an enlarged first letter in the left margin, and then by a mark called a *capitulum* or *pilcrow* (¶). By the seventeenth century, indentation became the standard way to signal to readers, "OK, here comes a new idea."

By the late nineteenth century, with the rise of public education, "paragraphing" was central to writing instruction. The purpose of a paragraph was simple—to develop ideas in depth, one at a time. Many writers numbered their paragraphs, marking an explicit progression from the first to the last idea.

These days, the paragraph has become something of an orphan. Harvard's rock-star linguist Stephen Pinker dismisses the very idea of the paragraph. "Many writing guides provide detailed instructions on how to build a paragraph," Pinker says in his book *The Sense of Style*. "But the instructions are misguided, because there is no such thing as a paragraph."

No such thing as a paragraph? Seriously? True, people disagree over when to end one block of text and start another. But it seems odd to dismiss such an important element of writing altogether. The best Pinker can do is note the paragraph offers "a visual bookmark that allows the reader to pause." But that's a copout. We can do better.

Language mavens before Pinker not only defined the paragraph succinctly, but also detailed a whole range of types of paragraphs. The best definition comes from Fred Newton Scott and Joseph Villiers Denny, in a 1902 book on composition:

> A paragraph is a unit of discourse developing a single idea. It consists of a group or series of sentences closely related to one another and to the thought expressed by the whole group or series. Devoted, like the sentence, to the development of one topic, a good paragraph is also, like a good essay, a complete treatment in itself.

Scholars identified a wide range of paragraph types: propositional (statement and proof of an assertion), amplifying (further developing an idea), preliminary (laying out the plan of analysis), logical (laying out an inductive or deductive explanation), periodic (saving the theme for the last sentence), and so on.

We can avoid these complications with this pithy definition:

> A paragraph is the statement and development of a single idea.

Whether narrative, summary, or analytic, the paragraph follows the Golden Rule of Writing: *Make everything a journey. Start strong, finish strong.*

Before we proceed, I need to make reference to one irregular form of the paragraph, which I call the "paracluster." A paracluster is a collection of lines from dialogue that, together, express one idea. Consider the following passage from F. Scott Fitzgerald's *The Great Gatsby*:

> "You're a rotten driver," I protested. "Either you ought to be more careful, or you oughtn't to drive at all."
>
> "I am careful."
>
> "No, you're not."
>
> "Well, other people are," she said lightly.
>
> "What's that got to do with it?"
>
> "They'll keep out of my way," she insisted. "It takes two to make an accident."
>
> "Suppose you met someone just as careless as yourself."
>
> "I hope I never will," she answered. "I hate careless people. That's why I like you."

In this scene, Nick discusses a woman named Jordan, a selfish woman who cheats and lies when it suits her. The collection of lines in this dialogue, with eight paragraph breaks, should be considered as one paragraph. This para-cluster expresses one idea: *Dishonest people exploit honest people.*

Enough preliminaries. For now, let's resolve to revive the idea of the well-constructed paragraph.

~

### Element 32
### Make Every Paragraph an 'Idea Bucket'

WHEN WE WRITE, our minds often wander. We start with one thought, which sparks a new thought—so we write it down. That new thought sparks another new idea—so we write that down. Then we think of something else again—so we write *that* down.

Before we finish any thought, we veer off course. And sometimes we never get back.

So I would like to issue a simple command: *State and develop just one idea in every paragraph.* Think of a paragraph as a bucket. Put one idea in each bucket, along with whatever information you need to explain that idea. Never put two or more ideas into the same bucket.

Figure out what point you want to make in every paragraph. Usually, the opening sentence states that idea. So ask yourself: Do the subsequent sentences all support or develop that idea? Or do you veer off in different directions?

If the paragraph contains more than one idea, cut the extra ideas. If you state three ideas in a paragraph, break the paragraph into three parts. Develop one idea per paragraph, with as much detail you need to develop the idea. Delete all extraneous ideas.

Writing one-idea paragraphs requires discipline and effort. So here's a simple trick: In your drafts, label each paragraph. In bold-face type, summa-rize the main idea in a short, zippy phrase. If anything in the paragraph veers away from the label, cut it.

Write labels that sound like tabloid newspaper headlines. To make those headlines sprightly, use punchy puns, exaggerated language, and plays on words. By writing tabloid headlines, you'll think harder about the point of each paragraph.

Let me give you an example. Here are the tabloid headline labels I might use for the paragraphs so far in this section:

- Wanderers
- Lost

- The Idea Bucket
- What's the Point?
- Ruthless Cutting
- Be a Label-Maker
- Tab It Up
- Tab Examples

Crafting tabloid headlines only takes a few moments but yields three major benefits:

- Making sure that every paragraph contains and develops just one idea.
- Testing whether each paragraph takes you, clearly, from the beginning to the end.
- Seeing all of the major ideas in a piece, instantly, in just a few moments.

Using tabloid-style labels can save you hours. Do you want to spend a few minutes tabbing your paragraphs along the way—or hours getting your piece wrong before getting it right?

Some writers kid themselves by thinking they can produce a stream of consciousness and "sort it out later." But if you lose control of one paragraph, the next one could get on the wrong track too. The ideas of one paragraph inevitably carry over to the next. If you state three separate ideas in paragraph one—losing the train of thought—you will probably stay off track in paragraph two. And the idea you develop in the second paragraph might be the one that doesn't belong anywhere in the piece.

So work hard, paragraph by paragraph, to state and develop just one idea at a time.

## Case Study
### Jonathan Manns's *Kaleidoscope City*

No city better illustrates grit and defiance than London during World War II. The Nazis pulverized the city, but under the leadership of Prime Minister Winston Churchill, London persevered.

In 353 words, Jonathan Manns describes the damage wrought by the Nazis in the bombing raids of 1940 and 1941—and how London suffered profound longterm losses in the years after the war. Like other catastrophes, like fire, disease, and extreme weather, the Blitz forced London to reinvent itself. Over the years, the city made lots of serious mistakes.

> Whereas the First World War had been a moment of productive aggrandizement for the capital, the Second World War was a near disaster. Inner London would

never recover its prewar manufacturing capacity, irredeemably knocked about by the German Luftwaffe. The housing problem, always acute in modern London's history, became critical as some 116,000 houses were destroyed or damaged beyond repair and another 288,000 seriously damaged. The Port of London, still the capital's mercantile and commercial powerhouse before the war, was severely damaged and would never recover from the technological advances made in wartime towards containerization and roll-on roll-off shipping. The 1940s would thus be the bleakest decade of the century, with vacant bomb sites scarring the landscape for years to come. It was from this moment, and for the next three decades, that London began to drastically hemorrhage both people and jobs. This was not so much the result of public policy, though decentralization and the building of New Towns, with restrictions on office building in central London, doubtless took their toll. More importantly, the flight from London was the result of the collective decisionmaking of hundreds of thousands of Londoners who felt their city could no longer offer them the quality of life they demanded and that could be obtained elsewhere. By the mid-1980s, the population of London had declined by over 2 million people, returning to something like the twentieth century and almost a million fewer than 1914. The effect of population loss on many inner city London districts seemed little short of catastrophic. Even worse was the deindustrialization of many parts of London, not just the inner traditional manufacturing districts of Islington, St. Pancras, Stepney, and elsewhere, but the wholesale destruction of the new industrial areas that had prospered so greatly in the 1920s and '30s, like Park Royal, the Lea Valley, and Thameside regions north and south of the river, including Dagenham. In the east, the closure of the Upper Port, the last ship leaving in October 1931, effectively marked the end of some 2,000 years of London's history, so long dependent on the Thames for its economic lifeblood.

I would break this passage into three paragraphs. Here's how the new paragraph begins, followed by the paragraph's key idea:

"Whereas the First World War ...": The destruction of London in World War II.

"It was from this moment ...": How London lost population and economic vitality after the war.

"By the mid-1960s ...": Summing up the losses that London had suffered by the 1980s, when the city began its comeback as a world city.

Jonathan Manns writes well. But I fear his readers get lost along the journey. Like bewildered tourists on a long excursion, readers peel away before the journey ends. What a shame. Manns has so much to offer. By breaking up his paragraph into single-idea buckets, he could hold readers for the entire journey.

~

## Element 33
## Follow the Golden Rule in Every Paragraph

EVERY PARAGRAPH DOES NOT JUST EXPRESS and develop an idea. Every paragraph offers a *journey*, which starts and ends strongly. Whatever you write—fiction or nonfiction, business reports or technical papers, for general or specialized audiences—take the reader from one specific place (the beginning) to another (the end).

The journey could depict physical movement, changes in emotions or other states of being, a new understanding. But somehow, something has to change from the beginning to the end.

When you map the journey, pay attention to the moments when you could go off track. Digressions pose the biggest challenge for most writing. We start on one route and get distracted. It's OK to take side trips, when they offer important information. But always—*always*—get back to the main road.

To chart your journey, remember the second part of the Golden Rule: *Start strong, finish strong.*

**Start strong**: In the first line, tell the reader something important, right away. Focus on the subject of the paragraph. Whether you want to explore a person, place, event, or idea, get right to the point. Be specific. Describe what's happening with that subject.

**Finish strong**: In your last line, clinch your point. Say what happens with the person, place, event, or idea. Make sure that something changes in this paragraph-journey. Sometimes, conclude with a memorable question or image, some worthwhile idea or phrase.

**Brackets and bridges in the middle**: Us the middle sentences to progress toward the final line of the paragraph. You might use a long series of sentences or just a few. Make sure every sentence leads to the next one. Try to make every sentence more important—with greater stakes and even tension—than the previous one.

In the discussion of the Landscape View, I suggested writing just one sentence per line. The main virtue of that approach, as we discussed, is focusing attention on each sentence, one by one. Just as a poet perfects his stanzas, one line at a time, a prose writer can perfect his sentences. The line-by-line approach helps you to track the *progression* of sentences, from the beginning to the end of every paragraph. You can tell—step by step, in every paragraph—whether you're making progress toward your goal.

Paragraphing is an art. Most writers have their own style for paragraphs, just as they have their own style for whole pieces. To develop that style, follow the Golden Rule. Take the reader, line by line, from one distinct place to another, different place.

**Case Study**
**Tom Vanderbilt's *Traffic***

We might expect that a writer about traffic would—consciously or unconsciously—make every element of his writing a journey. If we were talking about Tom Vanderbilt, the author of *Traffic*, we would be right.

In his wide-ranging report on cars and congestion in America—how vehicles move along highways and roads, how behavior changes in city centers, why parking is so hard, how congestion pricing works, what spurs battles between pedestrians and drivers, to name a few topics—Vanderbilt takes his readers on clear journeys in virtually every sentence and paragraph.

Consider this passage:

> Picture a highway during stop-and-go traffic. Like those drivers stopped at the light, each time we stop and start in a jam we are generating lost time. Unsure of what the drivers ahead are doing, we move in an unsteady way. We are distracted for a moment and do not accelerate. Or we overreact to brake lights, stopping harder than we need to and losing more time. Drivers talking on cellphones may lose still more time through delayed reactions and slower speeds. The closer the vehicles are packed together, the more they affect one another. Everything becomes more unstable. "All of the excess ability for the system to take in any sort of disturbance is gone," says Benjamin Coifman. He uses the metaphor of five croquet balls. "If you put them a foot apart and tap one lightly, nothing happens to the other four. If you put them all against one another and tap one lightly, the far one out then moves. When you get closer to capacity on the roadway, if there is anyone little tweak, it impacts a lot of the cars."

Vanderbilt opens by describing the issue: Stop-and-go traffic. A single driver's decision, he explains, can ripple throughout the highway, affecting many drivers. What decisions, specifically? Unsteady movement, overreactions, and talking on phones. Each of these decisions, Vanderbilt explains, can bunch cars closer together, exacerbating the impacts of decisions. Finally, Vanderbilt closes with the billiard-ball metaphor.

The paragraph takes us on a journey. Each step of the journey is clear. Of the paragraph's 13 sentences, seven begin with the subjects and verbs (e.g., Picture...," "We are distracted," "Or we overreact..."); the other six begin by setting the context for the action (e.g., "Like those drivers...," "Unsure of what..."). Never does Vanderbilt allow the reader get lost. The sentences all end strongly, too. Go back and read the last three to five words of the sentences. Each ending clinches the sentence's point. Most of them are vivid, showing the consequences of what happened before.

Most important, each sentence leads to the next. Because Vanderbilt knows the point of each paragraph, he progresses to that end with every sentence. Line by line he gets closer to his clincher.

Let me leave you here with two exercises. First, map this passage. Second, give the paragraph a tabloid headline. In a pithy three- to five-word phrase, state the essence of the paragraph.

Now, see how each sentence brings Vanderbilt closer to his ultimate point —that even small actions can upset the whole flow of traffic on a crowded road. Would you change the sequence of sentences in any way? If so, how?

Finally, take the challenge a step further. Ask yourself: Is this paragraph a complete story unto itself? Can you plot this passage using Aristotle's narrative arc? Try it. If you can't do it, read on ...

~

### Element 34
### 'Climb the Arc' in Most Paragraphs

THE PARAGRAPH OFFERS an opportunity to create drama in your writing. Whatever you write—a story, summary, or analysis—the paragraph is long enough to take your reader on a compelling journey.

So follow Aristotle's "narrative arc" in every paragraph. Open in the "world of the story," by introducing the reader to an important person, place, action, or idea. Then, line by line, move to increasingly dramatic or important moments or ideas. Finally, conclude by resolving the paragraph's issues.

If you give every paragraph a sense of drama, the whole piece will gain power. Readers will scarcely notice how you create such drama. But they will feel it—and be impelled to stay with you for the whole journey.

Sounds demanding, right? I can almost hear you responding: *Are you actually telling me to build an Aristotelian arc into every paragraph? Every paragraph?* But it's not so hard. Just take every paragraph, sentence by sentence. Structure your paragraphs to fit the three-part narrative arc.

World of the Story: In the first line or two, show the reader what you want to talk about. Preview the issues you want to explore. You can even hint or even tell the reader where the journey will end. Another words, show the beginning of the journey—setting the stage, raising the issues, "hooking" the reader.

Rising Action: Next, show the paragraph's journey in more detail. With each line, reveal something new. Raise the stakes of the story. Start simply, then move to more important and dramatic ideas. In the second sentence, then, take the first step—defining terms, naming the issues or players, or beginning an explanation. Then develop your ideas, showing complications and complexities, or revealing new dimensions of the issue.

Resolution: Finally, complete the journey. Take your reader to the end. Finish saying what you want to say. Conclude with something vivid, something that launches the reader to the next paragraph. With the final sentence(s), complete your idea and propel the piece forward.

You might not create a perfect Aristotelian arc for every paragraph. Some paragraphs, after all, just supply information. Other paragraphs take a reader along for only part of a journey.

But in every paragraph, you can create meaningful movement, from the beginning to the end.

## Case Study
## Thomas Campanella's 'Jane Jacobs and the Death and Life of American Planning'

The Golden Rule of Writing states that every level of writing—every sentence, paragraph, section, and whole piece—should take the reader on a journey that starts and finishes strongly. But we can ask even more. We can also create compelling drama at every level of writing.

To see how, look at this passage, which describes the rise and fall of the urban crisis in postwar America:

> The postwar period was something else altogether. By then, middle-class Americans were buying cars and moving to the suburbs in record numbers. The urban core was being depopulated. Cities were losing their tax base, buildings were being abandoned, neighborhoods were falling victim to blight. Planners and civic leaders were increasingly desperate to save their cities. Help came soon enough from Uncle Sam. Passage of the 1949 Housing Act, with its infamous Title I proviso, made urban renewal a legitimate target for federal funding. Flush with cash, city redevelopment agencies commissioned urban planners to prepare slum-clearance master plans. Vibrant ethnic neighborhoods — including the one my mother grew up in near the Brooklyn Navy Yard — were blotted out by Voisinian superblocks or punched through with expressways meant to make downtown accessible to suburbanites. Postwar urban planners thus abetted some of the most egregious acts of urban vandalism in American history. Of course, they did not see it this way. Most believed, like Lewis Mumford, that America's cities were suffering an urban cancer wholly untreatable by the "home remedies" Jane Jacobs was brewing and that the strong medicine of slum clearance was just what the doctor ordered. Like their architect colleagues, postwar planners had drunk the Corbusian Kool-Aid and were too intoxicated to see the harm they were causing.

Can you see a complete story here? Can you map the story using Aristotle's narrative arc? Let's plot the narrative graphically:

In this narrative arc, the "world of the story" is the postwar cities that are losing population with white flight and suburbanization. The "rising action" begins with "Help came soon enough from Uncle Sam." The feds used all kinds of tools—slum clearance, subsidies, tax policy, suburban-style design— to "fix" the cities. Alas, the policies only exacerbated the problem. In this telling, the story ends badly, with the continuing decline of cities in the 1970s and 1980s.

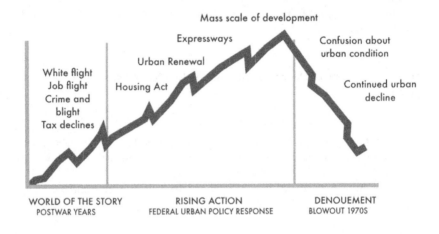

Bullets, alas, make us lazy. Bullets encourage us to make endless lists, rather than thinking through the logic of our ideas.

### And Another Thing . . .

Like other crafts, writing changes with technology. The paragraph has always played a leading role in the evolution of writing.

The paragraph, a creation of the printing press, transformed writing by breaking ideas into pieces that we could absorb, one by one. Now, the computer, Internet, and ebook revolutions are producing new formatting techniques. The trend is clear: The more you can break up text, the better.

The process started with bullets. People had used bullets for years in formal publications. But the rise of the personal computer made bullets ubiquitous. Why? Three reasons:

- People produce longer documents in professional settings. Bullets enable readers to skim the documents to find pertinent points.
- Software programs—from Word to standard email systems—make bullets easy to produce.
- PowerPoint has become the primary tool for making presentations in business and government.

Bullets, alas, make us lazy. Bullets encourage us to make endless lists, rather than thinking through the logic of our ideas.

Another product of the Information Age is the use of single-spaced paragraphs, separated by spaces. Some indent these paragraphs; others don't. This format looks odd in traditional publications like books and magazines. But it makes sense for web sites and professional documents.

The Internet also allows for hypertext, which allows readers to jump to a whole new document with a simple click. This enables authors to provide more detailed background information, references, and explanations. With hyperlinks, the author can give the reader choice about how much information to absorb.

> Writers like Joe Posnanski add another twist. While writing for *Sports Illustrated*, Posnanski used to make asides, right in the middle of the text. By indenting the aside, Posnanski marked it off from the main text. By putting it smack-dab in the middle of the text, Posnanski allowed us to experience his ruminations as they would occur in a conversation. Clever.

Whatever the format, writers need to compose paragraphs that explore a simple topic fully and take readers on a complete (if short) journey.

# IV

## DEPICTING ACTION

In our first two challenges, we explore people and places.

But we cannot really understand our work as placemakers until we understand *how people actually use places*. We need to understand the *actions* that shape places.

How, for example, do families use apartments or homes? What are their daily patterns? What do they do every day in the more "public" rooms (like the living and dining rooms) and in the more "private" rooms (like bedrooms and bathrooms)? How do people move around the place, from one room to another? Do these places allow people to relax? To connect with others? To feel "whole"?

How do people use parks and streets, museums and schools, riverwalks and gardens, transit stations and government buildings? To understand these questions, we need to observe people and things *in action*.

Places are not just static things. They are *interactive*. They not only *provide a container* for action; they also *shape* action.

So how do you describe action? Let me offer a simple formula:

First, ... Then, ... Then, ... Then, ... Finally, ...

To show action, break movements down into distinct motions. Every action is really a collection of smaller moves. If I take a walk in the park, I am really doing a whole series of motions—ambling in, surveying the area, zooming in on details, deciding whether to go down Path A or Path B, deciding whether to sit on a bench or grab a patch of the lawn, and so on.

One of my favorite planning studies is William Whyte's *City: Rediscovering the Center*. Whyte and his research team used time-lapse photography to capture how people use a variety of public spaces. They recorded people's actions, moment by moment, in parks, plazas, sidewalks, street corners, building lobbies, fountains, benches, chairs, and much more. By watching the action, they discovered what kinds of designs created the spaces that people wanted to use. It was data-based analysis at its best.

As a placemaker, you need to understand all of the elements of action. To do that, we have broken down action into two parts:

- Chapter 9: Action and scenes
- Chapter 10: Details

Once we understand how actions work, we need to deepen our understanding of writing techniques. And so we explore two new topics:

- Chapter 11: Grammar
- Chapter 12: Editing

I like to think of grammar and editing in terms of action. Grammar provides the rules for managing action, while editing provides the process for fixing glitches in the action.

When you walk or drive, for example, signs and other markers (e.g., crosswalks, speed bumps) indicate when you can stop, pause, yield, look forward, and more. Punctuation marks do the same thing. Periods tell you to stop, commas tell you to pause, colons tell you to look ahead, and so on.

The editing process enables us to fix what's out of order. When we find unnecessary words and phrases in our drafts—or when they don't work the right way—we rearrange them. Editing, in effect, is a process of fixing the actions in our drafts.

Ready? Let's go.

# ACTION AND SCENES

Human beings must have action; and they will make it if they cannot find it.

— ALBERT EINSTEIN

On February 26, 1972, a flood of water and waste overwhelmed the West Virginia community of Buffalo Creek. For decades, the Buffalo Mining Company had piled sludge from coal mines on the edges of town, creating a mountain 40 to 60 feet high and more than 450 feet long. The wall looked like a dam, but it could not resist the flood. One local likened the spongy mass to a "mound of mashed potato."

Suddenly, after days of late-winter rain, Buffalo Creek flooded and the wall collapsed:

> The entire lake of black water, all 132 million gallons of it, roared through the breach in a matter of seconds. It was already more than water, full of coal dust and other solids, and as it broke through the dam and landed on the banks of refuse below, it scraped up thousands of tons of other materials, the whole being fused into a liquid substance that one engineer called a "mud wave" and one witness described as "rolling lava." The wave set off a series of explosions as it drove a channel through the smoldering trough of slag, raising mushroom-shaped clouds high into the air and throwing great spatters of mud three hundred feet up to the haul road where a few men were returning from the mines. The rock and debris dislodged by those explosions were absorbed into the mass too. By now, there was something like a million tons of solid waste caught up in the flow.

This passage from Kai Erikson's *Everything In Its Path* offers a model for action writing. We see the flood overwhelming this community, hear the explosive sounds, and feel the power of the water and debris. We see the flood from the perspectives of workers, engineers, housewives, children, and retirees. The image of the mushroom cloud evokes disaster.

Erikson describes the scene, moment by moment. Rather than rushing into generalizations—a common habit for most writers—he breaks the action down into discrete pieces. He creates suspense by ratcheting the tension, moment by moment.

Reread Erikson's passage and pick out the action verbs. Then pick out the specific nouns. Look for the words that describe sensuality—the sights and sounds and smells. See how Erikson describes the scene with a flood of details. By focusing on details, Erikson makes the scene come alive.

With this rich description, Erikson has a powerful tool to explain the character—and breakdown—of the community of Buffalo Creek.

The flood rips up not just the physical environment, but also the community's social fabric. Before the flood, Buffalo Creek was considered a tight knit, caring place. Friends and neighbors left doors unlocked, loaned possessions to each other, gathered for supper and church. After the flood, they became suspicious and untrusting. Many bickered with old friends and neighbors. Some sank into alcoholism. Others left the area. Some even committed suicide.

Erikson's vivid scene raises a powerful question. Did the flood destroy the community? Or did the community's weak foundation undermine the people's ability to deal with the disaster?

~

### Element 35
### Depict Specific, Deliberate Actions

PEOPLE TAKE action countless times every day. The job of the storyteller is to identify which actions matter most for the tale, then to arrange them in a sequence that creates a whole experience for the reader.

Action always offers the potential of changing the world—in unpredictable ways. As the philosopher Hannah Arendt notes, action "has an inherent tendency to force open all limitations and cut across all boundaries." Whenever someone acts, they unsettle the world. Action makes stable things unstable. That's why stories need action. Stories are about discovery and change.

So just what is an *action*? Philosophers have debated the question since antiquity. Let's consider something an "action" when it involves a conscious person, making a deliberate choice, which directly influences some part of the world.

A Dutch linguist named Tuen Van Dijk offered three sets of sentences to explain action. Let's start with these four sentences:

Leaves are green.
Peter is ill.
The train from Paris arrives at 5 o'clock.
John recovered quickly from his heart attack.
Mary could not pay her income tax.

Something happens in these sentences, but we do not actually *see* anyone take any action. I would call these "summary statements." These kinds of statements offer important context for action. But they are informational, not action-oriented.

Now take a look at these three sentences:

Harry found a briefcase with ten thousand dollars.
George hesitated whether he would stay or not.
Laura stared out of the window.

In these passages, we get closer to action. We learn that Harry found a briefcase but have no real image of that moment. We see George in the moment before he *might* act. Laura staring out the window looks more like action. We can picture her, standing, looking intently. But she remains still.

Now take a look at four more sentences:

Ann carefully cleaned the windows.
Hans repaired my watch.
Barbara accused him of murder.
Larry refused to let him go.

We are getting closer. In each one, we can visualize someone putting his or body into motion in order to change something. We see Ann reaching up to get spots off the glass, Hans using tools as he leans over a table, Barbara pointing her finger, and Larry holding or blocking someone from leaving.

Let's take the last four sentences deep into action:

Ann leaned into the window, pressing hard with her soaked rag
    to wipe the dirt from the glass.
Hans peered through the magnifying glass and gently adjusted
    the spring of my watch.
Barbara stood, shaking, as she raised her voice and made her
    accusation: "You killed him!"
Larry blocked the door, preventing him from leaving the room.

Now we finally get what we need—vivid images of people performing some discrete action, in ways that affect other people or things.

As a storyteller, your job is to show the reader as much action as possible.

Here's a simple test for every scene you write: *Could you use the sentences to draw a picture?*

Don't summarize what people or think, how they're positioned, or what's happening around them. Get specific. Answer the following questions: *Who do you see—specifically? What do you see him doing—specifically? What is he acting on —specifically? What visible actions inform us about his goals—specifically?*

Show the sequence of movements needed to act. To describe a woman's commute, then, don't say: "She drove to work." Put details into a sequence, like this: "Leila balanced her leather briefcase and coffee while opening the door of her crimson Honda Civic. She tossed the briefcase onto the passenger seat and slid in behind the wheel. Then the car crept out of the driveway and into the street..." See the difference? The more specific the moments, with precise details, the more likely you will convey action.

To create action, get specific about who does what, *moment by moment.* Give your reader *moving pictures.*

## Case Study
## Jane Jacobs's *The Death and Life of Great American Cities*

Jane Jacobs became (arguably) the most important planning critic of the twentieth century not because of any academic degrees or professional standing, but because of her ability to observe what she saw.

Every day, while working as a writer and caring for her children, Jacobs paid close attention to the details of everyday life in Greenwich Village in New York. She was one of the greatest inductive thinkers in modern planning. With no grand theories, she developed her own analysis of urban life by observing.

Like a movie director, Jacobs starts at her own front stoop and gradually takes in the scene that unfolds before her.

> While I sweep up the wrappers I watch the other rituals of the morning: Mr. Halpert unlocking the laundry's handcart from its mooring to a cellar door, Joe Cornacchia's son-in-law stacking out the empty crates from the delicatessen, the barber bringing out his sidewalk folding chair, Mr. Goldstein arranging the coils of wire which proclaim the hardware store is open, the wife of the tenement's superintendent depositing her chunky three-year-old with a toy mandolin on the stoop, the vantage point from which he is learning English his mother cannot speak.

She turns to see movement from all directions:

> Now the primary children, heading for St. Luke's, dribble through the south; the children from St. Veronica's cross, heading to the west, and the children from P.S 41, heading toward the east. Two new entrances are made from the wings: well-dressed and even elegant women and men with brief cases emerge from

doorways and side streets. Most of these are heading for the bus and subways, but some hover on the curbs, stopping taxis which have miraculously appeared at the right moment, for the taxis are part of a wider morning ritual: having dropped passengers from midtown in the downtown financial district, they are now bringing downtowners up tow midtown.

Once people leave the neighborhood for work and school, she gets ready to begin her day:

> Simultaneously, numbers of women in housedresses have emerged and as they crisscross with one another they pause for quick conversations that sound with laughter or joint indignation, never, it seems, anything in between. It is time for me to hurry to work too, and I exchange my ritual farewell with Mr. Lofaro, the short, thick bodied, white-aproned fruit man who stands outside his doorway a little up the street, his arms folded, his feet planted, looking solid as the earth itself. We nod; we each glance quickly up and down the street, then look back at each other and smile. We have done this many a morning for more than ten years, and we both know what it means: all is well.

For Jacobs, the details told the story. Rather than jumping to quick conclusions, she observed each moment, each person, and each action. Those details provided the dots she needed to connect.

~

### Element 36
### Use Speech-Acts to Propel the Story

EVER LINGER in a bar or coffee shop to eavesdrop on a nearby conversation? Ever listen in on a conversation on a bus or in an office. Of course you have. And when you write stories, you need to give your reader the same guilty pleasure.

By showing two or more characters talking, you give your reader the pleasures of eavesdropping. You show your characters' private lives and thoughts. You reveal the characters' motivations, prejudices, loves and hates—in fact, all their emotions and thoughts.

But speech offers more than an illicit thrill. Speech is *action*. Just a few words can transform a story. When we say, "The Red Sox are playing the Yankees," we might simply convey a neutral fact. But speech does not just convey information; it also implies requests, questions, opinions, warnings, and more. In different contexts, "The Red Sox are playing the Yankees" could mean "Want to go?" or "I'm busy" or "Let's drive a different way to avoid stadium traffic."

Dialogue also reveals character. Dialogue shows how educated, cultured, friendly, and caring the characters are. Surprising speech patterns are especially revealing. Ever meet a rich, educated person who talks like a truck driver? Or a poor or working class person who speaks with exaggerated refinement? Such quirks tell us not just who these characters are, but how they want others to see them.

Dialogue would bore us if everyone spoke knowledgeably, directly, and honestly. In fact, people lie constantly—three times in every ten minutes of conversation, according to a study by a University of Massachusetts psychologist. Our parents teach us to tell the truth ("Did you break this bowl?"), but also to lie ("Tell Grandma how much you love visiting!"). Use dialogue to reflect this tension between lying and truth-telling.

When they don't lie, people often speak in ignorance. Showing a character with limited knowledge gives the reader a special thrill. The reader becomes part of the process of storytelling: "Of course that's not true," the self-satisfied reader says.

Here's a simple example of characters lying to each other, from Jon Krakauer's *Into the Wild*. In this scene, Chris McCandless, a young man who has decided to live in the wilds of Alaska, talks with Ronald Franz, an octogenarian who has hosted him for a few nights:

> One day in early February, McCandless announced he was splitting for San Diego to earn enough money for his Alaska trip.
> "You don't need to go to San Diego," Franz protested. "I'll give you money if you need some."
> "No, You don't get it. I'm *going* to San Diego. And I'm leaving on Monday."
> "OK. I'll drive you there."
> "Don't be ridiculous," McCandless scoffed.]
> "I need to go anyway," Franz lied, "to pick up some leather supplies."

Both Chris and Franz lied to each other in this passage—not out of a desire to manipulate the other, but to spare the other from concern or harm.

To reveal how characters deal with conflict, show them using speech to address their challenges. Why do the characters say what they say? What *don't* they say? How are others affected?

## Case Study
### Rhetoric of Occupy Wall Street

Cities have always been the centers of political protest. Dissidents can recruit activists easily in high-population areas. They can also put on a big show, using campuses, parks, streets and other public venues. They also have access to mass media eager for the sights and sounds of conflict.

The settings shape the dialogue that takes place in protests. The planners of the 1963 March on Washington understood that the National Mall would give the event a civic feel. The 1960s protests that took place in city streets and parks sometimes degenerated into violence. Campus protests—for the civil rights, free speech, and antiwar causes—sometimes had a more rarefied rhetoric. Protest settings—like Lafayette Park and the National Mall in Washington and Central Park in New York to Wenceslas Square in Prague, Red Square in Moscow, and Tiananmin Square in Beijing—have symbolic value.

The Occupy Wall Street movement, which began at the center of finance in New York and spread to hundreds of cities across the world, was rooted in parks and streets that symbolized the power of banks and financial institutions. These protests aimed to confront "the 1 percent," the catchphrase for the elites that dominate American society. Consider how these phrases shape the way people in the movement thought and acted:

*Direct action*: The essence of protest is direct confrontation of the opposition. Rather than debating legislation or government policies, direct action offers a way to "get in the face" of the opposition—forcing it to respond. Occupy Wall Street did just that at its protests in Zuccotti Park.

*Occupy*: Taking over space—parks, streets, buildings—ups the ante. By setting up tents and refusing to leave, protesters create a spectacle that challenges the power structure to respond. When you take over someone's space, it's hard for them to ignore you.

*Arab Spring*: Earlier in 2011, protests in Cairo's Tehir Square toppled President Hosni Mubarak and led to a wildfire of protests across the Middle East. The words "Arab Spring" buzzed around the Occupy movement, suggesting new possibilities for confronting power structures in the U.S. and elsewhere.

*General assembly*: Occupy Wall Street borrowed this concept from European protests. The general assembly is an ongoing, open forum to manage all aspects of the protest, from day-to-day logistics to political demands to strategy and tactics. From the Occupy movement's earliest days, the idea of the general assembly shaped every word and gesture of the protesters—and helped to avoid a takeover by "professional protesters."

*The 99 percent/1 percent*: With their location in the heart of America's financial system, the protesters confronted the political and economic elites who run the country—and who produced the 2008 financial crisis.

*"This is what democracy looks like"*: This slogan, borrowed from European movements, reframed political action from ordinary politics (elections, lobbying, legal action, etc.) to extraordinary politics (demonstrations, occupations, marches, boycotts, etc.).

*The people's mic*: Because city ordinances ban the use of electronic microphones in public parks, speakers conveyed their messages with "people's mics." After a speaker said something, the crowd would repeat it as a group. This call-and-response approach helped to bond the protesters.

The language of the protest movement grew out of its location in Lower

Manhattan—and its spread to the parks and squares across the country that symbolized the 1 percent's dominance of the political system.

~

### Element 37
### Build Actions Into Scenes

IF AN ACTION IS the smallest unit of a scene, then a scene is the basic unit of a story. A scene unfurls a complete set of actions; at their best, scenes take the form of Aristotle's narrative arc, with a beginning, middle, and end. A scene shows action and conflict, usually in a single place in a limited period of time.

Scenes take place in homes and workplaces, shops and restaurants, streets and cars, and churches and schools. They also take place on highways and shops, ballparks and legislative chambers, and about anywhere that people gather.

The range of possible actions is limitless—talking, arguing, canoodling, fighting, ignoring, playing, working, singing, fighting, loving, and more. What matters is what *changes* the story ... or what changes our *interpretation* of the story.

Every scene poses some dilemma that plays out in three stages, which we can plot on Aristotle's narrative arc. First, we survey the scene through a distinctive point of view. Second, the character debates whether to act. Third, the character takes action.

**A clear point of view**. The reader needs to know: Who's in charge of revealing this scene? Is it the main character, an opponent, a sidekick, or a mentor? Is it an invisible character, ignored by everyone else in the room? Or does an omniscient narrator hover above the scene?

An omniscient narrator hovers over every scene, knowing everything about everyone. He shows them in public and reveals details that the characters themselves might miss. And he shows them in private, revealing the thoughts and emotions that most other characters cannot see. He even gets inside their heads, revealing their internal thought processes.

The first-person POV offers a more intimate view. Through the eyes of one character—often the hero or his sidekick—we get a partial view of the goings-on. We see the hero sympathetically because we are so close to her, guessing her moves and responding to them with a sense of excitement or wonder.

Consider two classic examples. In Mark Twain's *The Adventures of Huckleberry Finn*, Huck narrates. We see this boy's character—his ignorance and his decency—through his unselfconscious comments about his abusive father, his overweening aunt, and his friend Jim. In the Sherlock Holmes series, Arthur Conan Doyle uses the first-person POV of Watson, the detective's sidekick. This view offers an intimate perspective but prevents the audience from getting ahead of the story.

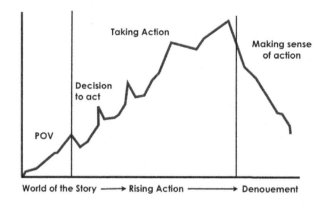

Taking Action

Making sense
of action

Decision
to act

POV

World of the Story ——→ Rising Action ————→ Denouement

Using more than one POV may confuse the reader. But if you make the POV clear in every scene, right away, different perspectives lend both intimacy and complexity. Truman Capote's *In Cold Blood* uses a number of different POVs—those of Herbert Clutter and his family, the murderers Dick and Perry, the detective Al Dewey, the townspeople at a diner and post office, even secondary figures like hitchhikers and the murderers' families. If you can frame each section clearly, the reader can follow whichever POV you provide.

Whatever POV you use, make sure the reader understands it right away—unless, that is, you want to surprise the reader.

**Moments of debate and hesitation.** Before people act, they need to *decide* to act. By considering the pros and cons of different options, they reveal their character. Choosing one option alters the course of the story.

Show the moment before the character makes his fateful decision—when he could stop or reverse course but decides to move forward.

In the "calm before the storm," we see the character's vulnerability. In these moments, the character is often more honest than at other times; at the same time, he lacks complete information. The moment of pause allows us to see the character's values, hopes, and fears.

The moment of decision could happen long before the story's action. In his account of the Buffalo Creek disaster, Kai Erikson explains how mining companies piled refuse from the mines high, then covered up evidence of the impending disaster. Company leaders knew they risked a disaster, but failed to act.

Show your reader that distinct moment of pause, which clarifies what's at stake.

**Irrevocable action.** After debate comes action. Once the characters weigh the pros and cons, they need to act—and they cannot go back. Deciding to go forward means abandoning the possibility of returning to old ways.

In taking a fateful action, characters can behave in one of two ways. They can either act with all their attention and energy, focusing on their goal without distractions and doubts. When you act with such commitment, solving problems becomes easier.

Or they could act distractedly and half-heartedly. This, alas, is how we normally act. Think of a time you made a gut decision to take a class or job, meet a friend or foe, pop in on a party, or take "one last" drink. We take actions like this every day, without fully considering the consequences. In fact, if we considered all the consequences of all our actions, we would become paralyzed. So the question is: When must we make decisions consciously and when can we act less deliberately?

### Case Study
### Malcolm Gladwell's 'The Science of Shopping'

When writing scenes, use this simple formula: Action + Action + Action + Action + Action … until you show how people produce change at a single time and place.

Paco Underhill, a pioneer in the analysis and design of retail shopping, uses detailed analysis of people's discrete, specific actions in order to understand their shopping behavior. Underhill learned how to analyze and design spaces from William H. Whyte. By using time-lapse photography to observe how people use streets, sidewalks, plazas, entryways, building edges, and other basic elements of public space, Whyte discovered how design affects people's use of space.

In this scene, Underhill and his team observe a couple, via closed-circuit video, as they shop for pants for their daughter:

> The basic steps of the shopping dance are so familiar to Paco that, once I'd grasped the general idea, he was able to provide a running commentary on what was being said and thought. There is the girl emerging from the changing room wearing her first pair. There she is glancing at her reflection in the mirror, then turning to see herself from the back. There is the mother looking on. There is the father—or, as fathers are known in the trade, the "wallet carrier"—stepping forward and pulling up the jeans. There's the girl trying on another pair. There's the primp again. The twirl. The mother. The wallet carrier. And then again, with another pair.

Each small action moves the story forward. Now see how Underhill confers with a colleague named Tom Moseman.

> "This is a very critical moment," Tom, a young, intense man wearing little round glasses, said, and he pulled up a chair next to mine. "She's saying, 'I don't know whether I should wear a belt.' Now here's the salesclerk. The girl says to him, 'I need a belt,' and he says, 'Take mine.' Now there he is taking her back to the full-length mirror." A moment later, the girl returns, clearly happy with the purchase.

She wants the jeans. The wallet carrier turns to her, and then gestures to the salesclerk. The wallet carrier is telling his daughter to give back the belt. The girl gives back the belt.

After operating in sync, the parents and their child reached an impasse. Should they buy the belt or not? Again, small, discrete actions determine the twist and turns of this shopping expedition. Moseman stops the tape to offer commentary.

He's leaning forward now, a finger jabbing at the screen. Beside me, Paco is shaking his head. I don't get it—at least, not at first—and so Tom replays that last segment. The wallet carrier tells the girl to give back the belt. She gives back the belt. And then, finally, it dawns on me why this store has an average purchase number of only 1.33. "Don't you see?" Tom said. "She wanted the belt. A great opportunity to make an add-on sale ... lost!"

As happens in almost every great scene, the actions follow Aristotle's three-part narrative structure. First, we get acquainted with the characters and the situation—the world of the story. Then we see the characters wrestle with various dilemmas, engaging in some back-and-forth and conflict—that's the rising action. Finally, the story winds down—that's the denouement.

∽

### Element 38
### Create a Mystery to Surprise the Reader

SURPRISE IS the secret sauce of storytelling. Humans make predictions, all day long, based on what happened before. We predict what family, friends, coworkers, neighbors, and even strangers will do, based on what they have done before. When predictions come true, over and over, we become blasé. So when surprise comes, we react emotionally. Surprise is the root of all learning and memory, all emotion and creativity.

So how do we give readers surprises? A simple formula, it turns out, shows how to create surprise of any kind—comedy or tragedy, farce or insight, subtle or raucous humor. The formula looks like this—

$$V/N$$

—where N stands for the expected, or normal, event, and V stands for a direct violation of that expectation.

Think of the great surprises in literature and art. Think of Oedipus's discovery that he killed his father and had sex with his mother. Think of Darth Vader's declaration to Luke Skywalker: "I am your father." Or think of *The Crying Game*, when Dil reveals to his lover Fergus that she was really a he.

History, Kurt Vonnegut once said, "is merely a list of surprises." Ponder some of them. Think of the Wright brothers, finally, alighting off Kitty Hawk. Think of the discovery, so improbable that it was denied for years, that mold produces antibiotic properties. Think of Eisenhower's deception of the Nazis to stage a successful invasion of Normandy. Think of the sneak attacks on Pearl Harbor or the Twin Towers.

Each of these events occurred when, at a specific moment, reasonable expectations were violated.

Now let's see if we can provide a simple process to create expectation and then violate it. It's simple, really. Just hide crucial information from whomever you want to surprise. Create a false understanding of the scene. Then reveal the truth.

Start by listing all the events or information that a person would need to understand the situation. Then shield one or more characters—or the reader—from knowledge of that information. The longer the sequence, the more opportunities to hide information and produce surprise.

You can embed surprise not just in sequences of action, but also in details of things. In the opening scene of Orson Welles's *Citizen Kane*, the New York publishing baron Charles Foster Kane utters the word "Rosebud" as he drops a snow globe. What does that mean? Only late in the story do we learn that Rosebud is the name of a sled that Kane owned in his troubled childhood, a symbol of his deep and abiding conflicts.

The more information you hide in a story, the more opportunity for surprises. Even a slow non-story, like *Oblomov* or *Waiting for Godot*, creates surprise when a long-ignored detail comes to light for the first time.

You can also create surprise by focusing attention on the wrong things. Detective stories often use such red herrings. In *The Mysterious Affair at Styles*, Agatha Christie offers two characters who so despise each other they would never collaborate on anything—except, as we learn at the end, they collaborate on a murder. In Christie's *The ABC Murders*, the obvious suspect for the murder of a shopkeeper is her drunken, threatening husband. But he's not the one, as a string of murders reveals.

Surprise comes from seeing some things but not others. As a writer, you have the power to conceal and to reveal, whatever and whenever you want. Make a list of all the people, places, things, and moments that reveal something about the subject. Then hide them—and reveal them, one by one, over the course of the story.

## Case Study
### Robert Caro's *The Power Broker*

Arguably, no force transformed twentieth-century America more than highways.

All across the country—from Boston to San Francisco—highways created a vast web that tied the country together. Highways also cut through the heart of cities, displacing millions and destroying vast swaths of old neighborhoods. Usually, a highway's design and construction followed a simple logic. To move traffic as efficiently as possible, traffic engineers were willing to sacrifice old neighborhoods. Displacement, then, was the price of progress. Robert Moses, New York's master builder, once said: "When you operate in an overbuilt metropolis, you have to hack your way with a meat ax."

The Cross-Bronx Expressway, a seven-mile connection along Interstate 95 to New Jersey, Long Island, and Manhattan, offers a perfect case in point. Overall the highway makes perfect sense; it was absolutely essential to connect the city to the larger region. But part of the expressway—a one-mile spur that runs through the old neighborhood of East Tremont—makes no sense at all.

Let's take a quick inventory of East Tremont and what got destroyed when Moses shifted the path of the expressway north:

> The neighborhood provided its residents things that were important to them. ... [I]t was only a few short blocks from anywhere in East Tremont to a subway ... [T]he neighborhood had jobs in a miniature garment and upholstery manufacturing district ...
>
> East Tremont was a bright bustling mile of bakeries, of kosher butcher shops, of delicatessens, of mama-and-papa candy stores ... You might go to Alexander's on the Concourse for clothes, but you didn't have to; Janowitz's on Tremont was just as good. ...
>
> And the Southwest border of the neighborhood was Crotona Park. "Beautiful. Lovely. Playgrounds. There was a lake—Indian Lake. Nice. We used to sit there, under the trees. We raised our children in Crotona Park." ...
>
> East Tremont had good schools. They were old ... but there were no double sessions and standards were high. ...
>
> "Those apartments were light and airy and cheerful." ... They [residents] loved them—and they could afford them.

To run through East Tremont, Moses detoured the highway to the north, away from its otherwise straight path through the center of the Bronx. Why? Usually, engineers create these twists to elude barriers. But this expressway faced no such barrier. The detour was much more costly in its disruption. A straight path would have required destruction of six buildings; the detour claimed 54 buildings, which housed 1,530 families and hundreds of small businesses.

Such heavy destruction did not need to happen. Why, then, did Moses ram the highway through East Tremont? Local activists tried in vain to find an answer. Caro offers a few possibilities:

• **An ideological statement**: Moses might have targeted East Tremont because its tight-knit community was the antithesis of his ideal of a modern, sprawling, car-dependent, Corbusian development.

• **Intimidation of future foes**: Maybe, like a mobster, Moses wanted to make an example of the neighborhood, to warn would-be activists elsewhere to submit to his rule. With all of his tactics—controlling politicians, blindsiding residents, destroying before building, tormenting opponents (like destroying upper floors of buildings while tenants still lived below)—Moses intended to intimidate people near and far.

• **Protecting and rewarding allies**: Maybe, like a machine politician, Moses simply wanted to reward and protect his allies. "One of [Bronx Borough President] Jimmy Lyons's relatives owns a piece of property up there and we would have had to take it if we used that other route, and Jimmy didn't want it taken, and RM promised him we wouldn't." Moses also knew that local politicians, who had financial stakes in the Third Avenue Transit Depot, located on the path of the highway.

So what was it? Caro never answers the mystery definitively. Probably, it was all of the above. But Caro lays out the tragedy in East Tremont with as much drama as an Agatha Christie mystery.

~

### And Another Thing . . .

WANT a surefire way to test whether the pieces of your scene fit together? Work backwards.

When we move backwards, we see the sequence of actions in a fresh way. Too often, when we read our own drafts, we fail to see kinks in the material. We have "familiarity blindness"—in other words, we cannot see flaws because we have seen the material too often.

So read backwards. Read your conclusion first—how the story is resolved. Then read the previous section, where the hero made a decision to change his life. Then, the previous section, where the hero recognized the issue that he has been denying all his life. Continue to work backwards, until you introduce the hero and the world of the story.

Read this passage from Martin Amis's novel *Time's Arrow* to see just how jarring—and revealing—backwards movement can be:

> First I stack the clean plates in the dishwasher. ... So far so good: then you select a soiled dish, collect some scraps from the garbage, and settle down for a short wait. Various items get gulped up into my mouth, and after skillful massage with tongue and teeth I transfer them to the plate for additional sculpture with knife and fork and spoon. That bit's therapeutic, at least, unless you're having soup or something, which can be a real sentence. Next you face the laborious business of cooking, of reassembly, of storage, before the return of these foodstuffs to the Superette, where, admittedly, I am promptly and generously reimbursed for my pains. Then you tool down the aisles, with trolley or basket, returning each can and packet to its rightful place.

Amis sustains this trick—telling the story backward, with the puzzlement of a naif—for 165 pages. We notice things we ordinarily would not notice because we see the scene running backwards.

By looking at events in reverse order, we can see details—about people and places, choices and actions, and the logic of the story—in fresh ways.

# DETAILS

When you walk into a room and you get a certain feeling or emotion, remember back until you see exactly what it was that gave you the emotion. Remember what the noises and smells were and what was said. Then write it down, making it clear so the reader will see it too and have the same feeling you had.

— ERNEST HEMINGWAY

**W**hat happens when you see? How do your eyes work? Can we train our eyes to see better? Can we train ourselves to observe better?

Before answering these questions, look at this chart. Read the letters, one at a time. Move from the first to fourth letters in each column, one by one. Then move from the third to fourth box in each column, one by one. Spend only as much time as necessary to notice what letter you have landed on.

$$
\begin{array}{ccccc}
\textbf{T} & \textbf{E} & \textbf{L} & \textbf{M} & \textbf{N} \\
\textbf{S} & \textbf{F} & \textbf{R} & \textbf{T} & \textbf{N} \\
\textbf{O} & \textbf{W} & \textbf{I} & \textbf{I} & \textbf{G} \\
\textbf{H} & \textbf{E} & \textbf{E} & \textbf{E} & \textbf{T}
\end{array}
$$

Now draw a box around any set of letters. Move your eyes inside, from one letter to another, inside the box. Then move around the outside of the box, again and again, until you have hit all the letters in the chart.

This is a variation of a game called Super Saccades. Eye specialists devised the game to help people exercise their eye movements so they can see better—or, to be more accurate, to *construct images* of what they see better.

When we view a scene, our eyes jump around three to five times a second, viewing tiny fragments of the scene at a time. These movements, about 15 degrees of vision, are called saccades. In saccades, our eyes jump to the most interesting pieces of the scene. What's interesting? Usually something with an unusual shape, color, or texture. As we quickly view these tiny pieces, our brain searches its memory for similar pieces and scenes. The brain creates a complete picture by combining the fragments it sees with the fragments of memory of past experiences.

"We can't perceive an entire visual scene simultaneously," University of Virginia psychologist Daniel Willingham notes. "We can pick out one object if it has some distinctive feature (e.g., a red car amidst a lot of white ones). But to appreciate a bunch of complex objects, you've got to serially process them."

Observation requires deliberate, patient work. We humans are not cameras, capable of recording all of a scene's details at once. What we see depends on what we look for—or what stands out. We have to scan, stop, look; then scan, stop, and look again; over and over, we scan, stop, and look.

∼

### Element 39
### Find Details By Looking Inside-Out

FINDING the right details requires learning to observe in new ways. A writer's job is to make the familiar unfamiliar and the unfamiliar familiar. When you find something that's familiar, don't write about what the reader would know already. Instead, find some details that would surprise the reader.

Start with a photograph of a fiddler from long-ago Asheville, North Carolina:

Right side up, you instantly recognize an older man, wearing a coat, poised to play a fiddle. You still recognize him upside-down, but it takes a moment of work. Without the picture's wholeness and familiarity, you process the image differently. Observed from an unfamiliar angle, you have to work to makes sense of the image. So you pay attention to shapes and shades. Rather than instantly thinking "fiddler," you look at the elements of the image, one at a time. And so you can find the telling details.

Betty Edwards, the author of *Drawing on the Right Side of the Brain*, teaches her students to draw by turning pictures upside-down so they pay better attention to the lines and shapes, the solids and voids, the colors and shadings.

You can also focus on details by envisioning a picture on a grid. Rather than paying attention to the whole picture, observe the shapes inside each of the boxes.

When you describe a person, scene, or action, break down your picture into segments. Observe the picture, square by square. Notice the colors, texture, shapes, and definition. Don't worry, right away, about the whole picture. Consider the image of the fiddler again, this time with a grid overlay.

Why do these strategies work? Because they slow down the brain's penchant for prediction. A brain researcher named Daniel Siegel explains:

> Our mental perceptions are constructed from [the brain's] drive to make disjointed reality into a fluid flow of experience. For example, our eyes blink frequently but our brains adjust to the gap in visual input and construct an unbroken picture. The brain has a bias for making the world appear solid and stable.

And whole. To find the telling details of any scene, break up the picture. Try not to pay attention to the familiar. Look, piece by piece, for the unfamiliar. Only then can you create a compelling image.

## Case Study
### Michel Foucault's *Discipline and Punish*

For most of human history, jails and prisons played a minor role in crime and punishment. Before the modern era, criminals and miscreants were held in jails only until they could be tried and punished. For the major form of punishment, beatings in public squares, people could gather and watch. This spectacle both affirmed the regime's authority and deterred criminal behavior.

Prisons offered a more rational and predictable means to control crime. Reformers like Benjamin Franklin in the U.S. and Jeremy Bentham in England believed that prisons provided a way to shape the criminal's mind. Bentham developed the concept of the panopticon, an "all seeing" prison that allowed guards to keep an eye on prisoners all day long.

In contrast with ancient dungeons—where prisoners were isolated in dark and invisible cells—the panopticon made prisoners visible. At the center of the panopticon stood a tower; around the periphery were cells. At any moment, the guard could peer into any cell and observe any inmate. Prisoners never knew when they might be under surveillance, so they were "disciplined" to behave at all times.

The French philosopher Michel Foucault describes the panopticon (the numbers in brackets are mine):

> Bentham's Panopticon is the architectural figure of this composition. We know the principle on which it was based: [1] at the periphery, an annular building; [2] at the centre, a tower; [3] this tower is pierced with wide windows that open onto the inner side of the ring; [4] the peripheric building is divided into cells, each of which extends the whole width of the building; [5] they have two windows, one on the inside, corresponding to the windows of the tower; the other, on the outside, allows the light to cross the cell from one end to the other. [6] All that is needed, then, is to place a supervisor in a central tower and to shut up in each cell a madman, a patient, a condemned man, a worker or a schoolboy. [7] By the effect of backlighting, one can observe from the tower, standing out precisely against the light, the small captive shadows in the cells of the periphery. [8] They are like so many cages, so many small theaters, in which each actor is alone, perfectly individualized and constantly visible.

The panopticon has set the standard for prison design—and the larger process of criminal justice—for more than two centuries. It also has informed design and construction for public housing, schools and college campuses, medical centers, town centers, and more. The panopticon, in fact, shapes every institution and experience of modern life.

Now let's examine this panoptic design. Take a look at the Stateville Correctional Center, a maximum-security prison in Crest Hill, Illinois.

Interior View of Cell House, new Illinois State Penitentiary at Stateville, near Joliet, Ill.—23

Move around the picture. Start with the biggest elements—the tower and the periphery. Then zoom in on the details. Step by step, identify what you see. Take just one element at a time. Describe each of the elements of the panopticon that Foucault describes, beginning with [1] and ending with [8].

This step-by-step process is how to *see*—and how to *describe* what you see.

〜

### Element 40
### Isolate Details to Make Big Points

"IN THE PARTICULAR," Anton Chekhov said, "is contained the universal."

Consider this great paradox. The more specific your writing—about characters, scenes, places, actions, moments—the more readers relate to it.

Specific details tap into your reader's memories and emotions. When you provide vivid details, the reader relates to these details. Your details prompt the reader to recall childhood moments, traumatic events, moments of ecstasy, images and sounds, feelings and emotions.

When you offer surprising details—the small nods and sighs, the light in the room and the color of the paint on the wall, the sound of the brook or the smell of the soil—your reader trusts you. Why? Rather than telling your reader what to think, you offer information that she can use to make her own judgments.

Details give authority to stories and arguments. Even if a character's paisley blouse, layered hair, or magenta lip gloss don't matter much, they show that the writer was attentive. And so the writer gains credibility.

To describe a person, place, or action, look for the aspects that are unusual —especially those that others might not notice. If you walk into a party, don't just look at the friends and family who shout "Surprise!" Look at the people on the edge of the room. Look for someone wearing an uneasy smile. Look for people and things that seem out of place, exaggerated, or understated. When you describe a familiar person—like Washington or Lincoln or FDR—don't repeat the details we know already. Show us something we don't know.

Look at this photograph of Richard Nixon. In most ways, Nixon was an ordinary looking man. He resembled most other middle-aged men of his time.

Nixon differed from most other men only in minor ways: the ski-jump nose, the beady eyes, the patchy hair, the bushy brows, and the jowls. Cartoonists exaggerated Nixon's distinctive features because they know that, to recognize something, we need to look for *what's different*.

Think about it. Has anyone every described someone like this: "Oh, you can't miss him—he's the one with two eyes, a nose, and a mouth"? To describe people, place, action, or idea, focus on what's *different*.

Cathy Davidson of Duke's Center for Cognitive Neuroscience offers a scientific explanation:

Attention is about *difference*. We pay attention to things that are *not* part of out automatic repertoire of responses, reflexes, concepts, preconceptions, behaviors, knowledge, and categories and other patterns both mental and physical (if we can make such a crude distinction) for which we have over time developed more and more efficient neural pathways.

So find the details that surprise the reader. Use colors, sounds, textures, shapes, and utterances that startle, amuse, or disturb the reader. Move from the predictable to the unpredictable.

## Case Study
## Wendy Lesser's *You Say to Brick*

We see with our eyes and even more with our brain. As our eyes dart around a scene, our mind fills in the gaps. Based on what we have seen before, we project details onto our scene. From this we create a complete picture.

That's when we need to take charge of the experience. Rather than just go wherever the eye and memory take us, we need to *direct* our attention to specific *details* of the scene. Only then can we notice what we're actually seeing —and why it matters.

Consider Wendy Lesser's assessment of the Kimball Art Museum in Fort Worth, Texas, designed by Louis Kahn. To begin, Lesser looks at the impact of an arched ceiling on the museum, in this passage:

> Take, for instance, the most distinctive feature of the interior, the arched ceilings that curve over the individual galleries, each shedding its measure of natural light from above. Being inside these long, high rooms makes you feel utterly at peace: a bit like the sensation you get in England's Dulwich Picture Gallery, perhaps, except that here Sir John Soane's elegant nineteenth-century materials and structures have been replaced by something distinctly modern. The concrete vault over your head is high enough to give you a sense of grandeur, not so high as to intimidate, with a gentle, unspectacular curve that holds the facing walls and all the paintings on them in its tender embrace.

Now that we understand the scene—the baths of light that the arched ceilings invite inside the museum—we can see how the setting affects the experience of viewing art. Here, Lesser examines how people look at paintings in Kahn's museum:

> Because the paintings are for the most part small, or at any rate human-sized, they are fully graspable when viewed straight on from a couple of feet away. They allow you to form an intimate, one-on-one connection with them. The portraits, too, are hung so that the faces are just about at face height (if you are roughly five foot six, which was Kahn's height), and this increases the intimacy

of the encounter. You may even get the feeling that some of these faces are leaning toward you, and that is not an optical illusion, for the paintings hanging on the travertine walls are actually suspended by nearly invisible threads that descend from above, causing the upper edge of each frame to jut out slightly while the bottom edge rests against the wall. This not only has the effect of making the image loom gently forward; it also makes the whole painting seem as if it were floating in air.

With this shift, Lesser brings us into the museum goer's world—more specifically, the space directly in front of the painting. With such a focus, Lesser can explore how that space works. The optical illusion of the painting, for example, comes from their hanging on threads from the wall. By focusing on a single subject, Lesser can find the details that make that experience possible.

~

### Element 41
### Use Status Details to Reveal Ego and Desire

AS SOCIAL CREATURES, we care about our place in the status system. We want to fit in, but we also want to stand out. So we send signals—in our dress, cars, homes, work, schools, hobbies, and speech—about how we want others to see us.

How important is status? So important that we sense pain and threat when it's challenged. To explore this point, Naomi Wiesenberger, a brain researcher at UCLA, asked study subjects to play a video game of dodge ball. Halfway through the game, two of the on-screen players turned away from the third to play a private game of catch. So how did the real-life player at the computer respond? The part of the brain that processes physical pain—the dorsal region of the anterior cingulate cortex—was activated. "Those who felt the most rejected," Wiesenberger reported, "had the highest levels of activity in this [pain] region." Even in a computer simulation!

Status comes both from conformity and difference. Conformity connects us to others. As social creatures, we depend on others for affirmation of our value. We need others to tell us that we're OK. Psychology experiments show that people begin to look like each other—and follow each other's rhythms—when they spend lots of time together. We need to say, in effect, *I'm just like you*. On the other hand, we need to separate ourselves from the pack. Lost in the sameness of the group, we lose our sense of self. So, while *fitting in*, we also want to *stand out*.

Some years ago, I worked with teachers at an independent school in Connecticut. While I waited for a meeting, I stood in a hallway and watched the teenaged students arrive. It was homecoming week, when students dress in different period costumes every day. One day they wore togas, another they wore colonial garb. On this day, they wore western clothing.

As the students climbed the stairway, they strutted in anticipation of their friends' *oohs* and *aahs*. One by one, they showed off their jeans and prairie dresses, plaid shirts and cowboy hats, headdresses and leather skirts and vests. What was different seemed to matter most. But look again. All these kids conformed to contemporary norms. They sauntered the way teenagers do. The boys wore baggy pants and styled their hair like Tom Brady. The girls wore tighter clothes and styled their hair like *Seventeen* models.

We want a sense of adventure, but we also want the stability of social norms. We care about appearances, about status and style, how we look and what people think about us. We want to look like the members of our tribes. We want to tell the world—with what we wear and drive, how we walk and talk—how we fit into the social order.

Tom Wolfe coined the term "status details" to describe the telling markers of social position. Status details, Wolfe says, involve

> the recording of everyday gestures, habits, manners, customs, styles of furniture, clothing, decoration, styles of traveling, eating, keeping house, modes of behavior toward children, servants, superiors, inferiors, peers, plus the various looks, glances, poses, styles of walking and other symbolic details that might exist within a scene. Symbolic of what? Symbolic, generally, of people's status life, using that term in the broad sense of the entire pattern and behavior and possessions through which people express their position in the world or what they think it is or what they hope it to be. The recording of such details is not mere embroidery in prose. It lies as close to the center of the power of realism as any other device in literature.

Status details offer a glimpse into the character's ego—and a community's swirl of egos, the tensions between individual expression and group conformity, and the deeper values that shape both individuals and groups. These details also tell us something about the time and place—the technologies, the trends and fads, and the zeal and the repression of the period.

## Case Study
### Steven Aronson's 'New York Apogee'

The leitmotif of Donald Trump's life, by all accounts, is the striving for success, adulation, privilege, and luxury.

As his biographers have noted, Trump's upbringing produced two often contradictory drives. First, Trump aimed to please his father Fred, a hard-driving developer in the Queens borough of New York City. Fred, a harsh and aggressive man, was known for his hard-edged business tactics, his brusque style with family, and his ties to shady business partners. Second, Trump sought to escape his father's world by graduating to the glamour of Manhattan, where he could build glittering skyscrapers that make his father's public-housing projects pale into insignificance.

Trump's greatest achievement, by all accounts, is Trump Tower, the 58-story, 664-foot building on Fifth Avenue, between 56th and 57th Streets. In his other business endeavors—in real estate, sports, casinos, "Trump University," airlines, food and spirits, even beauty pageants—Trump's attention wandered. But on this project, Trump stayed focused and clear about his vision, especially for the top three stories that became his home.

Trump brags regularly about his apartment and building. Trump Tower, he told *Architectural Digest*, is "the finest apartment in the top building in the best location in the hottest city in the world." He elaborated: "In the real estate business we have a generic term for the best location, wherever it is: the Tiffany location. And Trump Tower is literally that—it looks down on Tiffany's, which I purchased the air rights to a number of years ago."

The apartment itself is a seven-bedroom triplex penthouse with a two-story living room. *Architectural Digest* provides a seven-page tour of the apartment, filled with glossy images of the rooms and Trump posing with his first wife Ivana. Steven Aronson writes:

> Everything in the Trumps' two-story living room savors of the luxurious: from the understated chairs and sofas to a banquette covered with a fabric painted in 24K gold; to the antique Venetia-style mirror and the brown marble fireplace; up, up, up to the gold-leaf ceiling. "It's close to 20 feet," Donald Trump notes, "about as high as any ceiling in any new building in years." …
>
> The city literally ripples in the glass, flowing by day and flashing by night, its rivers and bridges caught in the crossweave of time and space. …
>
> [T]he bedroom … overlooks the living room and through that the city. "Ivana wanted a very feminine feeling up here," [the designer] Angelo Donghia said. "And she got it—peach-pink mirrors, peach suede walls. It's soft, comfortable, and modern." …
>
> The top floor offers guest rooms—not used very often since Trump owns the Grand Hyatt, the St. Moritz and the Barbizon Plaza hotels. The top floor also houses space for the three kids, with a nanny's quarters and kitchen and dining room. …
>
> "We're turning the entire roof of the building into a private park for our children," Donald Trump says. "It's going to have statues, waterfalls, gazebos, and everything else we can think of. We also own the duplex next to our triplex and we're converting it into a gym and play area for the kids. The space will also yield a huge library and a dining room for big buffets."

Every aspect of the penthouse expressed Trump's outsized aspirations and ego, his ideas about the good life, and his beliefs about success. To paraphrase Dorothy in *The Wizard of Oz*: "Toto, we're not in Queens anymore."

~

**Element 42**
**Put Details into Action**

WHEN YOU SEEK DETAILS, look for movement.

To observe movement, isolate the parts of a scene. Watch animals play in a field or marsh. Watch a crowd sway at a ballgame or concert. Watch the wind bend the trees. Watch the rhythms of people moving around a town square.

Movement activates the senses. By seeing movement, the reader can see, hear, feel, and even smell the action. Seeing details in motion reveals *relationships*. You get a sense of what causes what. You can also explain something complex, moment by moment.

Think back to the saccade chart. No matter what we view, our eyes dart from point to point to construct the whole picture.

To describe movement, create a "track" in your mind. Don't just assemble a mental picture of the scene; look for the elements that change over time. Focus on the subject—a person or animal, a car or other vehicle, a ball or other object of action—and observe it move across the scene. As you do so, notice how the action affects things nearby. Think of your subject like a motorboat moving through water. How and where does it move? What changes over the course of the movement? What kind of a wake does it produce? How does that wake affect other elements of the picture?

Even still pictures can be dynamic. A verbal snapshot of a moment in time can show all kinds of relationships. A sequence of those shots can tell a whole story.

**Case Study**
**Tony Hiss' *The Experience of Place***

Cities are, at their best, dynamic, sensual places. They bring people together in dazzling places to pursue countless dreams and projects. Urbanites develop a sixth sense for moving around in space. Anyone who has ever traveled through Grand Central Station in New York knows the amazing mixture of overwhelm and calm, confusion and focus, wandering and purpose.

Tony Hiss describes Grand Central Station first by detailing its physical attributes:

> The concourse is 470 feet long and the 160 feet wide, and it is 150 feet—15 stories, perhaps—from the floor to the peak of the vaulted ceiling. The room has arched windows 33 feet wide and 60 feet high, which are deep enough to have corners running through them—a series of walkways built between the outer glass and the inner glass in each window—and it has constellations painted on the ceiling, with 60 of the stars really glowing, because they are small light bulbs. A balcony

30 feet wide and 20 feet above the floor runs along every wall except the south
one. ...

Having oriented readers to the station's architecture, Hiss turns his attention to the way people move around and experience the place:

One recent weekday afternoon around 3:30, I entered the concourse from the
east, through one of the two long, nearly straight passageways that lead in from
Lexington Avenue. I came out of the east side IRT subway into the more
southerly of the two straightaways and immediately found myself part of a
stream of people, four and five abreast, all of them looking straight ahead and
moving at a fast New York clip toward the concourse along the right hand side of
the tunnel only twice the width of the stream itself. Toward me along the left side
of the corridor—which was well lighted, has a low white ceiling and a base
marble floor, and is lined with convenience stores—came a second stream of
people, just as wide, and moving at the same speed and with the same look.

Finally he considers his own place in this whirl of activity:

Though I could hear my own footsteps, nearby foot falls in normal tones of voice
registered as loud but blurred, indeterminate noises, and although no one was
touching me, or even brushing past, I kept feeling that I was about to be bumped
into. People sounded closer than they looked, and they seemed closer still,
because my eyes and ears couldn't determine whether the people I was looking
at where the people making the sounds I could hear.

By putting details into action—seeing how all of the elements of Grand
Central Station actually work, rush hour after rush hour—Hiss gives us a sense
of the station's grandeur.

∾

### And Another Thing . . .

WHEN I WAS a young reporter for United Press International in the 1980s, I
wrote a feature story about a Vanderbilt University medical researcher named
Pierre Soupart. A pioneer of *in vitro* fertilization, Soupart spent as much time
battling politics—the Reagan Administration's determination to block research
that might, in some way, offend the religious right—as working in the lab.
Soupart's story offered a fascinating glimpse into the politics of science.

When I submitted my article, my editor asked one question: "What's he
look like?"

I didn't understand why that mattered. Wasn't the article supposed to
explore the controversies surrounding Soupart's research? Shouldn't I focus on

the battles involving the Reagan Administration, the Christian Right, the medical community, and federal bureaucrats? Why did Soupart's *appearance* matter?

The reader needs to *picture* Soupart to *care* about him. The details I added— he was a short man with graying hair and a moustache, a chain smoker who always wore white lab coats—enable the reader picture Dr. Soupart moving around the lab, clipboard in hand, conferring with his young researchers. These details give him life.

Small details give us a sense we are in the subject's company. And remember, readers like to be in someone's company.

Observing carefully, in order to find telling details, requires slowing down the brain. You need to clear away distractions, so you can pay attention to the many elements of a picture you otherwise might not notice.

Psychologists call this quieting process "mindfulness." Mindfulness requires carefully observing thoughts, feelings, perceptions, and sensations. A mindful person works to avoid automatic responses. A mindful writer sees and describes each person, thing, or incident carefully, avoiding judgmental attitudes. By leaving behind judgment, you allow yourself to see things with a fresh eye.

# 11

# GRAMMAR

If you can remember all the accessories that go with your best outfit, the contents of your purse, the starting lineup of the New York Yankees or the Houston Oilers, or what label "Hang On Sloopy" by The McCoys was on, you are capable of remembering the differences between a gerund (verb form used as a noun) and a participle (verb form used as an adjective).

— STEPHEN KING

Noam Chomsky won fame a half century ago with his theory that language follows a universal grammar. How we use language—how we put words into sequences—is as basic to humans as how we eat or reproduce. Here are some of Chomsky's basic observations about the elements of grammar:

- All languages use vocabularies with many thousands of words.
- All languages use subjects and predicates.
- All languages use nouns and verbs.
- All languages use sets of sounds—but that set is just a small share of the total sounds that humans hear.
- All languages categorize distinctions in meaning in similar ways.

And so on. Still, how we apply grammar depends on our needs at any given time and place. Grammar started as a way to pace speech. The terms *comma, colon,* and *periodos* originally referred to the rhythm of speech. The point was to create meaningful pauses. At each pause, the speaker could impart as much information as the audience could take in.

Necessity, then, was the mother of punctuation. Communications requires that we adopt a common set of rules. Just as drivers need to follow the "rules of the road"—when to stop, change lanes, yield, turn, and so on—writers need rules to guide their own journeys.

~

### Element 43
### Make Sure the Parts of Speech Get Along

LIKE THE MEMBERS of a family taking a road trip, the different parts of speech need to get along. The nouns need to cooperate with the verbs and the pronouns. The modifiers have to stay close to the things they modify. Verbs and helping verbs also need to stick together.

A handful of simple rules will keep all your words working together. Think of them in three parts. Start by saying *who's who and what's what*. Then *show the action*. Finally, *make everything whole*.

**Rule 1. Say who's who and what's what**

Nothing matters more than the subject. So follow these simple rules to make the subject—*who and what*—clear.

• **Make nouns agree with verbs.** The principle is simple: Singular nouns get singular verbs, and plural nouns get plural verbs. But applying the rule can get tricky.

The greatest cause of confusion is the prepositional phrase, which modifies subjects and verbs. Prepositions are words that indicate relations, like *over, under, with, beside, next to, before,* and *after*. When we use prepositional phrase, we sometimes confuse the modifier for the subject. In the phrase "a group of children," for example, the subject is *group*, not *children*. Therefore, the verb should be singular: "A group of children is going to the playground." Focus on the subject and you'll always get it right.

Plural nouns also make noun-verb agreement tricky. Most words linked by *and* create a plural noun—and therefore require a plural verb. Thus: "The president and Congress *were* at loggerheads over the education legislation." But hyphenated words are considered a singular noun. Thus: "Give-and-take *is* required for passage of legislation." Some words ending in *s*, like politics, sports, and headquarters, seem plural but are actually singular. Some—like *politics* and *sports*—can be used both ways.

Use singular verbs for *each, either, everyone, everybody, neither, nobody, no one,* and *someone*. *None* is singular when it refers to a singular noun and plural when it refers to a plural noun: "None of the apartment was painted" says that no part of the *one apartment*—not the living room, not the dining room, not the bedroom—was painted. "None of the apartments were painted" says that none of the many *units* in a building—were painted.

• **Make nouns agree with verbs and pronouns**. We face a similar problem matching nouns and pronouns. People mistakenly treat a collective entity—like a school, team, or family—as a plural noun. So we see sentences like this: "In 2008, Vanderbilt won their first five games." But Vanderbilt is a single entity, so say "Vanderbilt won *its* first five games" instead.

The British use *their* in this situation, on the grounds that the subject—in this case, the team—contains multitudes. In fact, the British style was common in the U.S. until the eighteenth century. But we live in 21st century America now. Don't blur singulars and plurals.

• **Use possessives correctly**. The big challenge here is to avoid confusing possessive words with contractions.

To indicate a singular noun's possession of something, use an apostrophe and the letter *s*. For example: *Prince Charles's marital problems, James MacGregor Burns's study of leadership*, and *the witch's demise*. To indicate the possessive of a plural noun, usually just add an apostrophe. Thus: *The Democrats' electoral chances*.

With letters and digits, plurals look like singular possessives. So: *The A's have a good chance to win the pennant*.

Possessives get confusing when you talk about two or more people or entities. Consider the characters in the slapstick movie *Bill and Ted's Excellent Adventure*. Written this way, the title refers to a single adventure that both characters enjoyed. Bill and Ted comprise a single entity.

If this pair enjoyed several adventures together, say "Bill and Ted's Excellent Adventures." If each character enjoyed separate adventures, give both of them possessives: "Bill's and Ted's Excellent Adventures." If they separately enjoyed the same adventure—if, for example, each time-traveled to the French Revolution in separate time machines—say "Bill's and Ted's Excellent Adventure."

Now that we know how to use possessives, let's discuss the dangers of confusing possessives and contractions.

A contraction combines subject and verb. We use contractions to sound informal. Instead of saying, for example, "Bill Clinton is a native of Arkansas," we say "Bill Clinton's a native of Arkansas." Formal writing usually avoids such shortcuts; more casual writing doesn't hesitate a moment to use a contraction.

### Rule 2. Show the Action

The ultimate goal of all writing is to show action. Even when exploring ideas that we don't ordinarily see—like *freedom* or *fission*—we need to show something happening.

• **Get the tenses right**: Compared to other languages, English tenses are simple.

Start with inflections, the endings to verbs that change tense and meaning. English verbs use only four inflections for regular verbs. So we say, for example, that we *play*, he *plays*, he or we *played*, he is or we *are playing*. Simple enough: add *-s*, *-ed*, *-ing*, or nothing, and you can describe almost all action. By comparison, Latin verbs use 120 inflections.

Still, English poses its share of complications. Irregular verbs, for example, do not follow standard rules. Consider these examples:

**Base form—Past tense—Past participle**
Beat—Beat—Beat / beaten
Begin—Began—Begun
Blow—Blew—Blown
Fall—Fell—Fallen
Dive—Dived—Dived
Get—Got—Gotten
Keep—Kept—> Kept
Know—Knew—Known
Lay—Lain—Laid
Lie—Lay—Lain
Ring—Rang—Rung
See—Saw—Seen
Sink—Sank—Sunk

These verb forms are oddballs, with no obvious logic. Unfortunately, you need to memorize these—or at least be aware that you need to look them up.

• **Choose the tense that makes your writing clear**. Use tenses clearly and consistently. Specific historic events and past practices usually requires the past tense: *Martin Luther King rallied garbage workers in Memphis* and *Thomas Edison failed 10,000 times to develop a storage battery*.

To indicate an event that happened before another past event, use the past perfect tense. So you could say: *Martin Luther King* had gone *to Memphis when he was assassinated*. The past perfect tense talks about two different moments in the past at the same time. But when you litter your prose with past perfect, it gets hard to write simply. So use double-back tense sparingly, as a way to transition to that a simple past tense.

References to imagined past circumstances require a verb form known as the *subjunctive*: *If Abraham Lincoln had lived, the nation would avoided the bitter conflicts of Reconstruction*. Other imagined situations also require the subjunctive. I might say, for example, *If I were Superman, I would fly to work*. I will never be Superman, so the situation is purely imagined.

Also use the subjunctive to express extreme improbabilities: *If I were a Rockefeller, I would give away millions for cancer research*. Someone could become a

Rockefeller by marriage, of course, but it's not a real possibility for most people.

• **Avoid double negatives, usually**. Double negatives require the reader to spend too much time figuring out the meaning of a statement. Double negatives also say what isn't, rather than what is. So they leave too many possibilities open.

Take this statement: *Senator Patty Murray was not displeased with the education bill*. What does the senator think? The phrase tells us about the *absence* of something (displeasure) but not the *presence* of its opposite (pleasure). One thing's absence, after all, does not make its opposite present. Was the senator pleased? Thrilled? Indifferent? Intrigued? Uncertain? The reader cannot know.

Besides creating uncertainty, double negatives produce gloom. Psychologists report that using negative words actually depress people. Unlike math, where two negatives produce a positive, writing with double negatives multiplies negativity.

• **Avoid splitting infinitives, usually**. To understand a split infinitive, consider the distraction that occurs when a child interrupts a conversation or a when a cellphone beeps.

A split infinitive occurs when a word (usually an adverb) gets between a verb and helping verb.

Consider this: *Kate Smith liked to really sing loudly*. We know the meaning of this simple sentence. Kate liked to sing loudly. How much damage can *really*'s interruption of *to sing* cause? Not much, usually. In fact, a growing number of language mavens scoff at the old-fashioned ban of split infinitives. In her book *Grammar Snobs Are Great Big Meanies*, June Casagrande declares "only windbags fuss over split infinitives."

Split infinitives may, as Casagrande argues, add panache to a sentence. The *Star Trek* TV series opens like this: "To boldly go where no man has gone before." Getting to "boldly" sooner rather than later gives the passage panache. So we should not get too upset, right? Still, I wonder. Would "To go boldly where no man has gone before" lack pizzazz? What about "Boldly going where no man has gone before"? Both phrases work for me. Maybe we should heed the split-infinitive cops after all.

• **Use contractions, selectively**. Avoid contractions, unless you want to create a casual mood or quote someone else using contractions.

Formal documents like academic papers and legal documents usually avoid contractions because they sound informal. Using contractions in a formal document is like wearing Bermuda shorts to a wedding or funeral. Fit the style to the context.

In more conversational pieces, contractions help you sound real. You would not want to say "Let us suppose," would you? Don't irritate your reader with stuffiness. As a rule of thumb, use contractions when doing otherwise sounds stiff. That is (that's?) a judgment call.

### Rule 3. Make everything whole.

The best writing gives the reader a satisfying sense of wholeness. The story is not just a collection of events, but something that adds up to something complete and unified. An incomplete story produces frustration.

Likewise with grammar. When someone raises a point, but fails to complete it, we feel frustrated.

So consider a few grammatical tips to make sure you complete your thoughts:

• **Use sentence fragments and run-on sentences, only occasionally, for effect**. A sentence fragment is an incomplete thought. Like this. A run-on sentence goes on and on, often changing subjects, which gets confusing, because the writer should break it up into parts, and the reader will understand the thoughts better, and the writer won't confuse the reader.

These days, even academic writers use fragments to make writing conversational. Look how the Yale historian Edmund Morgan describes Benjamin Franklin trying to unmoor his ship:

> Franklin strips to his shirt and wades out into the water and mud up to his waist but finds the boat chained and locked to a staple in the stake. He tries to wrench out the staple. No go. He tries to pull up the stake. No go. Back to shore, and the three start looking for a farmer's haystack to sleep in.

Morgan uses these brief phrases—"No go" (twice) and "Back to shore"—to pace and redirect the passage. Morgan makes his youthful subject sprightly. But be careful. Too many short, telegraphic passages annoy the reader. If you're in doubt, tell yourself: *No go.*

Avoid run-on sentences, except, on rare occasions, when you want to describe long and meandering trains of thought that connect the present with the past or move from the here-and-now to some imagined or real past or even describe a place that meanders and weaves its way, like a path that winds up a steep mountain and ...

As your "default" style, write simple sentences. Only when you master the simple can you develop command of the complex.

• **Don't dangle your participles**. Participles are verb phrases that provide background information.

Consider this example: *Having served as supreme allied commander during World War II, Dwight Eisenhower understood bureaucracy.* The participial phrase "Having served as supreme allied commander during World War II" offers useful information about Eisenhower. You know it makes sense when you take out the prepositional phrase: *Having served, Dwight Eisenhower understood bureaucracy.*

But participial phrases often breed confusion. Sloppy writers often forget what phrase they mean to modify. Consider this sentence:

Winning the states of the old Confederacy, the electoral system tilted toward the Republican Party after Richard Nixon's 1968 campaign.

That participial phrase should modify the Republican Party, not the electoral system. So try this instead:

Winning the states of the old Confederacy, the Republican Party gained electoral dominance starting with Richard Nixon's 1968 campaign.

Do you know the political adage "Keep your friends close and your enemies closer"? Try this grammatical reminder: Nouns should keep their verbs close and their modifiers closer.

Writers err when they lose track of *what belongs with what.* They forget what subject goes with what verb, what modifier goes with what subject or verb, what noun goes with what pronoun, what noun or verb with what adjective or adverb.

At the end of every passage, just ask yourself what belongs with what. Move the pieces around until you find the right matches.

## Case Study
## Charles Bagli's *Other People's Money*

Charlie Bagli follows the three major rules of grammar in *Other People's Money,* his study of New York's real estate industry and the billion-dollar renovation (and takeover) of the Stuyvesant Town in Greenwich Village.

Let's see how he does it, in these passages about the construction of the massive apartment complex:

### Rule 1: Say Who's Who and What's What.

Like all rules, this one is easier to follow in simple situations. As the situation gets complex—as sentences get longer, with more topics and more complex action—it gets harder.

• **Match subjects and verbs**. We need to make sure the subject and verb agree with each other. Consider this passage:

In the fall of 1945, bulldozers, pile drivers, and steam shovels rumbled on to the Stuyvesant Town-Peter Cooper Village site to begin demolition of over 500 tenements, factories, warehouses, and storefronts.

The subjects and verbs do match here. Subject: *bulldozers, pile drivers, and steam shovels.* Verb: *rumbled.*

• **Match nouns and pronouns**. Things get tricky when you use pronouns. A pronoun removes the specificity. Consider this passage:

"We used to walk through the neighborhood," said Garcea, 77 and still marveling at the thought of it in 2001. "It looked like a war zone. It looked bombed out when they got through with it."

Again, everything is in order. Noun: *the neighborhood*. Pronouns: *it, it* and *it*. Because the noun and pronounce are so close together, we don't lose track of them. But using the same pronoun a sentence or two later might be confusing.

As the ideas accumulate, the challenges of grammar increase. In the following passage, we encounter a tricky possessive:

Metropolitan had acquired the land over two years, sometimes using intermediaries to mask their shopping spree so the property owners would not suddenly hike their prices.

*Their* is the possessive word. But what does it refer to? The way the sentence begins, you might think *their* refers to *Metropolitan*. But *Metropolitan* is a singular noun; *their* is a plural possessive. Does that mean Bagli goofed? I'm not sure. If *their* refers to the intermediaries, Bagli's in the clear. Maybe, to avoid confusion, Balgli should have done something like this:

Metropolitan had acquired the land over two years. The company's intermediaries masked their shopping spree so the property owners would not suddenly hike their prices.

Almost always, you can eliminate confusion by breaking up sentences.

### *Rule 2: Show the Action.*

In all good writing, something happens. Some form of action changes the world, in some way.

• **Get the tenses right, using the one that makes the action clear**: Most clear writing uses present and past tenses. But sometimes, for the sake of clarity, you need to use a different tense. Let's see how Bagli describes action in his work:

With the war winding down Europe, the insured judged that the moment had arrived to start building.

When a story takes place in two times—the major events, as well as the events that preceded them—you need to separate those times. So in this passage, Bagli distinguishes between the context (the war winding down) from the specific action (the insured judged).

Bagli avoids three common mistakes—using double negatives ("He wasn't without resources"), split infinitives ("He was strongly opposed") or unnecessary contractions ("Tenants didn't have enough money").

### Rule 3: Make Everything Whole.

Just as a house or neighborhood should have a sense of wholeness—a sense that all the pieces add up to something complete—so should sentences and passages. Almost always, that means giving every sentence a strong Subject-Verb-Object structure.

• **Limit use of fragments and run-on sentences**. Occasionally, to emphasize a point or create a mood, you can use a fragment or a run-on sentence. Consider Bagli's next passage:

> Some 765,000 veterans returned to New York City, exacerbating the existing housing shortage. The veterans were living in trailers, tourist camps, and Quonset hut, or doubled up with friends and relatives. Most of them could not afford to buy a house, which the city's Veterans Service Center said would require an income of $90 dollars a week, $34 dollars more than the average among veterans.

Bagli could have used a sentence fragment for emphasis or a run-on sentence to draw together a long string of thoughts. But he does not want to distract his own story. Good choice.

• **Use contractions only when you want to create a sense of informality**. Bagli also could have used contractions to make the writing more informal, like this:

> Metropolitan announced that it'd give veterans a preference at all of its housing developments.

Happily, Bagli stuck to simple and clear sentences, throughout his work. A consummate pro, Bagli lets his strong research and reporting carry the day. He avoids stylistic flourishes that would interfere with his narrative.

~

### Element 44
### Use Punctuation to Direct Traffic

IF ALL SENTENCES ARE JOURNEYS, which take the reader from one place to another, punctuation offers traffic signals to manage the traffic.

Punctuation tells the reader whether to stop (period), slow down (comma), look both ways (question mark), look forward (colon), yield (semicolon), or proceed slowly (ellipses).

Let's explore these signs in some detail.

**Use periods to stop the action**. The period is the writer's best friend. By marking the end of the sentence, the period gives permission to stop one thought and proceed to the next.

The British call the period the "full stop." The term is more than a label; it's also a command, with a theatrical air. The message is simple. If you can learn to make a simple statement, and then stop, you will become a good writer.

A liberal dose of periods would solve many writing problems. Most bad writing happens when the writer wanders off the subject. Mark Kramer used to hold out his cupped hands to his Nieman fellows at Harvard University. "Here's an unlimited supply of periods," he would say. "Use 'em all you want. No limits!" You could almost see those dots filling his hands, as dense and rich as black caviar.

**Use commas to pause the action**. If good writing depends on flow, the comma is the writer's second best friend. Commas create pauses, giving the reader a brief moment to sort ideas and images.

Commas serve two major functions. First, commas separate items in lists, so we do not get lost in a long train of nouns. Second, commas serve as parentheses that allow us to make side comments.

To make lists in a sentence, just insert a comma after every item. So: *Willie Mays could hit, hit with power, catch, run, and throw.*

Some editors say you can delete the last comma, known as a serial comma or an Oxford comma. I disagree. Without that last comma, "run and throw" sound like a single skill. Most people, of course, understand running and throwing to be separate skills. But why risk even a brief moment of confusion? Consider the line from Robert Frost's poem "Stopping By Woods on a Snowy Evening":

*The woods are lovely, dark, and deep.*

The line's meaning varies depending on the use of a serial comma. With the serial comma, *lovely, dark, and deep* refer to three separate attributes of the woods. Without the serial comma, *dark and deep* modifies *lovely*.

Commas also offer space for the writer to make a parenthetical comment. Therefore: *Willie Mays, a first-ballot Hall of Fame member, is baseball's greatest living player.* Mays's status as a Hall of Famer comes as parenthetical remark.

In both cases—separating items in a list and making a parenthetical remark —commas offer the pause the refreshes. But be careful not use commas to pause too often. With too many pauses, you lose tempo. Consider the following 70-word sentence from *The New Yorker*:

The first time that Sam Popkin, a political scientist at the University of California at San Diego, who, along with his wife, the China scholar Susan Shirk, has known Hu [Shuli] for many years, watched Hu report a story, it reminded him of the portrait of the *Times* reporter R. W. Apple in *The Boys on the Bus*, when "Apple used to make something like a hundred calls a day," Popkin said.

Nine commas shatter a simple idea (Hu is manic!) into a dozen pieces. Look how we might express the same idea with fewer commas:

With her frenetic pace, Hu Shuli resembles the legendary *Times* reporter Johnny Apple. As Hu's friend Sam Popkin notes, "Apple used to make something like a hundred calls a day."

In 29 words—two sentences, 12 and 17 words long, using two commas— the new passage says what matters. Surplus commas tempt the writer to go off on tangents. The new version avoids those tangents.

**Use colons to look ahead**. When you look through the viewfinder of a camera, you narrow your perspective to whatever lies in front of you. The colon acts in much the same way. Colons offer a way to pause a moment to look ahead. So:

Before he ran for president, Barack Obama had the same political experience as Abraham Lincoln: eight years in the state legislature and two years in Congress.

A colon also sets up a list:

Winter is coming, so get out your cold-weather gear: coats, hats, gloves, boots, and earmuffs.

When a sentence contains two passages that could stand alone as sentences, do not use a colon. Instead, use a period or a semicolon.

**Use semicolons to make a complex list; also use them to combine complete thoughts**. The semicolon's only mandatory function is to make lists within lists. In this sense, the semicolon acts as a super comma. Therefore:

To win the presidency, Democrats need to win Northeastern states, like New York, New Jersey, and Connecticut; Rust Belt states, like Ohio, Michigan, Wisconsin, and Illinois; and liberal bastions, like California, Oregon, and Massachusetts.

The semicolon's second function is optional. The semicolon creates a break —and a connection—between two complete thoughts in the same sentence. So:

William Buckley was a polymath; he was a writer, editor, speaker, activist, harpsichordist, and sailor.

Think of those independent thoughts as separate roads coming together. The semicolon provides the Yield sign that allows traffic to merge.

We could express those thoughts in two sentences or restructure the sentence with a comma (*William Buckley, a polymath, was a writer, editor, speaker, activist, harpsichordist, and sailor*) or a colon (*William Buckley was a polymath: a writer, editor, speaker, activist, harpsichordist, and sailor*). The semicolon offers a middle ground, with a pause longer than a comma but shorter than a period.

Some people hate this odd-looking little symbol. Novelist Cormac McCarthy calls it "idiotic." A copy editor at *The Washington Post* once called the semicolon "an ugly bastard." The novelist Kurt Vonnegut called semicolons "transvestite hermaphrodites representing absolutely nothing."

Mercy. Why such emotional revulsion to this little wink of ink? Why not put an extra tool into your toolbox? Sometimes you want to express two related thoughts without the period's abrupt, severe break. If so, the semicolon works wonders; it does the job. See?

**Hyphenate words to combine ideas**. Hyphens offer a great way to show how things relate to each other. Consider the following sentence: "East-coast liberals like Hillary Clinton differ from west-coast liberals like Jerry Brown." We could say, "liberals from the west coast," but that's not as pithy.

Of course, connecting too many things with hyphenation can get silly. Thus: "The first-term African-American senator from south-side Chicago made his first-ever run for the White House in 2008."

New words often arise by adding and then removing the hyphen. The word for the America's national pastime began as *base ball*, evolved to *base-ball*, and finally took the modern form of *baseball*. One modern example: *electronic mail* transmogrified into *e-mail* and then into *email*.

**Use em-dashes—like this—to make asides**. If you want to set off whole phrases or lists, use an elongated hyphen known as the em-dash. Look at this sentence:

> The Chicago Cubs' inability to win a World Series for 108 years—a period that saw 19 different presidents—caused angst among fans.

The em-dash helps the author make an aside. The em-dash tells the reader to pause, as if to say, "Hey, check this out."

Critics say the em-dash cheapens writing by encouraging a loose, informal style. To be sure, overusing any tool can be annoying. When we use the em-dash too much—like here—it distracts—and annoys—the reader. But in moderation—again, not like this—the em-dash offers a useful—and even fun—way to emphasize a point.

**Use ellipses to show thought trailing off ...** Every time I see an ellipsis, a set of three dots, I hear the sound of harp music. Ellipses (plural of ellipsis) suggest thought trailing off, pondering, open-ended ideas. Ellipses allow us to drift for a moment ...

A case in point: "Dorothy considered her challenge: 'If only I could see the Wizard of Oz ...'" We see the girl with braided hair, looking off into space, in her own world, lost in thought.

Ellipses also perform a more technical task: marking gaps in quoted passages. People rarely speak in compact packages, so writers need to stitch together comments made at different moments. To indicate gaps in a passage, use an ellipsis. So we might quote John F. Kennedy's inaugural address this way:

> Ask not what your country can do for you—ask what you can do for your country. ... Let us go forth to lead the land we love, asking His blessing and His help, but knowing that here on earth God's work must truly be our own.

Ellipses allow us to use just the words that convey the thought.

**Psst: Use parentheses to make asides.** Sometimes, you want to offer a tidbit of related information. That information might strengthen the argument (providing details or context) or simply offer an aside (as part of a conversation).

When you want to provide examples of a several things, use parentheses rather than saying "for example" over and over. When Barack Obama assembled his administration in 2008, he drew from America's elite universities. *New York Times* columnist David Brooks described the emerging team:

> January 20, 2009, will be a historic day. Barack Obama (Columbia, Harvard Law) will take the oath of office as his wife, Michelle (Princeton, Harvard Law), looks on proudly. Nearby, his foreign policy advisers will stand beaming, including perhaps Hillary Clinton (Wellesley, Yale Law), Jim Steinberg (Harvard, Yale Law) and Susan Rice (Stanford, Oxford).

Here an elite, there an elite, everywhere an elite. Brooks uses parentheses to make this point nicely.

Profligate use of parentheses makes writing choppy. On the other hand, sometimes you want to show just how choppy the world can be. "So are my parentheses part of my style?" Ben Yagoda asks (rhetorically). "Actually, yes. I am drawn to them in part because they express my belief that the world and language are multifarious, knotty, and illuminated by digression."

(Any questions?)

**Use quotation marks to say exactly what someone said.** To indicate the use of someone's exact words, use quotation marks. So:

> "Ask not what you country can do for you," President Kennedy said. "Ask what you can do for your country."

Always use the speaker's exact words. If you want to use bits and pieces of someone's speech, put quotation marks around the spoken words and use your own words to connect the phrases. So:

> After challenging the nation to "ask what you can do for your country," President Kennedy challenged other nations to "ask not what America will do for you, but what together we can do for the freedom of man."

In American English, punctuation marks usually belong inside quotation marks. Therefore: *"Ask not what your country can do for you," Kennedy said.*

Sometimes you need to quote someone quoting someone else. To do that, use single quotation marks inside double quotation marks, like this:

> "I went back to the doctor and he says, 'Henry, I told you, you can't make it, you're going to die in that mine.' I said, 'Well, Dr. Craft, let me try it one more time,' because I had some debts I wanted to pay."

What about a quote inside a quote inside a quote? Switch back and forth, from double quotation marks (") to single quotation marks ('), like this:

> "I met Joyce at the civil rights march, and she called out to me, 'Let's sing something. How about "Ain't Gonna Let Nobody Turn Me Around"? Let's do that one.'"

The power of quotation comes from our innate desire for inside information or intimacy. Whether we want to eavesdrop or hang on the words of an expert or wordsmith, quotations give writing extra depth and style.

**Use exclamation marks—rarely!—to show excitement or emphasize your points**. I once worked with someone who used exclamation marks, lots of them, all the time!!!! Even when discussing something mundane, she ended every sentence with a throng of these happy marks!!!! I guess it's not much different from someone who agrees with you all the time, or says "have a nice day" no matter what's happening!!!! But it's just too much!!!!

Sober wordsmiths avoid exclamation marks, except to show someone shouting. The novelist Elmore Leonard suggests using no more than two or three exclamation marks every 100,000 words (the length of a book). And I agree. Mostly! To evoke real emotion, tell a great story rather than use perky punctuation.

Every rule, of course, has an exception. I so admire Tom Wolfe that I admit the value of any and all of his exclamations. By one count, Wolfe's novel *The Bonfire of the Vanities* contains 2,343 exclamation marks in 659 pages. "I'm trying to restore punctuation to its rightful place," Wolfe once explained. "Dots, dashes, exclamation points were dropped out of prose because they 'reeked of sentiment.' But an ! shows someone getting carried away. Why not?

The writer carefully not using this punctuation doesn't bother to convey what's exciting to the reader."

Wolfe uses the exclamation mark cleverly, conveying excessive zeal or innocence or naivete or boorishness. It works for him. For most of us, though, it's like a sharp object best left in the drawer!

## Case Study
### The Crisis at Boston's John Hancock Tower

Compare two paragraphs, which explain the falling windows problem that delayed the 1976 opening of the John Hancock Tower in Boston for five years. First look at this:

John Hancock Tower provoked Boston's greatest architectural controversy before it attained the status of an icon. The opening of the 60-story structure designed by Henry Cobb was delayed for five years when its black windows rained down onto the streets of Copley Square. Scientists wondered whether the rhomboidal building could survive heavy winds. At first engineers believed that the windows popped because of the way winds twisted the building. Engineers later discovered that the double-layered windows were responsible. A thin strip of lead between the windows strained and then transferred pressure to the glass itself. The strain was too much and the windows snapped out of their frames and fell to the ground below. To fix the problem the engineers replaced all 10,344 original panes of glass.

Then read this:

Before achieving iconic status, Boston's John Hancock Tower provoked controversy (and fear!) when the steel-and-glass structure's black windows— double glass, sandwiched around thin sheets of lead—rained down onto the streets of Copley Square; at first, scientists wondered whether the rhomboidal building could survive heavy winds, but they eventually discovered the true cause of the popping: extreme pressures on the lead were transferred into the glass … which then dislodged from their frames and fell sometimes hundreds of stories below.

The first paragraph uses only one punctuation mark—the period. The second uses a bunch of them, in one sentence.

So what difference does punctuation make for a text's readability?

I like the first one better. Each sentence moves briskly. We never wait very long for the periods, so we know we can pause before exploring the next idea. The second passage twists and turns too much for easy comprehension. Reading it is like riding in a taxi with a driver who turns, stops, slows down, speeds up, and does U-turns. It's a little disorienting.

The ideal passage would use enough punctuation to offer a clear journey, with pauses to provide pacing and variety. Like this:

> Before achieving icon status, Boston's John Hancock Tower provoked controversy (and fear) when the steel-and-glass structure's black windows rained down onto the streets of Copley Square. What caused the windows to pop out? At first, scientists theorized that the height and shape of the rhomboidal building were at fault. Heavy winds would twist the double-glass windows, framed in thin sheets of lead, causing them to pop out of their casings. Scientists eventually discovered the true cause. Extreme pressures on the lead transferred into the glass. That pressure dislodged the windows from their frames.

Punctuation shapes how your prose twists and turns, looks ahead, casts a sideward glance, merges, and, finally, stops. Getting the punctuation right is one part technical mastery (knowing the specific tasks of punctuation marks) and one part play (trying out different combinations to give the passage clarity and flow).

~

### Element 45
### Select the Right Word

DETAILS MATTER. Any time you create the possibility of confusion—by bad spelling, syntax, or word choice—you risk losing the reader along the way.

A number of words sound alike, or get swapped with other words in different situations. As a result, writers misuse these words. For a comprehensive list, check a style guide like *The Chicago Manual of Style*. Meanwhile, learn the distinctions among the following sets of words:

**Affect and effect**: Used as a verb, *affect* describes how one thing influences another. So: *Hillary Clinton's popular majority did not affect Donald Trump's conviction that he won a mandate.*

Used as a noun, *affect* describes a person's emotional capacity. So: *Autistic children frustrate parents and teachers with their lack of affect.*

*Effect*, a noun, refers to consequences. So: *The effects of the Civil War included a stronger federal government and the end of slavery.*

**Alternate and alternative**: As a verb, *alternate* means taking turns. So: *Writers should alternate short and long sentences.* As a noun, it means a substitute for another. So. *His alternate taught the class.*

*Alternative* means a choice between two or more things. So: *Getting old beats the alternative.*

**Comprise and Compose**: Approach with caution; these two words confuse even the most careful writers.

*To comprise* is "to be made up of, to consist of, to include." The whole comprises the parts. So: *The United States comprises 50 states.*

*To compose* is "to make up, to form the substance of something." So: *The parts compose the whole.* To remember this, think of the musician who pulls together different musical ideas to compose a piece of music.

**Farther and further:** Use *farther* to describe physical space. Think of "far" to remember it as a distance word. So: *I ran farther today than ever before.*

Use *further* to refer to a figurative distance. So: *Walker advanced further in his violin lessons than Leila.* Or: *Let's examine this further.*

**Its and it's:** *Its* is possessive; it shows that something belongs to something else. So: *Its customer base includes senior citizens and boomers.*

*It's* is a contraction of *it is.* So: *It's a truism that Republicans have a "lock" on the states of the Confederacy.*

**Its and their:** *Its*, again, refers to the possession of a singular entity. So: *The University of Connecticut women's basketball team had its best years in 2009 and 2010.*

*Their* refers to the possession of a plural entity. So: *The Connecticut Huskies had their best seasons in the 2009 and 2010.*

**Lay and lie:** *Lay*, a transitive verb, refers to the act of putting something down. When you lay something down—a hammer, book, platter—you act on that object. *Lay* always takes an object. So: *I lay the book on the desk.*

*Lie*, an intransitive verb, does not take an object. *To lie* means to recline, or place your own body in a certain way. (The past tense is *lay*. Sorry. These rules do seem contradictory sometimes.) So: *Oblomov decided to lie in bed indefinitely.*

**Less and fewer:** *Less* refers to a smaller amount of something, without clear units of measurement. So: *After the 2008 election, Hillary Clinton had less power than Donald Trump.*

*Fewer* refers to smaller numbers of things that can be counted. So: *Donald Trump won fewer votes than Hillary Clinton in 2016.*

**Lose and loose:** To *lose* is to go down to defeat; *loose* means slackness. So: *The Mets got so loose at the end of the 2007 baseball season that they started to lose a lot of games.*

**That and which:** Quick, explain the different meanings of these two sentences:

> Bill Clinton favored welfare reforms that provided incentives to
> work.
> Bill Clinton favored welfare reforms, which provided incentives
> to work.

The first sentence, using *that*, is restrictive. It means that Clinton favored only those welfare reforms that went hand-in-hand with work incentives. *That* forms a bridge connecting the noun and the description. According to this passage, Clinton can support only reform with work incentives.

The second sentence, using *which*, makes a looser connection to the noun. In this example, *which* simply modifies "welfare reforms." We do not know whether Clinton would insist on the work provisions, only that work provisions are connected to welfare reform.

The comma offers the marker we need to make the distinction. A comma never precedes *that*; a comma always precedes *which*. Think of the comma as a pause for parenthetical information.

**There, their, and they're**: *There* refers to location, *their* to ownership, and *they're* a group in the state of being or acting. So: *As long as you are there, tell me if they're finished planting their gardens.*

**Who and whom**: Ask not for whom this question matters; it matters for thee.

*Who* acts as a subject, and *whom* as an object. If you are not sure which to use, rearrange the sentence to see who's doing what to whom—that is, who or what is the subject. If you need a reminder of when to use the "m," remember the title of Hemingway's book *For Whom the Bell Tolls.*

*Laissez-faire* grammarians do not care about the who/whom distinction anymore because, they say, we can tell what the writer or speaker means in either case. Use of whom, furthermore, sounds stiff, especially to the casual ears of 21st-century Americans. *Whom would you like to ask to the school dance?* Sounds a little prim.

When you see *who*, you know it's a subject. When you see *whom*, you know it's an object. I don't care who you are or for whom you write. Use these words precisely.

These grammatical distinctions sometimes seem picky. But they still matter. More precision trumps less precision.

## Case Study
## Thoughts on planning

Planning *affects* the way we think and act. When we *lay* plans on the table, we begin to map alternate futures. It's all about relationships: Should this park be closer or *farther* from the apartment complex? Do we want more or *fewer* fast food restaurants? What should *their* design features be? Should these rules be *comprised* of aesthetic standards? Should the zoning code be *loose*—or might that cause the area to *lose* historic appeal? Should *its* provisions be open to appeal? And who should *compose* these rules—community activists or city bureaucrats? To *whom* should they apply? *Further* down the road, should we consider changes to the code?

*There* will be many complex considerations, for sure. For example, what happens in an area with *less* population? What are the *effects* of population losses on real estate costs? If costs spiral, does *that* affect headquarters decisions? Do more jobs *lie* in wait if we offer incentives to major employers? What factors account for *their* decisions? Should we consider *alternatives*? *Which* makes the most sense: tax incentives or infrastructure investment?

~

### And Another Thing . . .

To succeed in any field—sports, music, speaking, writing, you name it—you need to perform as many actions as possible automatically. When you do, you free your mind for creative work.

Grammar should come automatically, almost all the time. When you construct a sentence, you need to use proper grammar and punctuation without thinking too much. If you must stop to think about the basics, you lose your focus on content and creativity.

Grammar offers a simple system to pace writing. When you know the building blocks of writing, and can pace your writing with periods, commas, colons, and other punctuation, you don't think too much. You can concentrate on the action or ideas you want to describe.

To be sure, rules of grammar sometimes seem arcane and pointless. George Eliot called grammar "the slang of prigs." Rules sometimes contradict each other—and sometimes make simple communication difficult. Winston Churchill rejected the ban against ending sentences with prepositions with this quip: "This is the kind of tedious nonsense up with which I will not put."

Grammar irritates and vexes almost everyone. But it also makes communication possible. It provides the rules of the road. If you follow the core rules, you can focus on reaching your destination.

## 12

---

# EDITING

Whenever you feel an impulse to perpetrate a piece of exceptionally fine writing, obey it—wholeheartedly—and delete it before sending your manuscript to press. Murder your darlings.

— SIR ARTHUR QUILLER-COUCH

A man arrives at his new apartment, eager to settle in. He looks around, imagining life in his new home. The movers arrive. They bring chairs, tables, wardrobes, a bed, boxes of books, and art. Quickly, the apartment fills up. But the boxes and furniture keep coming. Before long, the man can no longer move around.

> *Gentleman:* What is it that's left?
> *First Furniture Mover:* Wardrobes.
> *Gentleman:* The green and purple ones?
> *Second Furniture Mover:* Yes.
> *First Furniture Mover:* And that's not all. There's more to come.
> *Second Furniture Mover:* The staircase is jammed from top to
> bottom. Nobody can get up or down.
> *Gentleman:* The yard is cram-full too. So is the street.
> *First Furniture Mover:* The traffic's come to a standstill in the
> town. Full of furniture.

In his absurdist play *The New Tenant*, Eugene Ionesco captures this dilemma of modern society. We have too much stuff; we are, as one critic has noted, "stifled in a sea of inert matter." We do not know how to control our environments or lives. We let things and events control us.

The same problem happens in writing. In the age of the computer, we produce endless screens of words—emails and memos, texts and tweets, social media comments and more. *It just keeps coming.* Like the man in the apartment, we struggle to move through that clutter.

The writer's primary job is to help the reader see the world clearly. Only when you clear away junk can the reader understand your point.

Writers usually say too much in first drafts. The best writers revise their work, over and over, cutting and rewriting words, phrases, sentences, and paragraphs. William Faulkner once teased Thomas Wolfe for his wordy prose: "You're a putter-inner and I'm a taker-outer." Go ahead, put in all you want. But be a relentless taker-outer too.

All of which leads us to the most important single fact about writing. No writer just writes. A good writer needs to be a good editor too. As Fran Liebowitz has said, "all writing is editing."

Critique every word, sentence, and paragraph—over and over. You will be in good company. Ernest Hemingway rewrote the ending to *A Farewell to Arms* 39 times. James Thurber rewrote "The Train on Track Six," 15 times. "There must have been close to 240,000 words in all the manuscripts put together, and I must have spent 2,000 hours working on it," he said. "Yet the finished version can't be more than 20,000 words." Do the math. That's one hour for every ten words.

The goal of editing? To make every word do work. "Vigorous writing is concise," William Strunk and E.B. White say in their classic *The Elements of Style.* "A sentence should contain no unnecessary words, a paragraph no unnecessary sentences, for the same reason a drawing should contain no unnecessary lines and a machine no unnecessary parts."

Use only the words you need, and leave the rest behind.

Editing often feels tedious. But it offers an adventure, if you have the right attitude. Like a detective searching for clues, a good editor seeks out clumsy phrases, passive voices, unnecessary words and phrases. After finding them, he rewrites or cuts clumsy or superfluous passages.

Take time off after you write a draft. Clear your head before editing. You do not see what's in front of you because you've been looking at it for too long.

~

### Element 46
### Search and Destroy, From Big to Small

SUPPOSE you wanted to remodel your kitchen. Which approach would you take?

**Option 1.** Remove whatever walls, cabinets, and flooring you want to replace; rewire and replumb the room; replace the walls, cabinets, and flooring; install appliances; paint the walls; put in light and electrical fixtures.

**Option 2**. Paint walls, remove the walls, remove and replace cabinets, install fixtures, replace the plumbing, remove and replace flooring, retool electrical systems, and so on.

Option 1 works best. Why? First, by starting with the big tasks, you avoid repeating work. If you paint before removing and replacing walls and cabinets, you will need to paint it all again. Second, by moving from one discrete task to another, you avoid overwhelming your brain. We work well when we give a task our total attention. When we try to do more than one thing at a time, we struggle.

Most editors review drafts paragraph by paragraph, chapter by chapter. As they edit their pieces, they check for structure, word choice, noun-pronoun-verb agreement, accuracy, verb tenses, hanging participles, punctuation, spelling, style, and so on.

That's fine with short pieces or near-perfect drafts. But when we try to do too many tasks at once with rougher drafts, we get overwhelmed and lose focus. We simply cannot deal with the full range of issues—from the basic structure down to the minute details—all at once.

The brain loves simple, clear tasks. When you only search for one problem at a time, you stay sharp. You spot problems better and don't run out of energy.

Therefore, follow this simple approach to editing: Start big, working your way to smaller issues, one challenge at a time. Let's see how to do it.

**Start by blocking sections**. Most writing—even pieces as short as a two-page memo or a newspaper op-ed article—consists of a number of chunks. Each chunk presents distinct ideas.

Put a label on each major section. It's easier to manage a handful of well-marked sections, each with well-marked parts, than a piece with 75 unmarked parts.

For each section, express a clear "umbrella" concept. Everything in that section should fall under the umbrella concept. If any ideas veer off topic, cut it or move it.

Make sure your whole piece starts and end strongly. Make sure all its sections do as well. Consider writing the first and last paragraphs before anything else. If you know the beginnings and endings of your journeys, the pieces in the middle sort themselves out easily.

**Label ideas in paragraphs**. Every paragraph should take the reader on a simple journey, starting and finishing strongly. Make every paragraph a mini-journey, following Aristotle's narrative arc. Make sure you can explain this mini-journey with a simple tabloid headline. Make sure just glancing at your paragraph labels reminds you, instantly, about what journey it takes the reader. (More on this point in a moment.)

**Check sentences for the Golden Rule**. Make sure every sentence takes a journey, starting and finishing strongly.

**Find the modifiers that make sentences run on and on.** Sometimes it seems that crafting a simple sentence is the toughest chore of writing. As our minds whir with ideas, we get tempted to veer off track. Then we fail to make simple points.

Often, we get off track with prepositional phrases. Prepositions, remember, express relationships between things. The most common prepositions—*of, to, in, for, on, with, out, from, by*, and *out*—are among the 37 most commonly used words in the English language.

Prepositional phrases offer details about the subject. Notice how the prepositions work:

> Franklin Roosevelt was the son *of* a wealthy family *from* Hyde Park.
> Jimmy Carter came *from* a town *in* southern Georgia.
> I once lived *in* a house *by* the side *of* the Mississippi River.

These prepositional phrases provide useful information. But when you put too many of these ideas into a sentence, you lose sight of the main action—*who's doing what to whom*. The reader struggles to keep up with the twists and turns.

Let's look at an example from an academic history journal:

> After the Second World War, the general drift of American public opinion toward a more liberal racial attitude that had begun during the New Deal became accentuated as a result of the revolution against Western Imperialism in Asia and Africa that engendered a new respect for the nonwhite peoples of the world, and as a result of the subsequent competition for the support of the uncommitted nations connected with the Cold War.

In this 72-word sentence, the author uses 16 prepositions—*after, of, toward, during, as, of, against, in, that, for, of, as, of, for, of,* and *with*. Each one adds a new thought, but pulls the passage off course. It's overwhelming, like asking a driver to turn 16 times to travel a short distance. To rewrite that passage, I broke it up. Look at this new version:

> After World War II, Americans adopted more liberal attitudes about race. The New Deal began this process. Revolutions against imperial powers in Asia and Africa created new respect for the nonwhite populations. The Cold War also prompted the U.S. to consider how racial strife damaged America's image.

The revision breaks one monster sentence into three ordinary sentences. It uses 47 words, 25 fewer than the original. And it uses only five prepositions —*about, against, in, for*, and *in*—instead of 16. That's fewer than two prepositions per sentence—a more manageable number of twists and turns for the reader.

**Root out repetition and needless words.** Most drafts contain meandering, repetitious, and clumsy phrasing.

Too often, writers repeat ideas by using just slightly different words for the same thing. Politicians say they will care for "each and every" voter. Business executives tell us that "first and foremost," we have to cut costs. Advertisements offer a "free gift" for opening a bank account. We also hear people talk about *future plans, end results, armed gunmen, unconfirmed rumors, living survivors, past history, actual experience, advanced planning*, and *natural instincts*. Each of those expressions repeats a simple idea. So cut 'em!

**Eliminate hedges and emphatics.** Too often, when we want to emphasize a point, we use vague language.

A hedge limits or qualifies statements. By expressing conditions or exceptions, the hedge tells the reader, in effect, "I'm not *completely* sure what I'm going to tell you." Hedges include words like *almost, virtually, perhaps, maybe*, and *somewhat*. Such words pretend to modify a point, but give the reader little real information. Writers use them to avoid taking a clear, distinct stand.

An emphatic shows strength of conviction but lacks adequate evidence or certainty. Emphatics assert something without showing it. *As everyone knows* is a classic emphatic. So are *of course, naturally, understandably, usually, almost always, interestingly*, and *surprisingly*. Consider this passage from a portrait of Andrew Carnegie:

> The Carnegies were poor—very poor—but not quite destitute. Their home was a hovel, but not quite a hellhole. Allegheny, Pittsburgh, and the environs were ugly and just plain awful. But there were worse places in the world then, and there are now.

The passage tells us little. The author wants to emphasize points with locutions like *very poor* and *just plain awful*; he backs off his points when he refers to *a hovel, but not quite a hellhole*. The author would do better note the food the Carnegies ate, the clothes they wore, the size and furnishings of their home, and whether they had heat and water. Details, not emphatics and hedges, offer a clear picture.

**Address details, one by one.** Now address all the other problems: spelling and punctuation, noun-verb and non-pronoun agreements, adjectives and adverbs, dangling modifiers, passive verbs and imprecise nouns.

As you move from big to small problems, you'll see something amazing. By fixing the big problems, many smaller problems disappear. Why? When we structure a piece poorly—with the wrong chapters or sections, arranged poorly —we lose clarity about the smaller points. Because we're fuzzy on the big stuff, we're fuzzy on the little stuff.

If you get the big pieces right, the smaller pieces take care of themselves.

## Case Study
## Marie Kondo's *The Life-Changing Magic of Tidying Up*

We live in the age of excess. Westerners accumulate more material goods than previous generations could ever imagine. Overwhelmed, we struggle to organize our stuff. Over time, we lose control of our lives.

In extreme cases, hoarding creates a kind of madness, now listed in the *Diagnostic and Statistical Manual of Mental Disorders*. Hoarders refuse to throw away even useless junk—old newspapers and magazines, cheap SWAG, books and records, clothing, plastic bags, food leftovers, broken appliances and electronics, collectables, dead plants, old pet toys, broken dishes, empty bottles, you name it. I know an elderly woman whose children cleaned out her kitchen when she was in the hospital. Among the dozens of Hefty bags full of trash they cleared out was a frozen roast from the Clinton years.

Hoarders—and others who just have a hard time getting rid of stuff—develop an emotional relationship with their things. "I paid good money for that," people say. "I want to get some use out of it." So is fear of the future. "What if I need it?" We develop relationships with things, so we actually feel sorry for the things we discard: "That clock's been with me since my wedding day. It needs a home."

But when we keep too many things, they get in the way of living. In a cluttered home, we spend endless hours searching for things. We forget what we own, so we waste money buying more With an untidy home, visitors avoid us. We lose or ability to make distinctions between what's useful and what's not. Over time, the tyranny of stuff isolates us from the rest of the world.

To the rescue comes a Japanese woman named Marie Kondo, a consultant for people who struggle to get their stuff in order. With the discipline and unwavering commitment of a general, she moves into territory and clears out the mess. Her strategy is simple:

- "Before you start," Kondo says, "visualize your destination." Imagine the world where you want to live—where you know where to find everything, where every possession brings not only utility but joy, where you don't waste a minute looking for things. *Get specific.* Don't say, "I want to life a clutter-free life." Say: "I want to live a more feminine lifestyle." Or: "I want the kind of place my kids want to bring their friends." Or: "I want to hold dinner parties and sing songs around the piano."
- Undertake a massive purge of stuff. Take all your belongings out of closets and bureaus and other containers and lay them on the floor. Sort every single item.
- After laying your stuff on the floor, decide what items to discard and

192 | WRITING ABOUT PLACE

where to put the ones you keep. "Discarding must come first," she says. "Do not even think of putting your things away until you have finished the process of discarding."

- Keep only the items that "spark joy." If you have not used something for a long time, it's probably because it doesn't excite you. So discard it. "Keep only those things that speak to your heart," Kondo says. "Take the plunge and discard the rest." Love is the answer.

- Sort things by category, not location. You can never know how many things you have unless you bring them all together, in one place. Many of our duplicates are scattered into different rooms and containers. Only by bringing them out into the open can we see the absurdity of our accumulation. "In one spot, you can also compare items that are similar in design, making it easier to decide whether you want to keep them."

- Start with the items that are easier to assess. Begin with clothes, then books, then papers, then other supplies and equipment. Go from easy to hard. Getting rid of a garish or torn piece of clothing makes it easier to discard the artwork with sentimental value that doesn't belong anywhere anymore.

- If you have a hard time getting rid of something, for emotional reasons, pay your respects as you would with a friend who's leaving. Thank them for the joy and service they have brought you. Think of the good they can do elsewhere. "Let them go, with gratitude," Kondo says. "Not only you, but your things as well, will feel clear and refreshed when you are done tidying."

These same principles work for editing. Start by with a vision of what you want to give your reader. Lay out all your stuff—the good, bad, and ugly. Examine one category at a time, in the right order, from big to small—sections, parts of sections, paragraphs, sentences, and specific elements (quotes, stats, metaphors, observations, clever wordings). Solve your easy problems first; sometimes fixing easy problems makes tougher problems disappear; other times, it just makes them easier to handle. Keep only those passages that really work—those that truly say exactly what you want to say, simply and clearly and convincingly. And when you cut a passage you like, take a moment to appreciate how it helped you to understand your topic. Then let go.

Let's give the final word to Marie Kondo.

"As you reduce your belongings through the process of tidying," she says, "you will come to the point where you suddenly know how much is right for you. You will feel it as clearly as if something clicked in your head and said, 'Ah! This is just the amount I need to live comfortably. This is all I need to be happy. I don't need any more.' The satisfaction that envelopes your whole being at that point is palpable."

~

## Element 47
## Fix Problem Paragraphs With Tabloid Headlines

"WRITING, LIKE LIFE," Henry Miller once said, "is a voyage of discovery." In that voyage, we often get tempted to wander off the path.

You begin writing a paragraph with one idea in mind. That reminds you of another idea. That reminds you of yet another idea. And so on. Before you know it, you have veered far from the first idea—without offering adequate evidence for it. You might not even remember where you intended to go. And if you don't remember your destination, how can the reader?

How should we deal with unruly paragraphs? The solution is simple. Just *label every idea in every paragraph.* Come up with a short label—three to five words—that describes the idea. When a paragraph contains more than one idea, break it up into as many paragraphs as ideas.

Write your labels like tabloid headlines. At their best, tabloid headlines capture the essence of the story. They also give stories sizzle and intrigue. Consider these famous headlines:

> About President Gerald Ford's rejection of a federal bailout for
>     New York City: FORD TO CITY: DROP DEAD.
> About the Dalai Llama's visit to the U.S.: HELLO DALAI!
> About Congressman Anthony Weiner's sexting scandal: WEINER
>     IN A PICKLE.
> About a decapitation at a night club: HEADLESS BODY IN TOPLESS
>     BAR.

Labeling paragraphs *always* works. When I put pithy tags on paragraphs, I can quickly grasp all the ideas in a piece. When I repeat myself, I see it. When something doesn't fit, I cut it. When something is missing, I add it.

## Case Study
## Luc Sante's *Low Life*

The grid street design is both celebrated and reviled by urbanites. On the plus side, the grid creates neat sets of developable lots. It also makes it easy for ordinary people to navigate the streets. On the minus side, the grid often obliterates the natural contours of the city's topography. The grid also creates a monotonous cityscape, with few centers.

One solution to this problem, followed by cities like Barcelona, London, Paris, and Washington, is to disrupt the grid with major diagonal streets. Luc Sante explains:

Broadway's unorthodox diagonal thrust through Midtown created open plazas otherwise unprovided for by the procrustean grid plan. Union Square resulted from its collision with Fourth Avenue, and then Madison Square came up at Fifth, Greeley and Herald Squares at Sixth, Times and Longacre Squares at Seventh, and Columbus Circle at Eighth. The squares downtown—Washington, Stuyvesant, and Gramercy, in particular—were enclosed and protected in such a way that they became private parks for the tightly controlled residences that fronted them, but Broadway's plazas were open and overrun, and naturally became places of amusement. The theatrical nexus—or one of them, at least— began inching along Broadway after the Revolution, had reached the area around Spring Street just before the Civil War, and thereafter clocked in at each of the squares, one after the other, at approximately ten-year intervals, halting at Times Square at about the same time that the square was so named, when the *Times* building was erected between 1902 and 1904. Although the appellation the Great White Way did not come in until the twentieth century, it was noted much earlier that whatever stretch of Broadway happened to be hosting the greatest number of theaters was the most brilliantly lit area of the city.

So what's the major idea in this paragraph? I found two. First, Sante talks about how Broadway's unorthodox diagonal creates a series of squares and plazas where the intersect the prominent gridded streets. My tabloid headline for that discussion:

*Slash The Grid, Create Centers*

Second, Sante talks about the shifting locations of the theater centers (starting with "The theatrical nexus..."). Here's the headline I would use for that:

*Theater! Drama! On the move!*

Maybe this paragraph should remain as one. After all, both pieces deal with the impact of slashing grids with diagonals. But for my money, the passage explores two distinct aspects of this issue. I would break 'em up and develop the ideas more fully.

∿

## Element 48
## Edit by Reading Aloud and Backward

FOR MOST OF HISTORY, storytellers told their tales aloud. They recounted, from memory, great myths, histories, comedy, and tragedies. Audiences served as focus groups. When they responded well to a phrase or passage, the passage stayed; when audiences got bored or confused, the storyteller revised the piece.

These days, alas, most writers labor in isolation. We write our drafts, alone and silently. Sometimes we share drafts with friends and colleagues. But rarely do we read our pieces aloud.

When we read silently, we tend to glide over passages. Because of "familiarity blindness," we don't pay careful attention to the the details of what we know best. The more we know something, the less we pay attention to it. We skim. So we miss details. Did you notice, for example, that I used the word *the* twice in a row in this paragraph? Most people don't.

Consider two options for active editing. Read your drafts aloud, fast or slowly, to yourself or to others. Or work backwards.

**Read aloud**: Reading aloud helps you find clumsy or ungrammatical passages. Any time the reader stumbles, something's wrong. Something easy to overlook becomes noticeable.

When you read aloud, ask yourself: *Does one idea lead to the next? Can you follow the story or argument? Does the piece stay on track?* Also pay attention to the technical issues, like typos and clumsy, wordy, or vague passages.

Pick up a great book—a classic—right now. Read something by Truman Capote or John McPhee or F. Scott Fitzgerald. Find the poetry of Wordsworth or Shakespeare or T.S. Eliot or e.e. cummings. Or find a well-edited magazine, like *The Atlantic*. Read a passage aloud. Notice how the words glide.

Try reading fast. Readitfastrunningallthewordstogethertillyoustumble. Speed-talking reveals the clunky passages better than reading at a normal pace. You can read good writing fast, but flawed writing causes you to stumble. When you read fast, you are forced to activate your whole brain. You have to concentrate. Your whole body gets into it.

**Read backwards**. To combat familiarity, read backwards. Read the last paragraph first, then the paragraph before that, then the one before that, and so on. You will be surprised at how easily you can spot—and kill—bad and repetitive writing.

By reading backwards, you also see the piece's outline clearly. Does paragraph 17 follow paragraph 16 logically? Does paragraph 7 develop the ideas of paragraph 6?

To master skills, athletes often work backwards. They imagine the result they want—say, a tennis ball landing in the corner of the court, just beyond the reach of the opponent—and then think backwards to imagine the sequence of events leading to that result. After imagining the ball landing in the ideal spot, the player imagines the ball flying across the net ... then hitting the ball ... then bringing the racket back to hit the ball ... then getting into position, planting feet ... then seeing the opponent hit the ball over the net ... and so on.

The ancient Greeks knew the importance of building from the end. Herodotus said: "One should always look to the end of everything, how it will finally come out." Think of writing that way. Think of how you want to complete a passage, and then what came before, and then what came before that, and so on.

## Case Study
### Theodore Dalrymple's 'The Architect as Totalitarian'

If you have ever lost an object—and then retraced your steps to figure out where it happened—you understand the power of editing by reading passages backward.

When we retrace out steps to find a lost object, we are essentially working backwards, from the end to the beginning. In the process, we compel ourselves to pay attention to each and every moment we remember. Likewise, reading a passage backwards compels us to play close attention to every sentence and paragraph of our writing. Consider this passage, in which Theodore Dalrymple describes an exhibit of the architect Le Corbusier's work:

> At the exhibition, I fell to talking with two elegantly coiffed ladies of the kind who spend their afternoons in exhibitions. "Marvelous, don't you think?" one said to me, to which I replied: "Monstrous." Both opened their eyes wide, as if I had denied Allah's existence in Mecca. If most architects revered Le Corbusier, who were we laymen, the mere human backdrop to his buildings, who know nothing of the problems of building construction, to criticize him? Warming to my theme, I spoke of the horrors of Le Corbusier's favorite material, reinforced concrete, which does not age gracefully but instead crumbles, stains, and decays. A single one of his buildings, or one inspired by him, could ruin the harmony of an entire townscape, I insisted. A Corbusian building is incompatible with anything except itself.

Now look at the passage, with the order of the sentences reversed:

A Corbusian building is incompatible with anything except itself.

Both opened their eyes wide, as if I had denied Allah's existence in Mecca.

Warming to my theme, I spoke of the horrors of Le Corbusier's favorite material, reinforced concrete, which does not age gracefully but instead crumbles, stains, and decays.

A single one of his buildings, or one inspired by him, could ruin the harmony of an entire townscape, I insisted.

If most architects revered Le Corbusier, who were we laymen, the mere human backdrop to his buildings, who know nothing of the problems of building construction, to criticize him?

"Marvelous, don't you think?" one said to me, to which I replied: "Monstrous."

At the exhibition, I fell to talking with two elegantly coiffed ladies of the kind who spend their afternoons in exhibitions.

In a strange way, the paragraph almost makes as much sense backwards as forwards. As long as the author describes the events and ideas clearly, we can always follow along.

More important, though, reading it backwards helps us to avoid familiarity blindness and to pay careful attention to each sentence.

~

### Element 49
### Murder Your Darlings

SOMETHING EXTRAORDINARY HAPPENS when we write. We develop a relationship with our words.

When we write well—or just *think* we write well—we treat our paragraphs, sentences, and even phrases with affection. When we turn a phrase well, or offer a telling detail about a person or place or action, we look on our passages with reverence.

But sometimes we need to delete a well-turned phrase—or even a whole section, consisting of many well-turned phrases.

Why? As noted before, we often veer off track. The process of discovery takes us into unexpected territory. We might start a project thinking that X is the most important idea, only to discover that Y or Z are interesting too. And so we veer off track.

Eager to clinch our point, we sometimes overwhelm the reader with details or evidence. But don't think of your writing as a legal brief (unless you're writing a legal brief, of course). Make a point, offer evidence, and move on.

If you think you have written something beautiful, be careful. Your emotional attachment to that passage might signal danger. You might love a phrase or an idea so much that you don't realize that it ... *stinks*.

The ultimate test of any passage—any sentence, paragraph, or section—is whether it offers essential movement from the beginning to the end. All too frequently, we write passages that veer off the path. Track down those errant darlings and ruthlessly excise them. When you cut a passage, even one you adore, you give room for other passages to shine.

### Case Study
### NYCEDC's 'New York Works'

In the spring of 2017, I wrote a draft report for New York City's Economic Development Corporation, outlining a strategy to create 100,000 middle-class jobs in the next decade.

Writing government reports is a tricky proposition. The report's major goal is to speak to the people of the city—to create a dialogue about our common challenges and how we can work together. But every passage of a government report is fraught with political danger. Innocent-sounding words and phrases can alienate key constituencies. So you need to be careful what you say and how you say it. So if you write for government, you better be ready to murder your darlings. In my draft, this passage got cut:

> The area around Grand Central Station is one of the most important legal and financial centers in the U.S., with a growing tech sector as well. With 70 million square feet of office space, 200,000 workers, and the city's greatest transportation center, Midtown East is home of some of urban America's greatest landmarks, from the Lever House and Roosevelt Hotel to the Chrysler Building. But the area's office buildings have become outdated, with low ceilings and outdated technology. To compete with other Class A office centers around the world, the district needs to build new structures and update its existing stock.
>
> Rather than rezoning the whole area, the city and community have agreed to rezone a Grand Central subdistrict. The process comes at an auspicious time. Two transit projects—the Second Avenue subway line and the East Side Access—improve connections to the rest of the city and region. The Second Avenue line began operation in 2017 along six stops; it will expand in coming years. The East Side Access, scheduled to open in 2019, will bring the Long Island Rail Road lines from Penn Station to Grand Central.
>
> The strategy strikes a balance between historic preservation and the need for state-of-the-art Class A office buildings. To leverage this change, the plan uses air rights and FAR bonuses to provide incentives for new development and rehabilitation.

Now, here's how we replaced that section in the final report:

> The Greater East Midtown business district is one of the largest job centers in the region and provides many of the world's highest-profile business addresses. It contains more than 60 million square feet of office space, more than a quarter million jobs, and numerous Fortune 500 companies. However, the area faces a number of long-term challenges: aging building stock, limited recent office development (and few available office development sites), an existing zoning framework that hinders new office development, and public spaces and transit infrastructure that are stretched to capacity.

Gone is the background information about landmark buildings and zoning processes. When I drafted this report, I thought these details offered critical context. But the powers-that-be at EDC decided otherwise. Too much history, they figured, could detract from immediate challenges. To quote Joe Friday on *Dragnet*, the old TV series, they wanted "just the facts, ma'am." So we cut this passage. We murdered my darling.

～

### And Another Thing . . .

EDITING IS hard for two reasons. First, we don't like to admit our mistakes. Even when we want to catch errors, we get defensive when we realize that our writing is clumsy or confusing.

Second, when we read a text from beginning to end, we have a hard time spotting many problems. Why? Take a look at this sign and count the number of times you see the letter F.

> **FINISHED FILES ARE**
> **THE RESULT OF YEARS**
> **OF SCIENTIFIC  STUDY**
> **COMBINED WITH**
> **THE EXPERIENCE OF YEARS.**

Most people find only three F's because they glide over the three instances of the word "of." Hence the great challenge of editing: noticing familiar words, phrases, and punctuation.

If you have a hard time finding F's, you will experience even more difficulty spotting other problems. When you edit, after all, you need to check for a wide variety of issues—verb use, noun-verb agreement, punctuation, excess verbiage, precision of word choice, and a number of stylistic issues. It's just too much.

The answer? Break down the problem, from big to small pieces. Then search and destroy the little problems.

William Faulkner deserves the final word on editing. An interviewer for *The Paris Review* once asked him to provide a formula for becoming a good novelist.

"Ninety-nine percent talent," he said. "Ninety-nine percent discipline. Ninety-nine percent work. He must never be satisfied with what he does. It never is as good as it can be done."

So it takes 297 percent effort to be a great writer. Daunting, yes, but doable.

# V

# EXPLAINING A COMPLEX PROCESS

A century ago, a group of sociologists and their students at the University of Chicago fanned out into the neighborhoods to study the everyday life of the city.

That group, known as the Chicago School, closely observed how people lived and worked in the city. They studied the city as a complex organic system. To understand this system, they explored a wide range of processes in factories, homes, churches, unions, factories, bars, schools, museums, libraries, street corners, political parties, and more.

People's everyday actions in these places, moment by moment, made the city what it was. They added up to complex processes that reflected the city's identity and possibilities.

So how do we understand the complex processes of the city?

Start with actions. An *action*, remember, is just a sequence of things people do, which can be described thus: *"First, ... Then, ... Then, ...,"* and so on.

A series of actions comprise a sequence or a *process*: First, take this action; then, take that action; then, take the next action.

A *complex process*, then, would be a collection of these separate sequences.

Suppose we wanted to explore the complex processes that shape city parks —their uses, designs, support, meaning, and related matters. Think of the parks as a collection of a number of different processes. We might depict this complex process as a set of vectors. So a complex process might look like this:

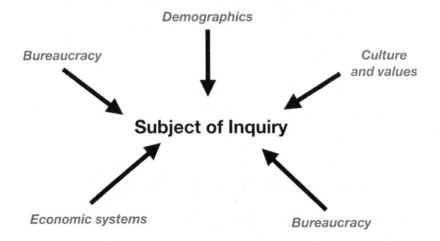

For each vector, we might describe a set of simpler processes, which themselves are sequences of actions. For demographics, for example, we might describe how different groups (male and female, young and old, professional and working class, students and visitors, and so on) use the parks—how they *act*. To explore culture and values, we might observe the interactions of people with different backgrounds, interests, group identifications, and so on.

Avoid too much generalization. Describe what you can observe, action by action. When those actions show a pattern, describe that pattern. But stay focused on what you can point to, what you can pick apart, moment by moment.

Here's the plan. We start by improving our skills as observers. We learn how to depict sequences of actions and ideas:

- Chapter 13: Questions and Brainstorming
- Chapter 14: Framing

Then we develop two new writing skills:

- Chapter 15: Composition
- Chapter 16: Numbers

One last point. Processes can be understood in both specific and general terms. We might describe that Boston residents used to hold a community charrette to save Fenway Park—or we might describe the process for holding charrettes anywhere, any time, on any topic.

Ready? Let's go.

# 13

# QUESTIONS AND BRAINSTORMING

If you ask the wrong question, of course, you get the wrong answer. We find in design it's much more important and difficult to ask the right question. Once you do that, the right answer becomes obvious.

— AMORY LOVINS

No one is dumb who is curious. The people who don't ask questions remain clueless throughout their lives.

— NEIL DEGRASSE TYSON

W herever we go, we ask questions. We spend all our days in dialogue, wondering about family and friends, community and cohorts, coworkers and merchants, and, especially, ourselves. We ask both profound and trivial questions. Teachers, research shows, spend 30 percent of the time in class asking questions—about 100 every hour.

Even when silent, we ask questions. We have 50,000 thoughts a day—many of them questions and answers to ourselves. We have a hard time shutting down our restless minds. Our natural tendency is to ask and answer questions day and night, even in our dreams. "I have a notion," Socrates said, "that when the mind is thinking, it is simply talking to itself, asking questions and answering them."

The best questions explore how people live their lives. What motivates people? How do we create a good health care system? How does the Internet affect the news business? What makes a successful baseball team? How can children be motivated to learn? How can addicts overcome their biological and psychological need for alcohol or drugs?

Even more important than any question is the string of followup questions. I might ask: What qualities make a person an expert? You might answer intelligence and hard work. So far, so good. But what do we mean by intelligence? Do we mean logic? Knowledge? Skills? How do we measure intelligence? What other qualities strengthen intelligence? Disposition? Interest? And what does "hard work" mean? Can we work hard and fail to gain expertise? Can we work more casually and get the skills we need? Can we quantify how many hours we need to practice to become an expert?

With good questions, we can build a strong story or argument. We know what kinds of issues to explore, what kinds of people to interview, what kinds of background research you need to do.

The sharper your question, the more information you'll find. With a focused topic, you know what information to look for—and that information is easy to spot. Looking for information about a broad topic is harder, because piles of information overwhelm us. With a broad topic, we're searching for a needle in a haystack; with a focused topic, we're looking for a needle in a sewing kit.

So how do you come up with a good question? The best way, in my experience, is to write down everything you know about your topic. Put it all on one piece of paper. That's critical. If you need a big piece of paper, that's fine. You can get an 11-by-17 piece of paper at Staples or Kinko's. Just be sure to put everything on one sheet, so you can see every idea that comes to mind.

How do you arrange these ideas on the sheet? Any way you like. Some writers group similar ideas together; others show connections between opposites. Others list data in one part of the sheet and general ideas or principles in another; others cluster major concepts with specific data. Always—*always*—draw diagrams and lines making connections among the ideas and data.

Thinking begins with questions. Our job, as analysts, is to ask the right questions and screen out distractions. To write well, then, aspire to become a modern-day Socrates.

~

### Element 50
### To Get Started, Spill Your Mind

TO EXPLORE A TOPIC, do lots of research. But also get your subconscious involved. Allow your lifetime of knowledge and insight to contribute to your analysis.

Your subconscious could either help or hinder your quest. If you relax, your subconscious will reveal all kinds of worthwhile insights. If you press, though, your subconscious will resist. Let me explain.

The subconscious is a complex web of memories, associations, fears, and desires. Many of these thoughts we repress—that's why they're *sub*-conscious —so they feel illicit. So they remain under the surface. How do we draw them out?

The short answer is: Be inquisitive. Even if you think you know the answers, pretend you don't. Research shows that the subconscious resists assertions. If I say, "The sky is blue," the subconscious looks for reasons to say it *isn't*. The mind also works like a search engine. When you ask a question, your mind Googles the brain.

Follow these nine practices steps to brainstorm ideas:

**1. Prime yourself**: Before brainstorming, do as much research as possible. When you read a book or article, write down a label for each major idea in the margins. That way, when you go back to brainstorm, you can review all the key concepts in a few minutes.

**2. Keep a notebook**: Bring a notebook wherever you go. Whenever you have an insight—especially about the topic of your writing—jot it down. Some people like an old-fashioned paper notebook. Others prefer to use their electronic devices. If you go electronic, try Evernote. This free app helps you jot down ideas wherever you are—on your phone, tablet, or computer. When you write in one place, it syncs automatically.

**3. See everything at once**: Too often we think serially. We have one thought, then another, then another, and so on. But you need to see all your ideas at once. So grab a big sheet of paper to hold all your ideas.

**4. Ask lots of questions**: The brain loves questions. When you ask yourself a question, the brain shifts into search mode. It comes up with all kinds of possibilities, rather than resistance.

Use the "divergence" strategy to generate as many creative ideas as possible. Businesses use "divergence tests" in hiring to find the most creative candidates. Here's how these tests work. Interviewers ask job candidates to list all the ways to understand a word or phrase. Narrow, literal-minded candidates list only obvious ideas; creative candidates list a number of surprising ideas.

Here's an example: *Name all the possible uses of a book.* You could say books offer reading materials, cutout pictures for posters, and goods to barter and sell. A more creative list might go far beyond the literary uses of a book. You could also use a book for a doorstops, kindling, weapon, writing surface, cutting board, straight edge, fan, noisemaker, blotter, coasters, Rorschach test, and symbol. How many more uses could you find for a book?

Divergence tests challenge you to leap beyond the obvious. That's a useful model for brainstorming. The more ideas you scribble on your page, the more creatively you can explore a topic.

**5. Rush**: Too often we suppress our good ideas before they have a chance to flower. We self-edit, deleting half-baked ideas when they might offer value. So let the ideas just flow. Don't worry if they're good or bad. You can sort out them later.

By rushing, we have a chance to make creative associations. Innovation occurs when we connect two things or ideas that no one connected before. As Einstein noted, "combinatory play seems to be the essential feature in productive thought." We cannot combine unlike things if we don't think of them first. So release all restrictions on your mind, at first anyway.

**6. Move from sloppy to ordered to sloppy**: Once you have filled your sheet with a mass of divergent ideas, see if you can spot patterns. Arrange items into categories. Draw lines to indicate connections between ideas.

Don't worry if all the ideas do not fit under your categories or groupings. That's a good sign. It means you have room to grow. So start to brainstorm again, with abandon.

Then look for ideas to eliminate, either because they are redundant or just uninteresting.

**7. Use idea prompts**: To discover ideas, sometimes we need a gentle push. We need the beginning of a thought, with the implicit challenge to complete the thought. Prompts provide those nudges.

Prompts put you right in the middle of a problem, like this: *Your company's energy costs are twice as much as your competitor's—so how to compete? Your hospital just cut its budget for critical diagnostic equipment—so how to serve patients just as well? Commuters can't take the main highway for a year during reconstruction—so how to accommodate the region's growing traffic?*

Every field—science, medicine, the law—offers sets of prompts to provoke ideas. Consider two of them. When he was working on a movie set, Alfred Hitchcock referred to *Plotto*, a 1928 book that three sets of story possibilities—protagonists, possible actions, and possible conclusions. Mixing and matching the possibilities produces a set of 1,462 possible plots. A world away, a Soviet inventor named G.S. Altshuller created a system of prompts for solving technical problems. The TRIZ system identifies contradictions in design—regarding materials, energy, size, shape, and more—to force the inventor to find alternative solutions to problems. Step by step, TRIZ suggests possible ways of combining possibilities.

**8. Mix Words and Images**: Whenever possible, draw charts and pictures. Show how ideas relate to each other. When you scribble images, you excite your mind. You move away from linear thinking. You see a whole bunch of ideas, and how they relate to each other, at a glance.

*Draw.* Simple stick figures work fine. Use them to illustrate the relations among characters (who), their passions and activities (what), the timing of actions (when), the location of activities (where), the reasoning behind activities (why), and their methods (how).

Try storyboarding. For every scene of section of your writing, draw a simple picture that expresses what's going on. Use 4x6 cards. Make a card for every idea. When you have all your ideas—or most of them—start arranging them into different formats. You'll discover at least a few ideas that are missing.

**9. Chunk and Sort Your Ideas**: Once you display your ideas, you need to arrange them. Grab another sheet of paper and create a schematic drawing of all your ideas. Try to identify the three or four major themes. Give each theme a memorable "tabloid headline." Create a hierarchy. Use arrows to show causality. Use big letters to show the fundamental ideas, smaller letters to show lesser ideas. Use bullets to indicate evidence.

After brainstorming, you will have a messy piece of paper with all you need to figure out complex problems. Think of the ideas on that brainstorming sheet as raw materials. With those raw materials, you can now design and build something of value.

## Case Study
## The Save Fenway Park Charrette

John Updike once described Fenway Park, the home of the Boston Red Sox since 1912, as

> a lyric little bandbox of a ballpark. Everything is painted green and seems in curiously sharp focus, like the inside of an old-fashioned peeping-type Easter egg. It was built in 1912 and rebuilt in 1934, and offers, as do most Boston artifacts, a compromise between Man's Euclidean determinations and Nature's beguiling irregularities.

But in the late 1990s, as a historic wave of stadium construction swept baseball, the owners of the Red Sox announced that they would raze Fenway Park and replace it with a modern facility. In response, a coalition of neighborhood activists, preservationists, policy wonks, and architects and planners made a bold play to keep and update the venerable old bandbox.

For more than a week, these dreamers held a charrette at Simmons College to develop plans to save the park, enhance the surrounding neighborhood, and meet the Red Sox need for more money. Dozens of concerned citizens brainstormed ideas, then subjected those ideas to the analysis of lawyers, architects, planners, environmentalists, tax experts, and politicos.

Did the charente work? Did its ideas make any difference? Eventually, the Red Sox were sold. The team's new management team decided to stay at Fenway Park and implemented a number of the ideas generated at the charrette. The recommendations they followed included:

- Build seats atop the famed Green Monster in left field. "You could sell these tickets for $100 a pop and it would pay for itself in half a season, said lawyer Dan Wilson, the effort's organizer. "Market them in a special way. Don't sell any season tickets there. It's a once-in-a-lifetime experience for everybody."

- Designate Fenway as a historic district, rather than just a historic building, to qualify for more tax benefits for preservation.
- Overhaul the nearby Yawkey Way subway stop, boosting service there and making it a transit hub.
- Close off Yawkey Way to expand the park's tight footprint for pre- and post-game meeting, shopping, noshing.

The charrette developed a number of other ideas that the Red Sox did not implement:

- Locate parking at peripheral areas with a 15-minute walk of the ballpark. Capture fans at facilities with empty lots at night, then offer jitneys to bring them the rest of the way to Fenway.
- Move home plate to the right field corner, in order to play games during the renovation process. The idea, dubbed Wayfen ("Fenway," rearranged), was the equivalent of moving the kitchen to the family room while renovating a house.
- Create a vomitory to bring fans into the upper deck of the park and to improve the park's overall circulation.
- Limit neighborhood traffic by embracing two initiatives—Nomore Garciaparka and the .406 Club. The first, an homage to star shortstop Nomar Garciaparra, would ban construction of new parking garages. The second, an homage to Hall of Famer Ted Williams, would set a goal of 40.6 percent transit ridership to the park.

Brainstorming helped to produce one of the most effective grassroots planning processes ever in an American city. The new Red Sox ownership group committed to staying in Fenway Park and renovated the lyric little bandbox. In 2004, the Red Sox won their first championship in 86 years.

~

### Element 51
### Ask This-or-That and W Questions

WE CAN ASK two kinds of questions, This-or-That and W questions.

This-or-That questions offer specific alternatives. For example: *Was Hemingway or Fitzgerald the better writer? Do you like Corn Flakes or Wheaties for breakfast? Are we going to eat before or after the movie?*

W questions begin with the words *who, what, when, where,* or *why*. While they focus on certain aspects of issues, they can be open-ended. You can answer these questions in countless ways.

Ask questions as if you are interviewing someone. When an answer doesn't satisfy you, ask another question. Push. Probe. Prod. Look for surprises.

For tips on asking great questions, let's turn to one of the great interviewers of the twentieth century. Here's how Studs Terkel, a master of oral history, describes his interviewing technique:

> I keep it simple: "What do you do? What is your day like?" Here's a good example: a gas meter [reader]. I ask: "What's the day of a gas-meter reader like? He says, "Well, it's dogs and women." And I say, "Dogs and women?" And then I realize the first is the reality, the second is the fantasy. You've got to know that. "Well, let's talk about the dogs first."

Terkel starts with the simplest questions, then goes deeper.

The best questions explore *how and why things happen*. What motivates a character? What incentives and arrangements produce a good health care system? What are the limits of free speech in a democracy? How will the Internet shape the news business? What makes a successful baseball team? How can addicts overcome cravings for alcohol or drugs?

If fact, you could combine This-or-That and W questions. Let's work through an example. Start by doing some basic reporting. Ask basic W questions, combined with This-or-That options.

- **Who** succeeds more—natively brilliant people or hard workers?
- **What** matters more—logical analysis or "big picture" thinking?
- **When** do we learn best? Reading? Studying notes and problems? Playing with different intellectual puzzles? Using our hands? Working with others?
- **Where** do we learn best? In the workplace? In school? Solving everyday problems? In groups? Alone?
- **What** does hard work mean—grinding for hours or organizing work into efficient, doable pieces?
- **How** does failure affect the learner—by discouraging or prompting more work?

A good question only begins the process. More important are the follow-up questions: *How come? When? What if ... ? But suppose ... ? I don't get it; can you explain, step by step? If that's true, then why ... ?* And so on.

When you combine This-or-That and W questions, you uncover a wide range of issues for your analysis. So let's take it the next step. See how we can weave your existing knowledge into questions:

- Who gains the most from raw intelligence—and who gains the most from hard work? Stereotypes suggest that academics, lawyers, and other "white collar" professionals benefit most from raw intelligence, while "blue collar" workers like factory and service workers people benefit the most from hard work. But is that true?

- What do we mean by intelligence? Is Howard Gardner right that there are multiple intelligences (e.g., logical-mathematical, spatial, linguistic, bodily-kinesthetic, musical, interpersonal, intrapersonal, naturalistic, existential)? What do we mean by hard work? Does it mean working hard without thinking—or working smart?
- When might we deploy these qualities of intelligence and hard work? Are there circumstances when intelligence matters more—and other circumstances when hard work matters more?
- Where do these qualities matter most? Where do analytic skills work best and where do more practical skills work best? Does intelligence matter more in affluent or poor communities? In bureaucratic institutions or intimate communities? In work life or family life?
- Why does intelligence sometimes trump hard work—but not always? Why do we think of intelligence and hard work as different qualities, when they are related?

One caveat: As you unfurl a series of questions, keep your eye on a North Star—the major issue you are exploring in the analysis. When your perspective changes, the North Star keeps you from wandering off course.

## Case Studies
### Brian Lamb's interview with Witold Rybczynski and Charles Euchner and Stephen McGovern's *Urban Policy Reconsidered*

In the age of celebrity journalism, too many interviewers spend too much time talking and not enough time listening. Their questions ramble, morphing into stories, theories, interruptions, and arguments, while the interviewee waits for a chance to interject an answer.

That's why I admire Brian Lamb, the creator of C-SPAN who interviewed authors on a show called "Booknotes" for 25 years. Lamb allows the author to answer questions. In an interview with Witold Rybczynski, about his biography of Frederick Law Olmsted, Lamb asked 83 questions. Those questions totaled 772 words, an average of 9.4 words. Rybczynski offered 92 answers, using 8,239 words, an average of 90 words. So Lamb's guest spoke about ten times longer. That's about what it should be.

Here is a representative sampling of Lamb's questions:

Where'd you get the idea for this book?
What did he have to do for Central Park in New York City?
Born in 1822, how long did he live?
And when he designed Central Park, or when he was
   superintendent, how old was he? ...

Where?
Who owned that?
Where did he get the name `Frederick Law Olmsted?'
What's this picture on the cover of your book?
Where's Prospect Park?
When did you start writing the book? ...
But where did you go, personally, what...
What did you see in Boston?
Where did he get the limp?
When did you leave Great Britain?

Asking simple questions not only allows information to flow. It can also provide a framework for writing. Years ago, I wrote a book on urban policy with my colleague Stephen McGovern. The whole book consists of questions and answers. When we first outlined the book, we figured that the right questions would create a good outline of the book. Here are some of the questions we asked and answered in a chapter about urban economic development:

What is economic development?
How did deindustrialization affect urban life?
Why didn't people in those communities just move away?
If cities were so strapped for resources, how did they pay for the
    redevelopment of downtown districts?
Why didn't affordable housing advocates object?
Was urban renewal an effective response to urban renewal?
What took the place of urban renewal?
Why wouldn't city officials divert more resources to areas that
    were most in need of help?
Wouldn't liberal city officials have favored a more neighborhood-
    centered approach?
So how did the downtown growth coalition go about
    implementing its downtown renewal agenda?
Dangling lots of incentives to businesses as a way to lure them to
    a city seems problematic? Isn't this corporate welfare?
How does a community-based model of development square
    with the reality of a global economy?

Since then, whenever I have written a long article or book, I have started with a series of question. The questions not only prompt me to cover all the essential topics. They also nudge me to keep an open mind. When you make a statement, you mind closes, just a little; when you ask a question, on the other hand, your brain goes into "search mode."

≈

## Element 52
## Always Ask: What Causes What?

PEOPLE ARE IMPATIENT. Whenever we tackle a complex problem, we want to leap to the conclusion. We want to know what's "best" or "fastest" or "smartest." It's as if life is a quiz show and we want to hit the button and answer before everyone else.

The problem is that the concept of the "best" begs the issue. It doesn't help us understand any problem or issue. Let me explain. Consider the following questions:

- What's the best form of government?
- What's the best business startup strategy?
- What's the best strategy for assembling a good baseball team?
- What's the best approach to acting?

Those questions are important, no doubt. Who wouldn't want to get simple, clear-cut answers to our problems, as fast as an answer on a quiz show? But what does "best" mean? When we say something is "best," we are begging the question: *Best for what?* So let's amend those questions to clarify matters:

- What's the best form of government ... *for engaging citizens*?
- What's the best business startup strategy ... *for identifying a market niche*?
- What's the best strategy for assembling a good baseball team ... *for creating and preventing runs*?
- What's the best approach to acting ... *for tapping into the character's deepest desires*?

Now we're reaching the nub of the matter. Look closely at these revised questions. Each question is really a search for *causality*. Each seeks to identify which elements *cause* what result.

I would venture to say that all analyses—and all stories too—make a causal argument. That statement can be stated simply:

$$X \longrightarrow Y$$

To understand any relationship—and even to make moral judgments—we need to understand what factors cause what outcomes.

Once we sharpen our thinking about cause and effect—once we know the specific question we want to answer; once we know what outcome we are trying to explain—we can get to work.

**Case Study**
**What Causes Urban Crime?**

For decades, in debates about public policy, the words *urban* and *crime* were considered synonymous—and for good reason. Cities, those great, smoldering melting pots, took on more of society's problems than suburbs and rural areas. Suburbs, in fact, were designed to exclude social problems like poverty and racial strife. So of course many of society's problems get left behind in cities.

So what causes urban crime? Why do people violate norms in cities? Why do people commit murder, assault, burglary, and arson in the city? The answer is as complex as these communities. Consider these four possible variables:

- **Density**: Packing people together creates tensions. In dense communities, people struggle over limited space. One person's enjoyment is another person's annoyance. In sprawling communities, people can avoid conflict by "doing their own thing," away from others. The wealthy and the middle class can create their own enclaves, in cities and suburbs alike. But when people need to share the same space—and when residents of that shared space struggle to get by—tensions may develop. These tensions spike when gentrification pushes poor and working class people to adjoining neighborhoods, exacerbating the competition for housing.
- **Hetereogeneity**: Humans are fundamentally tribal. We evolved to identify with "people like us" and to look suspiciously at others. All communities segregate their populations by class, race, and ethnicity. But what happens when people cross these physical barriers, when they move into "alien" territory? Usually, nothing. But in communities with longstanding racism—Chicago's Bridgeport and Boston's South Boston offer two historic examples— walking into the "wrong" neighborhood can provoke violence.
- **Class**: Inequality not only deprives poor and working-class people of the resources they need to live well. It also fosters resentment. In class-based communities, people resent groups both above and elbow them in the community's totem pole. They resent better-off group's wellbeing; they also fear that less-well-off groups might overtake them. These resentments can flare up in the day-to-day life of the street.
- **Policing strategies**: Police can either ease or exacerbate the dangers of crime. All too often, as incidents in Ferguson and Baltimore show, police take an aggressive, militaristic approach to communities of color. Over time, police and minority communities suspect and challenge each other's motives and actions. But police can play a positive role. Community policing brings together communities and police to work together. By fixing "broken windows"—the visible

signs of disorder, like unrepaired buildings and parks, graffiti on buildings and public places, and inappropriate public behavior—police can check disorder. Also, by using real-time data, police can confront "hot spots" of crime before they spin out of control.

Is this enough to settle the issue? Probably not. But it offers a good start. By investigating these variables, we will probably discover additional variables. Then we can gather evidence to understand what factors contribute to crime and disorder.

~

**And Another Thing . . .**

WE NEED the idea of causality to make sense of a complex world—to isolate the variables that help us to understand that complexity. But life is more complex than X causing Y. In reality, life is a booming, buzzing confusion of X's and Y's. As the philosopher Frederick Nietzsche writes: "Cause and effect: such a duality probably never exists; in truth we are confronted by a continuum out of which we isolate a couple of pieces."

When we search for cause and effect—and bring preconceived notions to the process—we sometimes mistake one for the other. Consider the conventional wisdom that education causes economic growth:

*Education —> Wealth and Economic Growth*

So politicians promote new initiatives—new spending, experiments like charter schools, standardized testing for accountability—to improve education. But in *Antifragility*, Nassim Nicholas Taleb argues that the opposite is true:

*Wealth and Economic Growth —> Education*

Education offers many benefits, Taleb acknowledges. But the experience of economic growth in places like Taiwan and Korea suggest that we misunderstand the dynamics of education and economic growth. Formal education did not boost growth there; in fact, Taleb suggests, formal education often *undermines* economic growth. Growth came first, then education.

These questions are complex. We need to isolate the variables. But we need to be careful, also, not to choose the variables and measurements that confirm our preexisting point of view.

# 14

## FRAMING

When you can measure what you are speaking about, and express it in numbers, you know something about it; but when you cannot measure it, when you cannot express it in numbers, your knowledge is of a meager and unsatisfactory kind; it may be the beginning of knowledge, but you have scarcely in your thoughts advanced to the state of Science, whatever the matter may be.

— LORD KELVIN

The world is a complex place. To understand that complexity, ironically, we need to pretend it's simple.

That's why we use maps. A map condenses reality into a small, manageable piece. A wall map of San Francisco, for example, reduces 47 square miles to about six square feet. By focusing on a few features—roads, parks, some landmark buildings—we can understand what we need to know. At the same time, we purposely ignore a lot more.

Could we do more? Could we add some lush details, like the size and shapes of homes or the pathways in parks? We could. But the more we add, the less useful the map would be.

Lewis Carroll expresses this dilemma in a story called "Sylvie and Bruno." Toward the end of the story, a character named Mein Herr explains his great innovation of a full-scale map:

"And then came the grandest idea of all! We actually made a map of the country, on the scale of a mile to the mile!"

"Have you used it much?" I enquired.

"It has never been spread out, yet," said Mein Herr. "The farmers objected:

they said it would cover the whole country, and shut out the sunlight! So we now use the country itself, as its own map, and I assure you it does nearly as well."

Like mapmaking, writing creates a simplified world in order to draw attention to a few aspects of that world. Stories focus on people, places, and action. Analysis focuses on categories of phenomena, and what they look like—what patterns they reveal—on a predictable basis.

The key to good analysis is finding the right "frame." A frame determines what we look at and what we don't. Just as a picture frame draws our attention inward, mental frames tell us where to focus. Whatever lies outside the frame is considered unworthy of attention, at least at the moment.

Suppose we go to a dinner party. When we arrive, we see the host greeting guests, with an exaggerated bonhomie. Meanwhile, her partner earnestly talks with other guests while he finishes preparing dinner in the kitchen. The couple's child, oblivious to both parents, sits in the TV room immersed in a video game.

What do we see? With one frame, we might see a happy family taking delight in having company. With another frame, we might guess that the man and woman are in the midst of a fight—separate from each other, pretending they're happy but doing everything possible to avoid each other. With another frame, we might see the child alienated from his parents . . . or as an autistic unable to engage other humans . . . or just as a happy kid doing his thing.

The frame we select determines the view we see.

Finding the right frame can be devilishly difficult. When you simplify the world, you leave out considerations that may matter. You might think you're focusing on the right aspect of the situation, but in reality you're not. A roadmap may work fine for drivers but not for runners, who need to know about sidewalks and hills. A figure ground map, which shows "solids" and "voids," does not distinguish the different kinds of buildings and open spaces. You can distinguish neither the solids (homes, businessses, parking garages, and so on) not the voids (parks, parking lots, streets, and so on).

When you analyze something, try different frames. Try to be conscious of the frame you use—and the ones you do not. Look for your frame's flaws.

∾

### Element 53
### Use Testimony of Experts and Others

SOMETIMES, the best way to begin a journey is to ask people who know the territory. Ask them to frame the issue for you. Then pay attention to what the frame excludes.

Let's consider a few issues. Does nuclear power pose too many risks to serve as a major source of energy? Will demographic changes unleash unprecedented waves of global migration? Does the human footprint threaten to species across the globe?

I don't know. I do know, however, that lots of brilliant minds are studying these questions. Many of them are not only knowledgeable, but also eloquent. When they speak, then, it makes sense to listen.

Testimony from experts often lends more insight than a long and detailed explanation. Think of quotes as shortcuts. You get the experience and wisdom of a trusted authority, in a pithy form.

When you quote experts, you tap years of their study and analysis. When Nobel laureate Paul Volcker discusses interest rates or deregulation, you listen. When Stephen Hawking describes the black holes, you listen. When Twyla Tharp talks about modern dance, you listen. Experts, of course, disagree on many issues. But expertise deserves respect. When hordes of experts endorse a point of view—when, for example, scientists affirm the dangers of global warming—their testimony deserves even more notice. Still, remain skeptical.

But don't just use quotations for exper-tise. Also use quotations just give your writing zip. George Wallace's statement that "there's not a dime's worth of differ-ence" between Democrats and Republi-cans provides a vinegary expression of an important point of view. Albert Einstein offers a chilling warning about the nuclear age: "I know not with what weapons World War III will be fought, but World War IV will be fought with sticks and stones." Ronald Reagan warns about the fragility of political liberty: "Freedom is never more than one generation away from extinction."

The worst quotations state the obvious. Tautologies—saying that one thing equals or causes that same thing—waste people's time. Athletes often say that "we just need to score more than the other side" to win. I have heard econo-mists tell us that "dis-saving" (also known as spending) reduces consumers' cash reserves. And I have heard psychologists explain that couples' arguing indicates danger for their marriages. Do we really need expert testimony on these matters?

(Well ... sometimes. Consider that last point about marital arguments. Psychologist John Gottman has found that arguing can improve relationships. Couples who argue, then negotiate their differences, do better than couples who do not argue at all. Gottman can predict a marriage's prospects by watching *how* couples argue, whether they attack each other personally or work to repair problems.)

To decide whether to use a quotation, ask yourself: Does the speaker lend special credibility to the issue? Does the quotation's language offer something provocative? Does the quotation reflect something unique about the speaker or issue? If the answers to any of these questions are yes, the quotation might add value to your piece.

### Case Study
### The Debate Over Global Warming

No issue sparks more controversy—and more invective—than global warming. To Al Gore and other environmentalists, climate change poses the greatest threat civilization has ever known. To Richard Lendzen and other skeptics, global warming is a hoax perpetrated by junk scientists, ideologues, and supporters of global government.

Here's what James Hansen, the director of NASA's Goddard Institute for Space Studies, says:

> Our global climate is nearing tipping points. Changes are beginning to appear, and there is a potential for explosive changes with effects that would be irreversible — if we do not rapidly slow fossil fuel emissions over the next few decades. Tipping points are fed by amplifying feedbacks. As Arctic sea ice melts, the darker ocean absorbs more sunlight and speeds melting. As tundra melts, methane, a strong greenhouse gas, is released, causing more warming. As species are pressured and exterminated by shifting climate zones, ecosystems can collapse, destroying more species.

Richard Lendzen, a geophysicist at MIT, disputes Hansen's argument:

> The notion of a static, unchanging climate is foreign to the history of the earth or any other planet with a fluid envelope. The fact that the developed world went into hysterics over changes in global mean temperature anomaly of a few tenths of a degree will astound future generations. Such hysteria simply represents the scientific illiteracy of much of the public, the susceptibility of the public to the substitution of repetition for truth, and the exploitation of these weaknesses by politicians, environmental promoters, and, after 20 years of media drum beating, many others as well. Climate is always changing.

What are nonscientists to think of his dispute? What pieces of evidence can we trust? Do these passages clear up any issues? Can these scientists agree on anything?

We quote experts and lay people not just to get their opinions, but also to see how they frame issues. To frame the issue of global warming, Hansen uses images of chain reactions and tipping points. Lendzen, meanwhile, scoffs that anything more than an "anomaly" is talking place. He frames global climate as a vast phenomenon, which has always experienced shifts over time—and not necessarily because of human influences.

Who to believe? Not for me to say. But when you gather the data, frame the issues well, you can move toward at least a provisional answer.

∼

## Element 54
### Consider Hypotheticals and Scenarios

HYPOTHETICAL SITUATIONS—IMAGINARY OR "WHAT IF" stories—often clarify complex problems. A hypothetical says something like this: *What if X happened? What if X happened at the same time as Y or Z?* Sometimes these imaginings are fanciful. But by imagining things that have not happened, you can open your mind.

Much of western philosophy is based on hypotheticals. Philosophers from Thomas Hobbes to John Rawls ask: What would happen if man were to create a government from scratch? What kind of government would people choose? Tom Perrotta's novel *The Leftovers* asks: What would happen if 2 percent of the population were to disappear one day? What would happen to people's psyches and relationships? What would happen to public order?

But hypotheticals go beyond philosophical what-ifs. Psychologists use hypotheticals to test how people think about choices in their lives. Consider these scenarios from the research of psychologist Daniel Pink:

- How do people respond when offered a choice between deluxe Lindt truffles for 15 cents and Hershey's Kisses for free?
- Why do people switch to a expensive coffee like Starbucks after playing pay less for a middling brand like Dunkin' Donuts?
- How does a consumer's past behavior affect future choices?

In these hypotheticals, Pink and others try to understand the drivers of people's behavior. Pink cares not whether you choose Lindt truffles or Hershey's Kisses. He cares about a bigger issue: When do irrational habits trump rational calculation?

Where hypotheticals attempt to tease out people's inclinations, scenarios gather troves of data and attempt to imagine a wide range of possible futures.

In a typical scenario exercise, people are asked to consider three possibilities.

- What would happen if everything went gloriously right?
- What would happen if everything went horribly wrong?
- What would happen if things stayed pretty much the same?

The point is to prepare participants—businesses, policy makers, communities, teams—for even the most extreme possibilities.

I once took part in a conference on media and the law. Fred Graham, the legal affairs reporter for CBS, created elaborate stories about dilemmas reporters face. Suppose, he asked, a nurse told you about wrongdoing at a hospital. What would you be willing to do to get the story? Would you read a private document lying on some else's desk? Take a document from a cabinet drawer? Sneak into an office? Change a source's identity?

Graham went around the room, asking journalists to make on-the-spot decisions. With each answer, the reporters shifted the narrative. Graham forced participants to make hard decisions about their ethics. It is worth lying and stealing to expose wrongdoing? Rephrase the question: Is it worth committing wrongdoing to expose wrongdoing?

Graham's secret? Pushing us to consider more and more extreme circumstances. If we said we would commit a minor ethical sin to get information, Graham upped the ante. He asked whether we would consider committing a more serious sin. By complicating the narrative, we explored different angles of these ethical dilemmas. That's how scenarios work.

Peter Schwartz, a leading theorist of scenario-building, explains in *The Art of the Long View*:

> Scenarios are not predictions. An old Arab proverb says that "he who predicts the future lies even if he tells the truth." Rather, scenarios are vehicles for helping people learn. Unlike traditional business forecasting or marketing research, they present alternative images of the future; they do not merely extrapolate trends of the present.

Policy analysts use scenarios to explore a whole range of important issues. What if terrorists target subway systems for chemical attacks? What if scientists discover a prohibitively expensive cure for cancer? What if global warming increases average temperatures around the world by 1 degree in the next 20 years? What if China's protectionist policies lead to U.S. retaliation? What if Americans do not get off their "SAD" diet of grease, sugar, and salt?

The scenario-building process moves through three stages:

- **Research**: Collect rafts of information about what you know: company records (investment, labor costs, sales, growth rates, use of technology, market shares) and customer information (demographics, geography, buying habits, brand loyalty).
- **Consider all possibilities**: Consider *all* possible events. Imagine the best and worst scenarios. Start with the worst-case scenarios.
- **Plan for all contingencies**: When you see all the possibilities, you know what you have to plan for. Devise a menu of responses for the worst- and best-case scenarios and everything in-between.

Consider the debate over energy policy. In the summer of 2008, U.S. gas prices passed $4 a gallon. Senator John McCain proposed expanding offshore drilling. Looser environmental regulations, he said, would produce enough extra crude to drive down prices. But would that happen? How much extra drilling would looser regulations allow? How much extra supply would drive down costs to, say, $3 a gallon? How about $2.50 or $2 a gallon? How quickly could that happen? Would this greater supply necessarily benefit American motorists, or might oil companies sell extra supply to Japan and other foreign markets? The answers, of course, depend on a number of complex questions about war and peace, world oil supplies, American conservation policy, breakthroughs in technology, and environmental issues.

By sketching several possibilities—great, awful, and neutral—scenarios create more room for the imagination. Scenarios help us to imagine a wide range of responses to future events.

## Case Study
### John Guinther, *Direction of Cities*

"All buildings are predictions," Stewart Brand notes. "All predictions are wrong."

No one ever really knows what will happen to even the best-laid plans, whether for a building, neighborhood, city, or region.

That's why hypotheticals and scenarios are so important. By constructing scenarios—possibilities that include unlikely possibilities (both positive and negative) as well as more realistic possibilities—planners can design projects that accommodate a number of scenarios. They can also understand these projects at a deep level.

Consider John Guinther's description of the dynamics of racial segregation in American cities:

> Assume an inner-city neighborhood in which Blocks A, B, and C adjoin each other. The deterioration is at its worst in Block A, where almost all the houses are unfit for habitation. ... The Block B people are nearly as poor as those on Block A, their housing conditions almost as bad and the drug culture nearly as prevalent, but they recognize that they are marginally better off than they would be if they lived on Block A. It is only when we get to Block C that we find any properties that are owned by the inhabitants. Although they are still quite poor and have meager job skills, fewer of them are on welfare; the Block C people are more likely to be victims of crime than perpetrators of it.
>
> Deeming Block A to be beyond repair, the city decides to raze it. Immediately, the Manhattantown effect sets in. The Block A tenants, because they are so poor, have very narrow transportation [options], and so most of them move no farther than Block B. The Bock B landlords subdivide their properties to get rentals from the newcomers. Seeing what is happening and not wanting to be neighbors with the Block A people, the Block B people head for Block C. The Bock C people see

the Block B people as being just as undesirable as the Block B people did those from Block A, and so they move out, too.

Step by step, Guinther shows how even simple actions can produce powerful ripple effects.

Without understanding a community's complexity, planners may make foolish assumptions. When we think of our world as a static place—where the impacts of certain actions are predictable and limited—we're likely to confront lots of unintended consequences. With a wide range of hypotheticals—from the tamest to the most outrageous possibilities—we can prepare in advance for many possible scenarios.

⌇

**Element 55**
**Find a Super Model to Guide Analysis**

CONSIDER THE MODEL AIRPLANE. It's a small version of the real thing. Done to scale, the plane actually looks like it could take flight. Of course, it can't. It lacks an engine and the distribution of its weight could not allow the wings to gain the right lift. The body and wings also lack the strength to last a flight. And forget about the glue holding the thing together under heat or pressure.

But we love model airplanes because they help us to envision the real thing. We hang them on a ceiling or hold them in our hands and imagine the real silver birds zooming at speeds of 600 miles an hour. And those models sometimes offer utility for non-hobbyists. During World War II, the War Department recruited teenagers to build models of Italian, Japanese, German, and Russian airplanes for use by American fighter pilots.

We might think of intellectual models the same way as model airplanes. We use models to simplify reality. Models can help us understand the world in fresh ways. Because they strip out many details, they can help us see the essence of complex situations. And we can use that insight to solve real-world problems.

Rather than providing countless details about a situation, a model picks out a few variables that matter most. A model makes a generalization: *If X tends to happen, Y tends to result.* Models help us to see the hidden logic of everything from a waiter's smile to the movement of stars and planets.

"We are pattern seekers, believers in a coherent world," says the Nobel laureate Daniel Kahneman. Simple models offer a powerful tool to begin to decipher a complex world. Before we can understand something complex, we need to simplify it; then we can look at its pieces and appreciate the complexity.

A toy airplane is a model. So is a map, a flowchart, and a picture of an atom. And so is a theory.

## Case Studies
### Vitruvius, Louis Sullivan, Le Corbusier, and David Harvey

Architecture and planning are ancient arts, which adapt to new circumstances. Over the years, placemaking has developed a number of super models, or simple ways of understanding complex challenges. Let's consider five of these "super models," which help us focus on the core elements of a problem and avoid getting lost in the details.

**Vitruvius**: The Roman architect Vitruvius argued that all great pieces of architecture satisfy three needs—commodity, firmness, and delight. Each of these qualities requires the others (see Chapter 9, "Numbers").

Commodity

Firmness        Delight

**Louis Sullivan**: "Form follows function." How should we design a building? According to Louis Sullivan, a structure's design should depend its specific purposes. "Whether it be the sweeping eagle in his flight, or the open apple-blossom, the toiling workhorse, the blithe swan, the branching oak, the winding stream at its base, the drifting clouds, over all the coursing sun," Sullivan writes in *The Tall Office Building Artistically Considered*, "form ever follows function, and this is the law." The purpose of a structure, then, should determine its design and details. Exhibit A is the skyscraper, which Sullivan pioneered. The skyscraper's purpose is to hold large groups of people; the purpose is not, like a church, to help us to commune with God. Skyscrapers, then, should efficiently provide for inhabitants and their basic functions, with little or no ornamentation.

**Christopher Alexander**: To build great architecture, Alexander calls on architects to make everything whole and organic. A building or place is not a collection of features; it is a unified system. To create a organic place—a building, park, square, or neighborhood—we need to allow it to evolve over time. The best design results from an ongoing process of discovery. People join together to explore the best designs, implement them, and adjust them as they discover how the designs work in real life. In the end, great design follows a limited number of "patterns," which have been used for millennia.

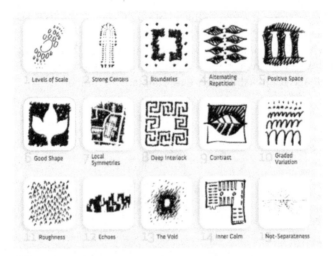

*Source: Sustainable Cities Collective*

**Le Corbusier**: To meet the needs of modern times—exploding populations, technology, global reach—requires wiping away the designs and patterns of old times. Instead of small, tight-knit communities, Corbu argued, we need to build vast towers that can house all our needs. Then we need to surround those towers with vast parks and connect them with modern road systems to other communities.

**The Roads Scholars**: In recent years, New York City has been blessed with two brilliant transportation commissioners. Sam Schwartz and Janette Sadik-Khan both understood that streets—their dimensions, layout, shading, uses, boundaries—determine the shape of public life in cities. The basic layout of streets, Schwartz notes, endures more than any other element of the city. "Vehicles come and go. Buildings go up and come down," Schwartz says. "Roads last forever." Maybe so, says Sadik-Kahn. But even minor changes—like narrowing lanes for cars or cordoning off space with painted lines—can transform streets and whole neighborhoods. Times Square's transformation, under Sadik-Khan, required just some buckets of paint and strategically placed bollards to reorient how people used the streets. For Schwartz and Sadik-Kahn, shaping the city begins with shaping the streets.

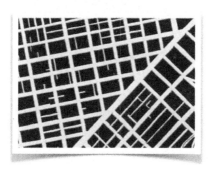

**David Harvey**: Modern capitalism requires constant "switching" between three "circuits" of capital. In the primary circuit, people buy and sell goods and services. In the secondary circuit, government provides financing and infrastructure needed to promote growth. In the tertiary circuit, the community invests in science, technology, and education to promote growth. When one circuit exhausts itself—for example, when the economy crashes because of overproduction or speculation—government develops policies in the other circuits to revive the economy.

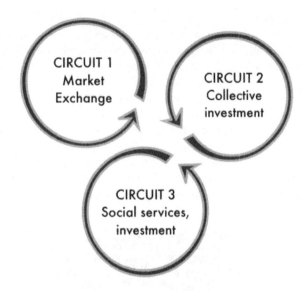

Each model helps us to understand, at a glance, a critical challenge in architecture and planning. By focusing on one pattern, we can sharpen our thinking. By starting simple, we can explore the world's complexity with a sharp eye.

~

### And Another Thing . . .

LET us close with a word of caution about the power of models and analysis. No matter how smart they are, experts often fail to predict events or see the underlying causes of complex phenomena.

For a case study of the limits of expertise, consider the Simon-Ehrlich wager.

Paul Ehrlich ignited a global debate about overpopulation with the publication of *The Population Bomb* in 1968. The world's population had doubled, from 2 billion to 4 billion, from 1930 to 1968. Without a global effort to reduce the birth rate, Ehrlich warned, the human race was doomed. The world, he warned, faced catastrophic shortages of food and natural resources. He predicted that the global crisis would cause the U.S. population to fall to 23 million by 2000.

Erhlich was using a static model. He assumed that humans could only mine and drill for the amount of resources then known to exist, with current technology and methods.

All this irked a California business professor named Julian Simon. Humans,

Simon reasoned, still occupied just a small portion of the planet. And as the population exploded, so did human ingenuity. Surely, Simon reasoned, we would find the resources we needed to sustain ourselves—and improve our standards of living—for centuries to come.

Simon's model was dynamic. He assumed that human ingenuity always finds ways to solve problems. If oil deposits are exhausted in Texas or Saudi Arabia, surely we could find new deposits elsewhere—or drill deeper to get at the deposits that now seem impossible to extract.

In 1980, Simon challenged Ehrlich to a $10,000 bet. Contrary to Ehrlich's prophesy of global shortages, Simon said, the prices of raw materials would not increase over the long term. Pick any set of raw materials, he challenged Ehrlich, and put your money on the line. If prices rose over ten years, Simon would pay Ehrlich the difference.

By 1990, the prices fell for all five of the five metals that Ehrlich bet would rise. Ehrlich conceded the bet and sent Simon a check for $576.07.

Julian Simon offered one last prediction before his death in 1998.

"The material conditions of life will continue to get better for most people, in most countries, most of the time, indefinitely," he said. "Within a century or two, most of humanity would approach the highest living standards of today's western nations.

"I also speculate, however, that many people will continue to *think and say* that the conditions of life are getting *worse*."

# COMPOSITION

You compose because you want to somehow summarize in some permanent form your most basic feelings about being alive, to set down ... some sort of permanent statement about the way it feels to live now, today.

— AARON COPLAND

Behold a great writer at work. Watch John McPhee, the Pulitzer Prize-winning writer for *The New Yorker* who has authored books on nuclear proliferation, geology, agriculture and oranges, trucking and shipping, Alaska, education, basketball, tennis, and writing.

Working in his office in Princeton, New Jersey, where he also teaches, McPhee assembles cards to organize his topics. He moves the cards around on his wall, pondering the right sequence. For his book *Encounters with the Archdruid*, McPhee used 36 three-by-five cards, each coded with a category. After figuring out how he wanted to start, McPhee studied the cards until key themes and moments stood out. Then, from his strong start to his strong finish, he organized them into the structure he wanted for his story.

The structure determines the reader's experience—emotional and intellectual—as much as the content. So McPhee tries to follow the wisdom he teaches his university students.

Two basic structures present themselves. He could use a simple chronology, with topical asides. Or he could explore a series of topics, with historical asides. Which approach works best depends on the audience, the subject, the narrative, and more. The best structure often takes time to find. McPhee explains:

The narrative wants to move from point to point through time, while topics that have arisen now and again across someone's life cry out to be collected. They want to draw themselves together in a single body, in the way that salt does underground. But chronology usually dominates. As themes prove inconvenient, you find some way to tuck them in. Through flashbacks and flash-forwards, you can move around in time, of course, but such a structure remains under chronological control and can't do much about items that are scattered thematically. There's nothing wrong with a chronological structure. On tablets in Babylonia, most pieces were written that way, and nearly all pieces are written that way now.

To find the best shape, collect the pieces and lay them out on a table or on a wall. Move them around. Pay attention to the beginnings and endings—not just of the whole piece, but of each of the parts as well.

When you figure out your blueprint, devise a plan to follow it. Some writers, like the biographer Robert Caro and the novelist John Irving, decide how they want to end the book and devote all their work to reaching that end. Others believe more in the power of a strong beginning. The novelist Jennifer Haigh once told me that if the opening passage faltered, the whole book would vector off course. Some people move the pieces around as they write; others hew faithfully to their outlines.

How do you know what approach works best? Try them all; see what works for you. Writing requires discipline, but you get to figure out which discipline works best for you.

∾

### Element 56
### Make Every Piece a Journey

EVERY PIECE of writing offers an opportunity to take the reader on a journey. No matter how ordinary or extraordinary the topic, every piece gives the reader a tour. Everything—every email, memo, report; every story, essay, or analysis; every article or book—takes the reader from one distinct place to another, different place.

Nothing excites the human imagination as much as change. We spend our days in routines, doing the same basic activities at home, work, school, and around town. So we come alive when something changes. As you give readers a journey, make sure they know what has changed by the end.

Think of the writer as a tour guide. Start by knowing your point of departure. Point out the sights along the journey. Get off the bus once in a while, if a detour will give the overall trip greater meaning—but don't stray too far. Conclude the tour by noting what's interesting about the new location. In every tour, start strong and finish strong.

Here's one way to make sure you create a journey for every piece: Write the first and last paragraphs first. Only after writing the start and finish should you write the middle paragraphs. Give yourself a roadmap. Make sure the map indicates the starting and ending points. Before you do anything else—taking as long as necessary—write your opening and closing paragraphs.

I discovered the magic of this approach while working on *Nobody Turn Me Around*, an account of the 1963 March on Washington. I had conducted more than a hundred interviews and explored thousands of pages of archival material before I started writing. One day, I panicked about my progress. So I decided to write the first and last paragraphs of about a dozen chapters.

As soon as I had my opening and closing lines, it was easy to compose and organize the middle material. Suddenly all those middle paragraphs lined themselves up. Without a clear destination, I would have veered off course. But I always knew where I was going—and I knew what paragraphs would get me there, step by step.

Pull one of your favorite books or stories off the shelf. Do the chapters have clear, definite starting points? Do they take the reader from one place to another, resolving the issues of the piece? Do the sentences and paragraphs unfold ideas, one by one? Do they move toward a conclusion? Does the piece feel whole and complete when you finish?

### Case Study
### William Cronon's 'The Trouble with Wilderness'

To Americans who grew up in the age of environmentalism—the Clean Air and Clear Water Acts, Earth Day, the EPA, recycling and organic farms, the Paris accord—the love of the great outdoors is a given. The natural landscape matters not just for our physical health, but also for our emotional and spiritual wellbeing. Only when we embrace nature can we appreciate the world's complexity and our duty to protect it. In the hippie crooner Neil Young's words: "A natural beauty should be preserved like a monument to nature."

But William Cronon takes exception to this sentiment. Don't get him wrong. He is as committed to the natural world as anyone. He devotes his life to the cause, in fact. But he is concerned that we have a misguided understanding of what it means to protect the wilderness. To explain his point, Cronon takes us on a three-part journey.

**The World of the Story**: Cronon begins with the idea that we need to "preserve" the environment. He quotes—then questions—Thoreau's famous aphorism that "in Wildness is the preservation of the World."

Cronon writes: "Far from being the one place on earth that stands apart from humanity, [the wilderness] is quite profoundly a human creation—indeed, the creation of very particular human cultures at very particular moments in human history. ... Wilderness can hardly be the solution to our culture's problematic relationship with the nonhuman world, for wilderness is part of the problem."

Let's see these ideas on a narrative arc:

The Rising Action: Now Cronon traces the rise of wilderness as a human creation. Step by step, he shows that we learn about nature not from our experience in untamed places, but in man-made natural areas (as oxymoronic as that might sound).

American ideals of the open frontier—as a vast expanse open to human settlement and exploitation—have shaped our ideals about nature. With the disappearance of the frontier, Americans tend to "look backward" and create monuments to nature. We isolate nature as a separate thing. That gives us permission to exploit everything else in our lives.

The decimation of Native American populations—civilizations that operated in harmony with nature—alienated us from a deep understanding of nature.

Postbellum settlement of the West, in dude ranches and hunting adventures, further warped our understanding of nature. Nature now means recreation, rather than truly natural places.

The rise of environmentalism, ironically, further separated us from nature. We see nature not as the most essential force of the world but as something to be "protected" as we might protect a child. We treated nature not as a complex system, but as a charity case.

The Resolution: So what is to be done? Cronin suggests that we discard the belief that the manmade and natural worlds are separate. "We get into trouble only if we see the tree in the garden as wholly artificial and the tree in the wilderness as wholly natural," he says. "Both trees in some ultimate sense are wild; both in a practical sense now require our care."

To survive, we need to apply an ethic of care to all our activities. We cannot romanticize nature while maintaining our destructive, unsustainable life in the manmade world. In both manmade and natural realms, we need to ask hard questions about the environmental impacts of our actions.

When we alter nature, Cronon says, we need to ask whether "whether we can use it again and again and again—sustainably—without diminishing it in the process." Are we killing off this piece of nature forever? Or can we maintain our natural resources while building communities?

The moral of the story is simple. As the philosopher John Locke argued almost a half a millennium ago, we need to take what we need from nature, but only if we leave "as much and as good" for others.

～

### Element 57
### Find the Right Shape

"THE GREAT BOOK OF NATURE," Galileo once said, "is written in mathematical language and the characters are triangles, circles, and other geometric figures."

The shape of your writing—straight line, circle, or triangle—affects what you say. Content follows form.

The straight line moves the piece in a clear direction—forward. Classic biographers begin with the hero's birth or background information about his family, then move, step by step, through his life. Consider the opening lines of this biography of Bonaparte:

> Napoleon Buonaparte was born at Ajaccio on the 15th of August, 1769. The family had been of some distinction, during the middle ages, in Italy; whence his branch of it removed to Corsica, in the troubled times of the Guelphs and Gibellines. They were always considered as belonging to the gentry of the island. Charles, the father of Napoleon, an advocate of considerable reputation . . .

And so on.

The circle structures the piece as a series of recurring patterns. In each cycle, the character moves through the familiar cycle of challenge, struggle, and discovery; when one circle ends, another begins. With each new circle, we confirm the familiar patterns but also gain deeper understandings. Machiavelli saw history this way. "All cities and all peoples are and ever have been animated by the same desires and the same passions," he writes. The circles of life repeat, again and again.

Finally, consider the triangle, which shows dynamic relationships among sets of threes. In one moment, the hero interacts with a villain and a sidekick; in the next, she interacts with a mentor and tempter; and so on. Just consider the most common relationship in all drama: the lover's triangle. The love relationship is always subject to change because of the existence of a third party. In philosophy, dialectics captures uses a similar triangle. Ideas move through three stages: *thesis, antithesis,* and *synthesis.* Nothing is forever. Change is always possible.

Politics and philosophy are full of threes. In politics we see battles between executive, legislative, and judicial branches; the U.S., Soviet Union, and Third World; and federal, state, and local governments. In philosophy, we talk about the body, mind, and soul; id, ego, and superego; and past, present, and future.

## Case Study
## Tracking Frank Gehry's Career

For decades, Frank Gehry has given modern architecture new, creative shapes. Combining his talents as a builder and an artist, Gehry uses the latest technology and materials in unusual ways. Gehry developed his talents at a young age. He absorbed influences from his father, a truck driver with some artistic abilities, and his mother, an autodidact who loved art and music. When the family moved from Canada to Los Angeles, Gehry reveled in L.A.'s scattered, dynamic chaos.

To his work, Gehry brings a desire to update modernism, a commitment to fitting structures into their gritty modern context, and an artistic flair to sculpt and create new forms. Gehry draws throughout his design process. By sketching out ideas, he conceptualizes all aspects of his projects. For Gehry, building is a process of never-ending learning and daring.

Consider six distinct moments of Gehry's career:

- **Education**: Gehry struggled, in his early years, to find his passion. Was it driving trucks? Announcing on radio? Working in chemistry? When he realized how much he loved museum expeditions with his mother, Gehry took up art and sculpture. He then got an architecture degree from USC and a planning degree from Harvard.
- **Early projects**: Working for Victor Gruen's firm, Gehry began to develop his style as a sculptor and architect. In The David Cabin, Gehry showed his love of context and gritty building materials by exposing beams, rich with texture, both inside and outside the structure. Gehry loved, as he put it, "the hammer marks on the wood." Another work, for Lou Danziger, involved two oblong boxes, "positioned as carefully as pieces of minimalist sculpture," in the words of critic Paul Goldberger.
- **Renovation of his Santa Monica home**: In his breakthrough project, Gehry returned to art. He wrapped his house in metallic sheets, allowing the bones of the industrial building to remain visible. In this work, Goldberger finds "a subtly asymmetrical arrangement of solids and voids."
- **Growing his capacity**: A relentless learner, Gehry took advantage of his growing fame to develop his distinctive approach to architecture. When billionaire Peter Lewis gave him $5 million to build a house, Gehry created ever-expanding visions. He never realized those

visions—Lewis halted the project after he spent $82.5 million on the project—but Gehry developed his unique style during those years.

- **The Guggenheim Museum**: In 1997, Gehry won global acclaim for his masterpiece in Bilbao, an old port city in northern Spain. Philip Johnson called it "the greatest building of our time." Located on the waterfront, the museum is wrapped in shining titanium waves. This vast work of art connects with the surrounding area, practically expanding the museum's grounds to the whole waterfront district.
- **Walt Disney Concert Hall**: This massive structure looms above the streets of Los Angeles. The Bilbao-like exterior draws attention from all sides, giving Angelinos both a living sculpture—great for viewing while stuck in traffic!—and a world-class music hall.

So how do you tell this story? It could follow a simple line, describing events with a straight chronology:

The story could also be structured into a triangle. At every phase of his career, Gehry struggles to find a vision … then embraces his artistic powers, using natural and industrial materials to fashion sculpture-like buildings … then works with the challenges posed by the project site and plans. We might look at each phase of his career like this:

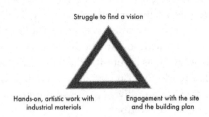

Finally, we might see Gehry's career as a series of circles, which reveal the recurring patterns of Gehry's life and career. For each circle, we see Gehry applying his three-part methodology (see the triangle, above) to different challenges:

Education   Early projects   Renovation of home   Growing capacity   Bilbao   Disney

I like the idea of the circles—showing the recurring patterns in Gehry's work, how he moves through similar processes and "comes full circle," again and again.

How about you?

~

### Element 58
### Slot Your Paragraphs

WITH THE BASIC shapes of composition—straight lines, circles, and triangles, in addition to Aristotle's narrative arc—let's explore how to organize information within those shapes.

The key unit of all pieces is the paragraph. So let's begin with a quick review of the skills you need to write a good paragraph.

- Make every paragraph a journey, which takes the reader from one place to another.
- State and develop just one idea in every paragraph.
- Give each paragraph a three- to five-word label. Cut anything in that paragraph that does not support idea expressed in that label.
- Write these labels as if you were writing a headline for a tabloid newspaper.

Now we need to arrange those paragraphs, put them in the right order. I call this process "slotting." Think of the way you put files in slots on desk organizers.

To slot paragraphs, first decide where you want to start and finish your piece. If you don't know that, as we have already discussed, you cannot figure out how to organize anything else.

Once you know the starting and the finishing points, look at all your tabloid headlines. You might have dozens of headlines and paragraphs. So what's the best sequence for them? What's the best road to travel from the beginning to the end? You might be surprised how easy it is to arrange these paragraphs, if you have labeled them all and know where to start and finish.

Work from the outside in. Figure out what paragraphs best support the opening paragraph; then figure out what paragraphs best support the closing paragraph. Once you arrange clusters of paragraphs at the beginning and end, you can easily arrange the paragraphs in the middle.

Some years ago, I wrote a mess of a book draft. "There's a lot of great stuff in here," my editor, Hillel Black, told me, "but I don't see where you're going." So I made a stack of three-by-five-inch cards that identified the book's main ideas. We ordered lunch and then spent an hour or so moving the cards around on a table. Finally, we arranged the cards into a workable plan for the book.

That's what you can do with paragraphs. When you give them punchy labels, you can survey all your ideas at a glance. Then you can determine the order that works best.

## Case Study
## Malcolm Gladwell's 'The Terrazzo Jungle'

To illustrate this idea, look at the work of Malcolm Gladwell, America's most successful nonfiction writer.

What's Gladwell's secret? Partly, it's his structure. Each paragraph offers a coherent mini-essay. Because he writes such tight paragraphs—just one idea per paragraph—Gladwell never loses the reader even when talking about obscure or abstract topics. Then he slots his pieces well.

Gladwell's article "The Terrazzo Jungle" models the idea of slotting. The piece describes the evolution of shopping malls in America, focusing on the career of a developer named Victor Gruen. The story jumps around in time, moving from sweeping historical statements to comments about the characters' appearances and temperaments.

Here's the backstory. As a young man, Victor Gruen revolutionized retailing with his creation of the modern mall. This innovation won him fortune and fame. Gruen—and, later, another developer named Al Taubman—attended to every detail to make malls not only profitable but exciting and safe as well. And in the end, Gruen was shocked by the ugliness that his innovation created.

Now here's an outline of the 26 paragraphs in this piece. Think of each paragraph as a bucket for one idea. See how the buckets line up in a sequence.

1. **Victor Gruen's story**: His life, from Austrian immigrant to mall mogul.
2. **Gruen's Southdale model**: The design of the modern mall.
3. **A media sensation**: How Gruen's work excited journalists and others.
4. **Southdales everywhere**: Developers copy the Southdale model thousands of times.
5. **Al Taubman**: A Michigan developer takes the model to the next level.

6. **Short Hills Mall**: A description of Taubman's signature mall.

7. **Details matter**: Taubman's attention to details—flooring, handrails, and visibility—to overcome "threshold resistance."

8. **Details matter, continued**: The design of corridors in malls.

9. **The power of anchors**: Exploring the case of Nieman Marcus.

10. **Other details**: Why malls have two stories, use ring roads and multiple entrances, and provide more parking at the second level.

11. **Control**: How developers manage mall environments.

12. **Old-style control**: The limited control of old-style downtowns.

13. **Vienna backstory**: How Gruen hoped to remake old Vienna.

14. **Suburban chaos**: Gruen's attack on unplanned communities and his plans for a community with apartment buildings, houses, schools, parks, a medical center.

15. **Lonely critique**: Developers and others ignore Frank Lloyd Wright's critique of Gruen.

16. **No mall community**: Gruen's mistake in assuming that he could impose Viennese mass planning on suburbia.

17. **A failed mall**: The failure of Framingham's Shoppers World.

18. **Tax breaks**: Depreciation transforms the economics of malls and strip development.

19. **Tax break impact**: Why building now trumps the stock market for investing.

20. **Logic turned on its head**: How malls transform regional economies.

21. **Gotham vision**: Gruen's vision for a Corbusian city in New York.

22. **Gotham vision, continued**: Gruen's vision, continued.

23. **Malls transform America**: Postwar America's embrace of the mall as a social as well as economic place, depopulating public spaces and older communities.

24. **Private versus public good**: The belief that merchants can produce something good for all.

25. **Too big**: Taubman's critique of Gruen.

26. **Malls maul**: Gruen is shocked by the ugliness of the mallscape.

Gladwell takes us on a journey from innocence to disillusionment, from creativity to stagnation.

By giving each paragraph a label, you can slot the whole story, from beginning to end, with short tabloid-style labels. Then you can review the whole piece at a glance—and decide whether passages need to be moved or removed from the piece.

~

## Element 59
## Make Transitions Lightly

IMAGINE TAKING a train trip for a couple hundred miles. As the train glides and bumps on the tracks, you peer out the window. You notice a variety of spaces along the way—farm houses, suburban tracts, storage sheds, manufacturing buildings, parking lots, city centers—as they pass. Watching the changing landscapes, you don't need anyone to narrate transitions. You easily jump from scene to scene. The one common thread is your journey.

Making transitions as a writer is not much different. To direct the reader to a new idea or place, we don't need to announce that a move is about to happen. We simply need to make the move. Usually, simply changing the subject is usually enough to shift from one idea to another. When that doesn't work, a simple word or two signals the reader to shift perspective.

To make most transitions, all you need to do is change the subject. One or two words usually offer enough of a traffic signal to the reader. Here are some other simple tactics (with specific words) to make transitions:

- *Continue the discussion:* Also, again, as well, another, in addition, furthermore, likewise.
- *Show location:* Above, below, by, near, under, over, alongside, in front of, behind, in the back.
- *Show time:* When, then, before, after, suddenly, during, finally, later, lastly, meanwhile, until, then, when.
- *Pivot words:* However, but, after, before, more than, less than, likewise, also, likewise, even though, despite.
- *Clarify:* So, for example, consider, put another way, to clarify.
- *Question:* So why ...? How ...? When ...?
- *Emphasize:* Again, because, on the other hand, again, frequently, in fact, surprisingly, often overlooked, seriously.
- *Conclude:* Finally, lastly, and so, as a result.

Your high school English teacher probably taught you to use wordy, blunt transitions, like this: *The second major cause of the French Revolution was ...* Or: *As we have seen in this paper ...* That's fine for high school, when you are learning how to connect separate fragments into one piece.

To be sure, readers often need help moving from one subject to another. But you can do it simply. Words and phrases like "so" and "because of" and "after" and "before" and "as a result" usually suffice to direct the reader to a new aspect of the piece. Like drivers flicking on turn signals, transitions indicate the next phase of the journey.

Our brains naturally jump, quickly and easily, from one idea to another. In

our video age, we jump countless times a day without noticing. Moviemakers call it "quick cutting." When a movie shifts from a bedroom scene to an outdoors action scene, the viewer understands the shift. Why? Because once you've completed one idea or scene, you are ready for a new one. We are always ready to jump.

### Case Study
### Witold Rybczynski's *Home*

LET'S see how one skilled writer, Witold Rybczynski, makes transitions. Randomly, I selected his chapter on the changing technologies of the home.

Most often, Rybczynski simply introduces a new subject to signal a transition:

> The American interest in reducing housework ...
> The Victorian effort to improve domestic comfort ...
> The rooms in a French eighteenth-century hotel were carefully located...
> Compare this house with one that Christine Frederick chose...
> Henry Rutton was a Canadian engineer who ...
> Interior decorators, even more than architects, were ill equipped
>    ...
> The first use for electricity ...
> The popularity of electric appliances ...
> Mechanization in the home ...
> The lesser number of servants in the United States...
> The great American innovation...

Frequently, Rybczynski simply continues the previous paragraph's discussion, as these paragraph openings show:

> What was needed to make these devices practical ...
> Beecher was expressing a point of view ...
> What she was reacting against was ...
> It might have ended there...
> Technology helped, elsewhere.
> The answer is, probably few. ...
> This design was the work of ...
> What she was reacting against ...

At other times, Rybczynski uses pivot words to introduce new thoughts by making comparisons with previous thoughts:

Ventilation affected the fabric of the house *even more than* gaslight. ...
The main motive power, *however*, remained ...
A *less visible* but *equally important* benefit ...
The *lesser number* of servants in the United States was not ...
The American housewife's reliance *on fewer* servants was not only ...
A *greater* interest in domestic efficiency ...
Of course, these *early* pioneers...
For *a variety* of reasons, ...

Rybczynski also transitions by marking a change in time, as these paragraph openers show:

The lack of interest of most architects in new technologies *marks a watershed* ...
*Until* the eighteenth century ...
*Once* electricity had entered the home it was available for other uses. ...
Gaslight had taken *more than 50 years* ...
*By 1900*, electric lighting was an accepted ...
The ability of electricity to provide direct heat *was quickly*...
More than half of the electrified homes *in 1927*...
Wartime encouraged...
*The same year* that *Housekeeping Engineering* appeared ...
Some of the suggestions of the domestic engineers *now* seem pedantic and forced. ...

Sports officials understand say they perform best when no one notices. "As soon as you notice the umpires," one major-league umpire told me, "they're getting in the way of the game." Like umpires, transitions should be unobtrusive. They should keep the game going, without much notice.

### And Another Thing ...

MAN IS A PATTERN-SEEKING ANIMAL. To understand anything—from brewing coffee in the morning to understanding Samantha Bee's jokes on late-night TV—we need to identify patterns. When we "get" the pattern, we can introduce complications to the piece.

The catchier the pattern, the easier the reader can follow—and get invested emotionally.

Consider Beethoven's Fifth Symphony, the most famous piece of music in

the western world. The piece has been imitated everywhere, from the Beatles' song "Because" to the disco classic "A Fifth of Beethoven." The Allied forces in World War II used the piece as its victory march, since the opening motif spells out V (for victory) in Morse code. Everyone knows the opening, the foreboding four notes that announce, as Beethoven said, "death knocking upon the door."

Go anywhere in the world, whistle or hum those four bars, and you will get an instant look of recognition. Why?

It's not just that Beethoven makes such a bold statement. Think about how he does it.

We could also look at Beethoven's Fifth as a simple march of notes and themes, one leading to the next. The music moves in a straight line, with clear movement in one direction.

Or we could see the piece as an endlessly repeated cycle, with the same themes varying only in details. The piece moves back and forth, from heaviness to lightness. We experience power, energy, excitement, and dread from the pounding notes; then we experience lightness, sweetness, and hopefulness from the light notes.

Finally, most powerfully, Beethoven gives us a series of triangles: DA da da DUM. That three-part structure looks and feels like Aristotle's narrative arc. We experience a clear beginning, middle, and end.

You see this pattern in all great pieces of writing. Writes move forward, one moment after another … with a recurring cycle, shifting back and forth, from heaviness to lightness, from specificity to generality … three steps at a time, like a triangle or an arc.

An interesting thought, anyway: Beethoven's Universal Theory of Composition.

# 16

# NUMBERS

Throughout recorded time, there have been three kinds of people in the world, the High, the Middle, and the Low. They have been subdivided in many ways, they have borne countless different names ... but the essential structure of society has never altered.

— GEORGE ORWELL

In the age of multitasking, consider this question: How many things can you pay attention to at the same time?

How about seven? For years, the "rule of seven" dominated thinking in education and business. The idea originated with experiments in the 1940s, which found that people remember seven digits before their brainpower falters. Other studies say we can focus on only two or three things at a time. Still others say we can focus on just one thing at a time. When another idea enters our consciousness, we switch tasks—we don't multi-task.

With the rise of the Internet, we are inundated with information. As writers, our job is to sort that information for the reader. Rather than just dumping mountains of statistics and observations and logical arguments, we need to pick out and focus on essential images and ideas.

Just as a computer crashes when overloaded with data-heavy programs, so the human brain crashes when overloaded with too many demands for memory or action.

Consider the "Jam Test," an experiment at an upscale grocery store in Menlo Park, California. Researchers from Stanford and Columbia set up two displays. One offered customers a choice of six varieties of jams; the other offered a choice of 24 varieties. Customers at the small display bought a jar of jam 30 percent of the time; customers at the larger display bought a jar just 3 percent of the time.

Overwhelmed by choice, people stop trying to figure things out. They forget what they want, lose focus, and wander away.

What to do? Use numbers to organize the world. Use ones to create spotlights, twos to present contrasts and complements, and threes to show dynamic relations. Just about every idea you want to explore can, somehow, be organized with these three numbers.

Because readers can picture small numbers, it's easier to remember them. Take a moment to visualize the numbers one, two, and three. Close your eyes. Imagine what those numbers look like. The number one may look like a dot in the middle of a vast open space. The number two probably shows two things, close enough for comparison but far enough to be separate. The number three probably displays the corner of a triangle.

We see these images every day, so we have a quick grasp of any ideas that fit into those schemes. Whatever you write, offer these basic groupings. Avoid overwhelming readers with too many categories, choices, examples, evidence, and details.

~

### Element 60
### Use Ones to Highlight People, Places, and Issues

ONE MAY BE the loneliest number, as Three Dog Night says in its hit song of 1969, but it's also the most powerful. When you focus on one thing, everything else fades into the background.

Oneness suggests, above all, wholeness and unity. When something is complete, it does not need outsiders. One is also simple; in fact, the Latin root of simple, *semel*, means "a single time" and "for the first time." Oneness also stands for integrity. If there is one way to do something, it is usually the best of many different ways.

History books overflow with stories of singular characters—Christ, Cleopatra, Napoleon, Lincoln, Keller, and Gandhi, to note a random half-dozen—who stand apart. We learn a lot by looking at the world-changing powers of such singular characters.

Singular events also fill the history books. The Declaration of Independence, Gettysburg, the murder of Archduke Ferdinand, the Great Crash, Pearl Harbor, Hiroshima, JFK's assassination, and 9/11 mark turning points in history.

In a sense, oneness defines the march of human history. Religion shifted from polytheism to monotheism with Judaism, Christianity, and Islam. Government shifted from congeries of small city-states to unified nation-states;

in modern times, dreamers from Woodrow Wilson to Bill Gates have aspired to create some form of global government.

Oneness appeals to people because it sweeps away the confusion and clutter of manyness. When Thomas Hobbes wrote the *Leviathan*, in the aftermath of the English Civil War, he could see no other way to create order—and, ironically, liberty too—than to install a Sovereign with absolute power. Two centuries later, John Stuart Mill's *On Liberty* outlines "one very simple principle"—the idea that people ought not interfere with other people's affairs—as the essential rule of human communities.

We use the number one to make sweeping claims about people, events, ideas, everything. Consider these passages:

> Only Brendan could rally all the troops.
> The guru could say what life meant, and what his role in it ought to be.
> Washington was the one leader who could bring order out of chaos.
> Since Villa was the one man who could raise an army large enough to defeat the *federales*, Obregon had him assassinated in 1923.
> Only she could reform his wicked ways.

Talking about "the one" focuses attention. But it always—*always*—oversimplifies. So follow a statement of oneness with a deeper explanation of how things work.

### Case Study
### Christopher Alexander's *The Nature of Order*

How, Christopher Alexander asks, can architects and planners make designs that foster a sense of "wholeness"?

The answer comes with a mind experiment. Take a blank piece of paper, Alexander urges, and put a dot anywhere.

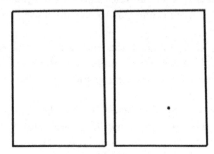

The dot creates a number of possibilities for organizing and understanding space. Alexander's exercise reflects larger truths about how we view the world. When we create a center—when we focus on one thing—everything else changes around it. Alexander writes:

> Although the dot is tiny, its impact on the sheet of paper is very great. The blank sheet of paper is one whole, one kind of wholeness. With the introduction of the tiny dot, the wholeness changes dramatically. We begin to experience a subtle and pervasive shift in the whole. The space changes throughout the sheet of paper (and not only where the dot is), vectors are created, differentiation reaching far beyond the dot itself occur within the space. As a whole, an entirely different configuration has come into being, and this configuration extends across the sheet of paper as a whole.

A good place is really a collection of centers, positioned alongside and sometimes overlapping each other. Each center has its own character—not just scale and materials and shape, but also feelings of warmth and character and naturalness. To succeed, each center defines and enhances other centers.

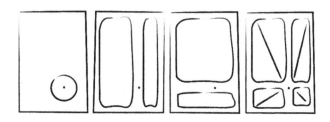

Consider the centers that help orient us in a simple house. The front door provides the center to the front of the house; everything relates to that focal point. Once inside, a prominent window provides a new center. So does an arch. So does a fireplace. So does a prominent piece of furniture. So does a piece of art.

Ones shape everything around them, if they're somehow different, well placed, important for some purpose. Your greatest challenge as a writer, really, is to figure out which *ones*—which ideas or feelings, images or relationships—you want to highlight.

Christopher Alexander's dot is similar to Wallace Stevens's famous jar:

> *I placed a jar in Tennessee,*
> *And round it was, upon a hill.*
> *It made the slovenly wilderness*
> *Surround that hill. ...*

Amazing, isn't it, to see how a whole landscape can be transformed with a focus on a single object. So when you write or design, ask yourself: *What's my dot? What's my jar?*

~

## Element 61
## Use Twos for Oppositions and Complements

WHEN NOAH FILLED the ark with pairs of animals, he had a specific purpose: Allow the reproduction of species. Writers use pairs for two different reasons—to show opposing and complementary ideas.

First, using pairs sets up an opposition. When you put two characters in a scene, the two often battle each other. When you set up two ideas—like capitalism and socialism, men and women, science and the humanities—they reveal themselves by showing, clearly, what they are not. The author Christopher Vogler offers these oppositions:

Sloppy *vs.* Neat
Brave *vs.* Cowardly
Feminine *vs.* Masculine
Open *vs.* Closed
Suspicious *vs.* Trusting
Optimistic *vs.* Pessimistic
Planned *vs.* Spontaneous
Passive *vs.* Active
Low key *vs.* Dramatic
Talkative *vs.* Taciturn
Living in the past *vs.* Forward-looking
Conservative *vs.* Liberal
Underhanded *vs.* Principled
Honest *vs.* Dishonest
Literal *vs.* Poetic
Clumsy *vs.* Graceful
Lucky *vs.* Unlucky
Calculated *vs.* Intuitive
Introverted *vs.* Extraverted
Happy *vs.* Sad
Materialistic *vs.* Spiritual
Polite *vs.* Rude
Controlling *vs.* Impulsive
Sacred *vs.* Profane
Nature *vs.* Nurture

People often define themselves by contrast with some "other." The Crips and Bloods get their identity as much from what they *aren't* as from what they *are*. So do residents of city neighborhoods, schools, cities and regions, and whole nations. Racial, ethnic, and religious tensions arise from this same kind of negative identity. Bigots fear intermarriage because it undermines their identity as a negation of the other.

In your stories, look for the characters who understand their own identity *in opposition to* something else. "Anti" people are everywhere. Because people usually operate according to their "loss aversion," we care more about keeping what we have than gaining something new. Hence the cliché: "A bird in the hand is worth two in the bush."

Pairs don't just oppose each other; they also reinforce and complete each other. According to the ancient Chinese idea of yin and yang, opposites complete each other. Even in opposition, yin and yang come from the same world and need each other. Together, two sides provide a balanced approach to the world. Examples of yin and yang include male and female, emotion and reason, power and finesse, work and ease, and art and science.

Think of some potent examples. Muhammad Ali and Joe Frazier, while fighting for the heavyweight championship of the world, also battled for each other's respect. Bill and Hillary Clinton, partners in life and power, clashed behind the scenes over policy and personal affairs, but defied all the tabloid predictions of divorce. And don't forget the great rivalries of sports: Yankees-Red Sox, Celtics-Lakers, Notre Dame-Michigan.

Twos give stories energy. Nobody doesn't enjoy a love story: Romeo and Juliet, Anthony and Cleopatra, Tristan and Isolde, and Odysseus and Penelope. And don't forget Rhett and Scarlett in *Gone With the Wind,* Jeff and Lisa in *Rear Window,* Nick and Amy in *Gone Girl,* or Philip and Elizabeth *The Americans.*

As long as the tug-of-war continues—or as long as the characters' differences reveal interesting things—pairs work fine.

### Case Study
### Witold Rybczynski's *How Architecture Works*

If ones orient us toward singular way of seeing and organizing the world, twos teach us about the give-and-take of life. We tend to compare things, automatically, without thinking much. Witold Rybczynski writes:

> Our language and our way of seeing the world are influenced by our bodies, which have fronts and backs. Thus, we approach a person openly from the front,

and sneak up on them from the back; we present a brave front to the world, or turn our backs on it; we tell someone to their face, or whisper behind their back. It is important to know which is which (that's why double-faced carnival masks are so disconcerting). This is all the result of practical considerations: houses need places where you take out the trash; museums need truck docks where works of art are unloaded; office buildings need delivery bays. The back is the place for mailrooms, temporary storage, garbage rooms, and access to parking, trash bins, and Dumpsters.

Once you understand the importance of fronts and backs in architecture, you better understand how buildings succeed and fail. Here, Rybczynski uses this idea to assess the Seagram Building in New York:

> The Seagram Building definitely has a front, which faces Park Avenue and whose entrance is reached by crossing a spacious plaza. In the vantage point of the plaza, the 39-story shaft looks like a perfect prism. In fact, the other side—the back—is a full-height spine, one bay deep, whose solid walls brace the slender tower. These sheer walls are covered on the exterior by a grid of bronze mullions, just like the rest of the building but filled with Tinian marble rather than glass.

Which brings me to a pet peeve. The city of New Haven has embarked on the most impressive school-building initiative in the country. Between 1995 and 2013, the city built or renovated 37 schools for the district's 20,000 students. But many of these buildings lack a true front. The most egregious example is the Worthington Hooker School, a handsome brick structure that sits on the city's greatest street, Whitney Avenue.

Every time I pass the school—by foot, bike, bus, or car—I sigh with regret. I expect a grand entrance to greet me to this grand school. Alas, the main entrance is tucked to the side, lost in the parking lot off the main road. In the front, the school should greet the community: *Come in! Explore! See our civic treasure!* Instead, it murmurs: *We're not here. Find us if you can. We're not going to help.*

~

### Element 62
### Use Threes to Reveal Dynamic Relations

THE FILMMAKER MARTIN SCORSESE was once asked for advice on how to write a good scene. His answer: *Put three people in a room.*

As architects and builders attest, triangles offer the sturdiest shape for construction. Unlike rectangles, which collapse under pressure, triangles maintain their its shape and strength. Builders use triangles in skyscrapers, bridges, tunnels, and other big facilities. For this reason, one design expert has called for changing the shape of bricks from rectangles to triangles.

Trios offer the most dynamic grouping for a story or analysis. Threes offer never-ending combinations. Everything two characters do affects a third; that third force, in turn, shifts the balance of power among all three. Any time one of the parties shifts, the other two must respond. The alignment of power changes constantly; every shift offers new dynamics and insights.

Ancient peoples found holy mystery in earth, wind, and fire. The Bible teaches us about the Father, Son, and Holy Ghost. Photographic reproduction uses three basic colors, red, green, and blue. Traffic lights have three colors. Urban economist Edward Glaeser explains successful cities with a different triad: sun, sprawl, and skills.

Andrew Hodges points out the centrality of three in conflict:

> Three is the number of dividing and ruling. Three is the number of fighting an ally over how best to oppose an enemy. Three is the number of triangulation, which seems to mean doing what your enemies want, while leaving your friends with nowhere else to go."

Power struggles organize in threes, with two main contenders often hostage to the demands of a third contender who can make or break them. In the two-party system of American politics, the Democrats and Republicans win or lose depending on how well they appeal to the third force—the great mass of independents and undecideds. In the multi-party systems of France, Israel, and England, the leading parties usually need one of the outside parties to assemble governing coalitions.

How important are threes to drama? A literary theorist named James Stiller once examined the structures of ten Shakespeare plays and ten classic films. Almost always, three or four characters play the active role in the scenes. Stiller's findings make sense. Most of our everyday conversations and interactions involve three or four people. Even when bigger groups get together—when teenagers hang out at a pizza joint or when their parents host dinner parties—people cluster in smaller groups and the conversation usually drifts to small knots of two or three people.

Literature offers countless triangles. Consider this partial list: Oedipus, Laius, and Jocasta (Sophocles's *Oedipus Rex*); the three daughters vying for Lear's legacy (Shakespeare's *King Lear*); Daisy, Tom, and Gatsby (F. Scott Fitzgerald's *The Great Gatsby*); and Santiago, the boy, and the townspeople (Ernest Hemingway's *The Old Man and the Sea*).

In fact, triangles give such power that we might consider using triangles to structure all our stories and analyses. So Aristotle's narrative arc might look like this:

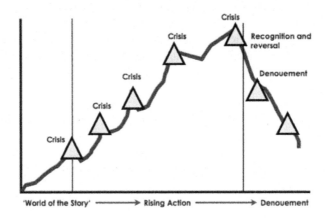

By using triangles to advance a story—or analysis, as we'll discuss later—you create dynamism in every scene. But you don't overwhelm the reader with complexity. And you set up the next scene by leaving some issues unresolved.

## Case Study
### Vitruvius's *The Ten Books of Architecture*

Marcus Vitruvius Pollio, a first-century roman architect and engineer, identified three qualities of great structures—*utilitas, firmitas,* and *venustas,* or, in English, commodity, firmness, and delight. Each of these qualities is necessary; each contributes to great works of architecture, from a humble cottage to a landmark civic building. If even one quality is missing, the other two are diminished.

Let's examine them, one by one.

*Utilitas* (commodity): What is the function of a building (or bridge, road, or even garden)? Why is it created? What does it allow users to do? When we think of a school, for example, we think of learning. But what kind of learning? Is it a severe, top-down learning that focuses on rote knowledge and skills? Or is it an open, collaborative kind of learning that helps students to discover truths and understand them in context? Architects will design a school differently, depending on the ultimate goal.

*Firmitas* (firmness): Great structures are strong, resilient, and enduring. A building must stand up against the elements and provide a solid and enduring place for people to thrive. As Stewart Brand suggests, great buildings "learn" and evolve. They provide strong "bones" that can be adapted to the every changing users and their desires. Aesthetic desires often cause architects to create buildings that lack this quality; Jefferson's Hall of the House of Representatives and Frank Lloyd Wright's Fallingwater are two examples. Truly great structures, though, do not require extraordinary efforts to maintain.

*Venustas* **(delight)**: For both casual onlookers and intense users, a great structure evokes delight. This delight, as Christopher Alexander notes, comes from its human scale, its ability to relate people to each other, and its embrace of vernacular materials and styles; each of these factors contributes to a sense of wholeness. Architecture is not just a practical tool, but also a form of art. So a certain amount of ornamentation and style is important for buildings.

These qualities are like the legs of a stool. Each leg works better with the other two in place. Firmness and commodity makes delight more possible; firmness and delight make makes commodity more possible; and so on. In fact, these three qualities are infused in each other. Centuries after Vitruvius, Louis Kahn famously said that "form follows function." Nothing new here: form refers to firmness, function to commodity. Vitruvius simply adds that delight matters just as much.

～

### Element 63
### Use Lists to Show Complexity

LISTS REVEAL a wide range of experiences and ideas. With a list, you offer the reader a survey of people, places, events, or ideas. The tour might not offer much focus. But that's OK. Sometimes we need to survey a long list before we can isolate the two or three key elements.

Long lists sometimes make it hard to decide what really matters. Consider, for example, the voting blocs that Democrats need to win national elections: blacks and Hispanics, college students and other first-time voters, educated and working class whites, soccer moms and office-park dads, high-tech business interests, environmentalists, churchgoers, feminists, disgruntled Republicans, and maybe even supporters of the Green and Libertarian parties. Did I leave anyone out?

Such long lists, alas, do not foster sharp analyses. You might as well say Democrats need lots of votes from lots of groups. But of course! You could make the same point about Republicans. Better to focus on critical blocs of voters—e.g., minority groups, unionized workers, and suburban women—that could tip the election.

When we make lists for chores, shopping, meetings, and procedures, we avoid taxing our memory. In a busy world, trying to remember too much often results in mistakes. Atul Gawande, a doctor at Brigham and Women's Hospital in Boston, has found that simple checklists of procedures save lives in the operating room. Any good doctor, in the midst of a tense and complex workday, might forget one or two actions he needs to take. Even one mistake can be fatal. Gawande explains:

> The checklists provided two main benefits... First, they helped with memory recall, especially with mundane matters that are easily overlooked in patients undergoing more drastic events. (When you're worrying about what treatment to give a woman who won't stop seizing, it's hard to remember to make sure that the head of her bed is in the right position.) A second effect was to make explicit the minimum, expected steps in complex processes.

Writers don't face such life-and-death situations. But lists offer a great way to summarize the essential parts of any complex situation, which you can then break down and explore in more detail. Long lists can be unruly—but not as unruly as scattered, easily forgotten ideas.

## Case Study
### Robert Kanigel's *Eyes on the Street*

How does a city die?

To explore this question, consider what happens when a vast public housing complex replaces a small, tightknit community. Think of the loss of thick networks, developed over generations. Think of the loss of identity that occurs when people move from three- to five-story structures to modernist towers. Think of the disorientation and isolation that results when basic needs and activities no longer take place in the community.

Bill Kirk, who ran the Union Settlement in East Harlem in the 1950s and 1960s, watched the destruction of old tenements to make way for the 1,200-unit Franklin House public housing project. Kirk gave tours of the area, with a focus on a five-block area where a dense little neighborhood once stood. Kirk tallied the area's losses with a simple chart:

> Across the top of the page ranged five columns, for the five blocks of Manhattan street grid that where the old neighborhood, labeled I through V. Running down the page were 44 classes of business, from appliances and baby carriage storage tissue stores, toys, and travel agencies. It was a Tabulation of the Lost: not long before, the streets circumscribing Block I were home to three fruit stands; now there were none. There'd been three cleaners in Block II, two meat markets in Block III, five grocers in Block IV, three barbers, a beauty parlor, and a radio and TV repair shop in Block V, and 14 candy stores in the area as a whole, among scores of others. All were gone. So were 13 hole-in-the-wall manufacturers, two union offices, three churches, one political club, and eight social clubs. All told, across East Harlem, the projects had eliminated more than 1,500 retail stores, with virtually none built in their place. Pity the poor capitalists? Maybe. But if you took your eyes off their troubles and looked instead at the neighborhood

they served, you'd see not only entrepreneurial livelihoods lost, but social glue weekend—the community, as Jane would put it, replaced by a dormitory.

The inventory is revealing. In the name of creating new communities to accommodate the city's growing population, policymakers and planners have stripped life out of the communities.

∿

### And Another Thing . . .

ALL WRITING, ultimately, isolates one or two or three subjects from the complex world. Why? Experiments on attention offer the answer.

In a famous experiment at Harvard University, subjects watch a video of basketball players passing a ball. Researchers tell subjects to count the number of times players wearing white pass the ball. Half of the viewers do not notice a student dressed in a gorilla costume who walks into the middle of the scene, stops, and beats his chest for the camera.

So what's the action in that scene—the players or the gorilla? It depends. Are you looking at just the players with the white shirts? Or the two teams? Or the two teams and the ball—or the two teams and the gorilla? Or everything in the picture, all at once?

How we organize our experiences—in ones, twos, threes, or lists of four or more—shapes how we interpret the world.

# VI

## ANALYSIS

As placemakers, we have one final task—analyzing a complex issue.

Here's where we develop all our knowledge and insights. Rather than just understanding *particular* people, places, and actions, we now explore the *general patterns* of human and natural phenomena.

Consider, for example, the question of affordable housing. Planners explore a wide range of issues, like:

- What kinds of structures do developers produce? When do apartment buildings get built? When do other kinds of housing, like multi-family buildings or single-family houses, get built?
- Where do developers locate different kinds of housing structures? What accounts for these decisions?
- Who finances development projects? Who designs them? Who actually *builds* them?
- Who tends to live in what kinds of structures? How do people chose different communities? How do the community's laws, codes, prejudices, banking systems, and racial and ethnic identities produce segregation?

Analyzing these kinds of complex issues involves more than asking *who, what,* and *when.* It demands answers to the questions *how* and *why.*

Sometimes it makes sense to begin analysis with some case studies. To explore the difficult process of neighborhood integration, for example, we might explore moments when blacks attempted to integrate all-white neighborhoods. We might consider the experiences of people like Jerry Peppers, a black man who moved his family to the all-white neighborhood of South Fairfield Avenue in Chicago in 1990. His trials and tribulations—the resistance he faced, his responses, how his struggle changed over time—have much to teach us about the issue.

That historic moment is fascinating. It's a great way to start. But as analysts, we want to explore a broader question. We want to understand not just Jerry Peppers, but the experiences of whole groups of blacks (or other groups) who moved into different kinds of neighborhoods (e.g., middle class, white, central-city, etc.) over a longer period of time (e.g., after World War II, after the passage of civil rights laws, during periods of gentrification)?

When you talk about particular people, places, and events, you are a *storyteller*. When you talk in general terms about people, places, and things, you are an *analyst*.

All analysis is, ultimately, a statement about causality. To understand a complex topic—who lives where, what groups use parks, why neighborhoods fall apart or experience revival, how businesses locate their operations, where violence and crime occur, what areas give rise to creative industries, to name just a few—we need to examine *what factors cause what outcomes.*

To learn how to write an analytic piece, we start by exploring storytelling for analysis and then how to make a causal argument:

- Chapter 17: Storytelling for Analysis
- Chapter 18: Making a Case

Now that we understand how to describe and analyze place-related issues, we develop two new writing skills.

- Chapter 19: Rhythm and Beats
- Chapter 20: Wordplay

The best writing blends the particular and the general—the stories about specific people and places, on the one hand, and the more general patterns of people and places. That's what we'll do in this section.

Ready? Let's go.

# 17

# STORYTELLING FOR ANALYSIS

Here's the Law of Universal Specificity: You can't write about everywhere or everyone, only about one person or one place. If you want to write about everybody, start with one person, in one place, doing one real thing.

— THOMAS FOSTER

To explain his life as a scientist, Rodolfo Llinas tells stories of his youth, rich with metaphors.

As a boy, his visited his grandfather, who was a psychiatrist. Once he witnessed one of his grandfather's patients have a seizure. "I thought he was going to die," Llinas says. His grandfather explained that the patient didn't want to do what he did, but "there's something wrong with his brain."

That incident posed the ultimate questions of Llinas's career. What's the relationship between a person and his brain? Is the brain separate from our being? Or is the brain, in essence, the whole self? How do we understand—and shape—how the brain operates?

Later, Llinas tinkered with a Victrola, taking it apart and putting it together again. "All of these [parts] by themselves had no property," he recalled. "But as a whole, they would make music." When he rebuilt the record player, he understood the "elegance" of the machine. Simple outside, it was complicated inside. "Once you understand something at that level, it's yours."

The Victrola gave Llinas, a neuroscientist at New York University's School of Medicine, not only a metaphor to understand the brain but also a North Star for his research. The whole, he understood, is greater than the parts. But to understand that whole, you need to understand each of the parts. Back and forth the researcher goes—from the parts to the whole, then back again, over and over.

Colleagues of Llinas at NYU also look to stories and metaphors to make sense of their work.

"At the end of the day, the scientist is a storyteller," says Gordon Fishell, a cell biologist at NYU. "Back in prehistoric times, we had a group of cave dwellers, and they didn't have a hell of a lot to do than tell stories. Whoever holds the big stick gets to talk. You get to hold it as long as you hold the audience."

Scientific investigations often create a similar kind of suspense. Researchers ask tough questions and develop a collection of answers—some right and some wrong. In their labs, at conferences, and in their writing, researchers "iterate stories." They try out one possibility, then another, then another. They gather data to see which storyline merits support. The wrong answers are just as important as the right ones, for the same reason that false clues lend drama to a good book or movie—they force people to think harder.

At professional conferences, Fishell makes a practice of guessing what speakers are going to say. "There's a rhythm to it," he says. "People are going through details, and I know where story's going. But I'm bored if that's what they do. I'm more interested when they say, 'We did this but didn't get the result.'"

"Whether you're Spike Lee or Ingmar Bergman or a scientist, its all the same thing," Fischell says. "Creative people create. Why did I want to do science rather than fiction or being a lawyer? In science, there's *truth* there."

The lesson for writers: Analysis is just another variety of imagination and storytelling. You cannot analyze any issue—no matter how abstract it seems—unless you can picture it and make it part of a narrative.

Whatever problem you explore—the challenge of regional sprawl, the debate about global warming, the process of Darwinian evolution, the effects of music on the brain, or the causes of organizational failure—start with stories.

∾

### Element 64
### Narrate Complex Issues

IN MY WORK with business groups, we use stories and characters to analyze the challenges of designing products and services, finding talent and financing, and marketing and selling. Whatever issue you face, good analysis begins with stories.

Still, many sober-minded business people and scientists, resist storytelling. It seems so ... *soft*. In one seminar of Fortune 500 executives, I noticed one COO squirm in his seat as we talked about character types in *The Wizard of Oz*.

"We're not telling stories in my business," he said with exasperation. "That's fun, but we're trying to solve *problems*."

Another one called out: "Can we talk about grammar and emails?"

I never thought I'd hear anyone make that plea. But I could see the point. These executives wanted to write better emails and memos, not tell stories. Still, I wanted them to see how stories could help to analyze difficult business problems. When I work with non-writers, I ask them what situations matter to their work and lives. They describe these scenarios like this:

- An executive at a manufacturing supply company considers strategies for growth. To make smart decisions, he needs to understand labor costs, equipment and other capital investments, advertising and marketing strategy, strengths of competitors, earnings-to-debt ratios, new product launches, and so on.
- A housing developer debates whether to build an apartment building near a commuter station or outside the city. To make the decision, he needs to understand the interplay of land and building costs, local wage levels, vacancy rates, interest rates, and the like.
- A health care provider creates fitness programs for major corporations. Her goal is to cut the company's rising insurance costs. To create the best program, she wants to understand the effects of exercise, nutrition, medications, emotional wellbeing, and age.

As we explore these situations, stories take shape. Type A executives can see themselves dealing not with abstract, isolated problems, but as actors in a larger drama.

In that meeting with Fortune 500 executives, I asked seminar participants to identify people at their companies who fit the eight character types. After scribbling for a few minutes, the mood in the room changed. Then one executive said something like this:

I've been thinking about my company battling for market share, struggling to keep prices low, keep the workers happy, all that. And all that *is* important.

But you need to see the situation as a story too. We're the heroes of the story. Our competitors—actually, just a couple of them—are the villains. In our company we have both rational and emotional types. They always seem to line up against each other, and too often I try to please them both. And we have our mentor, the founder of the company, and these new investors who are trying to get us away from our traditional business. It just goes on and on.

I *get* it. My job is to figure out: *What are we meant to become?* And how can I line up all these characters to be on my side, or at least help me when I need them? And when they're against me, how can I deal with that? I knew that before. But now I see the patterns underneath the spreadsheet numbers and product strategies.

When you can see the characters—with different motives and strengths, desires and habits—you can understand complex concepts better. All analysis, after all, is just storytelling at a higher level of abstraction.

## Case Study
## Eugenie Ladner Birch's 'From Flames to Flowers'

During the 1978 World Series at Yankee Stadium in the South Bronx, as the Yankees played the Los Angeles Dodgers, ABC TV's cameras shifted away from the stadium to the surrounding area. The camera panned over burning buildings, most probably the result of arson. "Ladies and gentlemen," Howard Cosell announced with his famous nasal drone, "the Bronx is burning."

What was happening? How did the Bronx get in such dire straits?

To understand the crisis, return to the Bronx's heyday, when the Bronx's "urban villages" buzzed as the city's melting-pot populations blended into their communities. Immigrants lived, side by side, with multi-generational families and communities. Industry and commerce thrived. Jobs were plentiful. The "Beautiful Bronx," a natural idyll for those leaving the cramped quarters of the Lower East Side and Hell's Kitchen, was a successful experiment in urban living. By 1950, the Bronx was home to a fifth of the city's population.

Bronxites, in other words, got along. "Differences between Bronxites were real but in a larger sense they were not substantial," said the historian Lloyd Ultan. "In many ways the people were very much alike. Rich or poor, Catholic, Protestant, or Jew, living on a farm, in a small house, or apartment, they were all middle class and embodied middle-class values."

Then came the disruptions. The city built block after block of public housing in the Bronx; unlike other boroughs, the Bronx lacked the political power to fight them. At the same time, when Manhattan undertook 15 urban renewal projects in the 1960s, displaced families moved north toward the Bronx. Meanwhile, redlining shoved the borough's racial minorities into ever-distressed corners of the city—like, you guessed it, the Bronx. Around the same time, as new highways slashed through the tight-knit neighborhoods, the Bronx became a place to drive through. The flight of business and the middle class picked up momentum.

Sometime in the 1960s or 1970s, the destruction reached a tipping point. Mixed neighborhoods segregated. Orderliness turned into mayhem. Buildings were worth more from insurance than their rents or equity, so landlords hired gangs to torch them; between 1970 and 1975, the Bronx averaged 33 fires a night. Crime was rampant. Presidents Jimmy Carter and Ronald Reagan vowed change but could not break the momentum of destruction. Mayors came and went. At one point Ed Koch shrink-wrapped the burnt-out buildings along the Cross-Bronx Expressway with images of well-tended homes.

For years, no one knew what to do—or to care enough to figure it out. Planners sometimes dreamed big. A massive project called Co-Op City, for example, aimed to create a Corbusian idyll amid the mayhem. Planners envisioned a new subway line to replace an elevated line. But these grandiose ideas could not end the Bronx's decline. In many ways, they exacerbated the troubles.

Eventually, the planners and residents created projects that produced "small wins." A project in Charlotte Gardens, for example, focused on rebuilding the community, building by building and block by block, using the timeless patterns of urban villages. Residents worked to recreate human-scale communities, where neighbors knew each other. Mayor Koch, meanwhile, devoted historic sums to build and rehab housing—$5.1 billion over 10 years for the city's most troubled areas.

Alas, these efforts did not halt the momentum of disinvestment and decline. The Bronx continued its slide into extreme segregation. The poorest of the poor—including homeless, unemployed, single-parent households—continued to struggle. Drugs and gangs held sway over many neighborhoods. The flight of industry and jobs continued.

This story highlights a number of questions for analysis. What causes decline? What's the role of government? Of prejudice? Or deindustrialization? What can be done to reverse the decline? Lower taxes? Special districts? Major development projects? Infrastructure? Training? Affordable housing? The story clarifies not only the human element of urban decline, but also the key issues to explore.

As thinkers from Socrates to Einstein knew, narrative is an essential part of analysis. So to understand any complex issue, start with stories.

∾

### Element 65
### Use Beats to Make Arguments

A BEAT IS A DISTINCT MOMENT—a small or large physical action, piece of dialogue, or any change in a scene. Every beat creates change. Every beat invites a response. With every beat, you push the story forward.

Plato and other Greek philosophers called the process of exchanging beats *dialectics*. One person would make a statement ("thesis") and a second person would counter ("antithesis"); after some consideration, they'd combine the best of both sides ("synthesis"). They moved from positive to negative and back again. In the process, they advanced, steadily, toward the truth.

Consider one of the most famous exchanges in philosophy. In Plato's *Republic*, Socrates and Thrasymachus debate justice. Thrasymachus declares justice to be "the interest of the stronger." Looking for a crack in his logic, Socrates asks whether bullies ever make mistakes about their best interests. Yes, Thrasymachus admits. Then Socrates asks: Since bullies don't always act in their own best interests, how can we say that the actions of the stronger party are always just? Here's how the debate concludes:

> *Socrates*: Have we not admitted that the rulers may be mistaken about their own interest in what they command, and also that to obey them is justice? Has not that been admitted?
> *Thrasymachus*: Yes.
> *Socrates*: Then you must also have acknowledged justice not to be for the interest of the stronger, when the rulers unintentionally command things to be done which are to their own injury. For if, as you say, justice is the obedience which the subject renders to their commands, in that case, O wisest of men, is there any escape from the conclusion that the weaker are commanded to do, not what is for the interest, but what is for the injury of the stronger?

Beat by beat, the argument proceeds. One positive beat prompts a negative beat, which prompts a positive beat, and so on. Every argument produces a counterargument. I say X, you say not-X, and we adjust. You say Y, I say not-Y, and we adjust.

Raise a question and offer an answer. Then look for that answer's assumptions, as well as possible flaws in that assumption. Then look for a way to respond to that flaw. Then consider an alternative approach. On and on, Socratic dialoguers look at issues from all perspectives. They move back and forth, considering both positive to negative aspects of the question.

Beat by beat, you move toward some kind of truth.

## Case Study
### Nassim Nicholas Taleb, *Antifragile*

If every story is an argument, the major job of storytellers is to direct the reader's attention: *Pay attention to this, not that.* The storyteller aims to coax the reader into seeing the world in a certain way.

If so, it makes sense to apply storytelling techniques to works of analysis and argument. Nothing creates rhythm, engaging the reader moment by moment, better than beats. Look how Nassim Nicholas Taleb, describes his rumination on city planning:

> I was recently stuck in a traffic jam in London where, one hears, the speed of traveling is equal to what it was a century and a half ago, if not slower. (–)
> It took me almost two hours to cross London from one end to the other. (–)
> As I was depleting the topics of conversation with the (Polish) driver, I wondered whether Hausmann was not right, and whether London would be better off if it had its Hausmann

razing neighborhoods and plowing wide arteries to facilitate
circulation. (−)

Until it hit me that, in fact, if there was so much traffic in London,
as compared to other cities, it was because people wanted to
be there, and being there for them exceeded the costs. (+)

More than a third of the residents in London are foreign-born, and,
in addition to immigrants, most high net-worth individuals on
the planet get their starter *pied-a-terre* in central London. (+)

It could be that the absence of these large avenues and absence of
a dominating state is part of its appeal. (+)

Nobody would buy a *pied-a-terre* in Brasilia, the perfectly top-
down city built from scratch on a map. (−)

Each moment in Taleb's brief narrative advances an argument about city
planning. We listen as Taleb talks with his cabbie and ponders the congestion
of London. By putting us in the cab, Taleb prompts us to think of our own frustrations in traffic. He pulls us into the story.

In the process, Taleb also makes an argument. He skillfully moves from
beat to beat. He alternates positive and negative ideas. To begin, Taleb offers
three negative ideas about traffic in London. His third beat raises a radical
idea: Why not clear away London's messy street design to make travel easier?
To respond to this question, Taleb offers three positive beats. Maybe traffic is a
good sign if it indicates that people want to spend time in London. Finally,
Taleb concludes with a negative beat about urban clearance programs. Who
wants to be in Brasilia, the antithesis of London?

By the end of the narrative, Taleb has made his argument: Maybe traffic
congestion is a small price to pay for the vibrancy of urban life.

∾

### Element 66
### Use Cliffhangers to Drive Analysis

IF YOU CAN TURN an analysis into a suspense story, you'll *own* the reader. And
you'll be able to offer a balanced and powerful critique.

In mysteries or suspense stories, the cliffhanger comes at the ends of chapters or episodes. A character has just been put in a perilous situation. Can he
survive? Will he? How?

When you leave the resolution of an issue hanging, you invite the reader to
play a guessing game. David Rock, a business consultant who uses the latest
research on the brain to suggest strategies for his clients, explains: "Think of
the brain as a *prediction machine*. Massive neuronal resources are devoted to
predicting what will happen each moment."

To keep readers involved—whether you're penning a murder mystery, a biography, a sports story, or a technical or political analysis—create cliffhangers. Create situations where the reader frantically tries to predict the outcome.

Think of arguments as intellectual stripteases. Reveal only enough to pique the audience's interest. Raise a question, then tease readers with possible answers. When you conclude one point, tease your readers on another point.

Sales people have an expression: "Don't spill all your candy in the lobby." Too often, in their eagerness to win a contract, sales people rush into a detailed explanation of all the costs and benefits of their product. Before even hearing about the needs of their prospect, they offered detailed explanations of why their vacuum cleaner or car or heating system—or whatever—works better than the competition's.

Better to reveal ideas deliberately, one by one. Better to tease the reader, create a guessing game. Better to keep the prospect intrigued.

When you use suspense to make an argument, you not only keep the reader engaged. You also explore all sides of an issue. By lining up a number of possibilities, you make it easy to give each possibility its due. If you treat each possibility fairly—showing how much it contributes to the outcome—you will earn the reader's respect and engagement.

## Case Study
### William Whyte's *City: Rediscovering the Center*

If public life is important—if the joy of city living involves people coming together to share the parade of urban life and to struggle together—then what makes a public space work?

City planners struggle to create great public spaces. William H. Whtye observes that some parks and plazas "work"—they attract diverse crowds, where people gather for coffee, lunch, and other get-togethers—but others fail. Why? "If places such as Seagrams and 77 Water Street could work so well," he asks, "why not others?"

Whyte set out to answer that question, to discover what specific factors cause public spaces to succeed or fail.

To begin his analysis, Whyte considered a series of "common sense" ideas about public spaces. Then, over a period of three years, he used time-lapse cameras to track where people gather, how they cluster, and what they do. Then he examined the data from the video images to answer a series of questions.

Women, Whyte discovered, are the key to the liveliness of public spaces. The greater the percentage of women users, the more viable the place. Why? The obvious factor might be safety. But we need to explore more to find out.

When do people use public spaces? Eighty percent of plaza use comes around lunchtime. Very little comes after 5:30. That suggests two possible approaches to boosting public life: (1) Improve the lunchtime scene as much as possible to take advantage of a natural desire to enjoy public space or (2) Try to extend usage by catering to people's social needs beyond peak lunch hours.

How? It depends. First, explore who uses the park, how, and when. Men, Whyte observed, prefer "front stage" spots and women favor more secluded areas. What about couples? Surely they prefer privacy, no? Actually, no. "The most fervent embracing [takes] place in the most visible of places, with the couple oblivious to the crowd."

So why do people use public space? People need a place to meet, so what works for that? Some like gathering near building walls, others near fountains or flagpoles or sculptures. But you can't count on any pattern of behavior for meeting. "Patterns of this sort may last no longer than a season—or persist for years." Surprisingly, people also gather in the most inconvenient places—directly in the flow of traffic.

Let's explore location in more depth. For lunch, you might think that people would walk for several blocks to get to a perfect place. Wrong. "People *ought* to walk [but] the effective radius of a good place is about three blocks," Whyte discovers. Still, even big populations close to parks and plazas don't insure success. Why? Was it the sun? A hot bright sun can drive people away, right? Not really. "The sun ... did not explain the differences in the popularity of plazas." How about aesthetics? Again, not so much. Architects care about the beauty of a building or a square, but ordinary people look at what's happening at eye level.

If location is not critical, what about design? How does a space's shape affect its usage? Some design professional believe that "strip plazas," long and narrow spaces, "are little more than enlarged sidewalks" and therefore could never accommodate people who want to linger a while. "Our data do not support such criteria." What about the amount of space available? That makes sense, in a Goldilocks way. Parks require enough space to accommodate people but not so much that people will feel insignificant in a large canyon. "Once again we found no clear relationship."

With his endless time-lapse tapes, Whyte has upended much conventional wisdom about public spaces. Almost as if grasping at straws, he asks: "What about the amount of *sittable space*?" Eureka! Finally, the evidence seems to support Whyte's hypothesis: "People tend to sit most where there are places to sit." But what does that mean?

You might think that the supply of chairs and benches determines sittability. But—again, surprise!—that's not what the evidence suggests. "The most basic kind of seating [in most parks] is the kind that is *built into* a place, such as steps and ledges." Too often, otherwise sittable ledges are topped with sawtooth points, jagged rocks, spikes, metal balls, slippery angles, or railings that hit you in the small of the back. Many fixed seats, like park benches, are uncomfortable or don't allow the kinds of conversations people want."

What basic standards, then, would ensure maximum sittability? "By recording over time how many people sat at what heights, we would get a statistical measure of preferences. We didn't." People don't care about seat heights as much as set depths. "Rarely will you find ledge or bench that is deep enough to be sittable on both sides. Some aren't deep enough to be sittable on one. ... For a few additional inches of depth, a developer can double the amount of ledge-sitting space."

If most plaza users come in small groups, their angles matter. Most groups "like to position themselves so they are catty-cornered from each other." Alas, too few seats allow such arrangements. Benches are especially troublesome. For comfort, people need to be from 18 to 30 inches away from each other. Too often, benches fail this simple test. "Designers can move them ... [but] it is highly unusual for this to be done."

What about a kind of theater in the round? People love gathering in semi-circles to watch musicians and performers and the passing crowds, right? Yes, but amphitheaters usually set the seats too far from the action. People want to be close to the action. Tightly packed theaters-in-the-round work; bigger theaters-in-the-round just create a lot of dead space.

Finally, Whyte arrives at his grand conclusion—his ultimate finding about creating sittable spaces. First, use movable chairs. Most people like to move wire chairs before sitting in them—not just to get into a comfortable position, but also to establish agency. "The possibility of choice is as important as the exercise of it." Second, use grass. "While it is not the most comfortable seating, it is fine for napping, sunbathing, picnicking, and Frisbee throwing. Like movable chairs, it also has the great advantage of offering people the widest possible choice of sitting arrangements."

~

### Element 67
### Use the Senses in Arguments and Rhetoric

CAN you *see* justice or fairness? Can you *see* economic growth, productivity, or inflation? Can you *hear* relativity? Can you *feel* a normal distribution or a margin of error?

You might see little room for sensory experience in the abstract ideas of philosophy or scientific inquiry. But, in fact, we can't understand even the most abstract concepts without appealing to the senses.

To understand the concept of fairness, for example, we visualize equal portions of things ... or people taking turns ... or people bargaining with a mediator. To understand power, we visualize something physical, like muscles or machinery. To understand leadership, we envision a president in the Oval Office, a manager at a meeting, a football coach or symphony conductor running a practice.

*The more we use real-life images to understand abstract concepts, the better we understand and explain those concepts.*

And so we enter the realm of rhetoric, where reason and emotion join together. Politics often gives rhetoric a bad name. When demagogues twist facts and manipulate emotions, the worst kind of misinformation results. When used honestly, though, rhetoric offers the best way to appeal to both hearts and minds.

Let me take it one step further. *We need emotions to think logically.* Emotions tap into our experiences—what felt good and bad in the past. They also tap into our capacity for empathy. When we imagine how our actions might affect other people, we think more rigorously. People who lack emotions, like people on the Asperger spectrum, often lack the ability to make hard decisions. Lacking emotional affect, people struggle to sort through information and make a "gut" call.

"Reduction in emotion," the brain researcher Antonio Damasio says, "may constitute an important source of irrational behavior."

Think of it this way. Emotions are whole-body distillations of our experience. They give us ways to analyze things, instantly. When a toddler touches a hot stove or an electrical outlet, the reaction is physical and emotional. That toddler knows, immediately and forevermore, that he does not want to repeat that experience. So when he approaches a similar situation, he knows—instantly—what to not do.

The longer we live, the more experiences we have. We remember those experiences—and make sense of them—because of their physical or emotional elements. The more we can connect emotions to ideas, the quicker and more fully we can make decisions.

The bottom line is that writers need to use sensual language to analyze and convey ideas.

## Case Studies
### Witold Rybczynski's *Looking Around* and Christopher Alexander's *The Timeless Way of Building*

To evoke the senses in writing, observe closely how places engage your vision, hearing, and tactile sensations. This is what Witold Rybczynski does in his description of Seaside, Florida, the New Urbanist community built by the Walt Disney Company:

> A visitor walking its narrow streets at dusk can just make out the broken outlines of pitched roofs, balconies, and lookout towers against the sky. Light from the porches fills out and illuminates the brick pavement. The night stillness is interrupted by the unmistakable murmur of domestic life: the clink of glasses, conversation, a sudden laugh. It is easy to imagine that one has been transported to the town of Thornton Wilder's imagination. And, in a way, Seaside is our town. Not our town as it exists today, but as we want to be: small, comfortable, safe, friendly.

In this short passage, Rybczynski helps us to see, hear, and feel what it likes to be in Celebration. To see what I mean, pick out the words that evoke each sense. With this background, you can make a case for how the New Urbanist city operates.

But to evoke the senses, you do not need to string together a whole series of words and images. Sometimes, the most sensuous writing lingers on a moment. Consider this passage, in which Christopher Alexander argues that architecture should "act as nature does":

> To act as nature does is the most ordinary thing in the world. It is as ordinary as a simple act of slicing strawberries.
>
> One of the most moving moments in my life, was also one of the most ordinary. I was with a friend in Denmark. We were having strawberries for tea, and I noticed that she sliced strawberries very very fine, almost like paper. Of course, it took longer than usual, and I asked her why she did it. When you eat a strawberry, she said, the taste of it comes from the open surfaces you touch. The more surfaces there are, the more it tastes. The finer I slice the strawberries, the more surfaces there are.
>
> Her whole life was like that. It is so ordinary, that it is hard to explain what is so deep about it. Animal almost, nothing superfluous, each thing that is done, done totally. I learned more about building in that one moment, than in 10 years of building.

When we imagine Alexander's friend slicing strawberries, we experience the world sensuously. By focusing on those thinly sliced strawberries, Alexander brings us into a special world where people take care, where they don't rush, where details matter. Even though Alexander does not describe the kitchen, we get a sense of what it might be like.

Why does this matter for analysis? By identifying the factors that usually get ignored, Alexander recovers an important truth. Sometimes, when we operationalize a variable, we neglect to see it in ways that do not fit our definitions. By staying open to narrative experiences and the senses, Alexander deepens our understanding of what makes places come alive.

∽

### Element 68
### Allow Ideas To Unfold, One by One

A GOOD WRITER works like a tour guide. The guide does not point out everything on the tour. He selects a few telling details and avoids irrelevant details.

When giving your reader a tour of a topic, remember to focus on just one or two things at a time. The more complicated your topic, the simpler your explanation should be. So let ideas unfold, one by one, so the reader follows every step of the process.

Too often, writers pack lots of background information into a paragraph or two, tight as a tin of sardines. But too much information, too soon, overwhelms readers. Your job is to *unpack* the many complex aspects of an issue and explain them, one by one. Use simple, familiar terms.

Remember Louis Malle's film *My Dinner With Andre*? Andre Gregory holds forth at a restaurant, with Wallace Shawn as his rapt audience of one. He talks about his adventures in Tibet, England, the Sahara. For most of the film, Shawn just asks questions: "What do you mean, exactly?" and "What would you actually do?" and "Well, tell me about it" and "You *did*?" That's how explaining works.

Recipes offer another useful model for explaining. Cooks must perform their tasks one at a time, in the right order. To make a dish, you must move deliberately, step by step. Preheat the oven to 350 degrees. Then gather the eggs, flour, vanilla extract, sugar, chocolate chips, and so on. Then whisk the flour and baking soda. Then beat the butter and sugar. Then add the eggs, salt, and vanilla. Then ...

> Preheat oven to 350 degrees.
> In a small bowl, whisk together the flour and baking soda; set aside.
> In the bowl of an electric mixer, combine the butter with both sugars.
> Beat on medium speed until light and fluffy.
> Reduce speed to low.
> Add the salt, vanilla, and eggs.
> Beat until well mixed, about 1 minute.
> Add flour mixture; mix until just combined.
> Stir in the chocolate chips.
> Drop heaping tablespoon-size balls of dough about 2 inches apart on baking
>     sheets lined with parchment paper.
> Bake until cookies are golden around the edges, but still soft in the center, 8 to
>     10 minutes.
> Remove from oven, and let cool on baking sheet 1 to 2 minutes.
> Transfer to a wire rack, and let cool completely.
> Store cookies in an airtight container at room temperature up to 1 week.

Take one step at a time. If you get the order wrong, you might create a disaster.

I once convened a writing class in a kitchen, where we made an apple pie. The students narrated the process into a digital recorder. As students sifted and whipped and rolled, they offered their own thoughts about cooking. They talked about family traditions, special kitchen tricks, and likes and dislikes. Afterwards, I transcribed the conversation. The result was a good first draft of an essay on cooking. From that point, the students knew how to explain anything well.

Writing requires the same process as cooking: take your time, do one thing at a time, in the right order, illustrating and explaining as you go.

**Case Study**
**Robert Gannon's 'Buildings That Keep Their Balance'**

How do tall buildings stand up against the pressures of wind and earth-quakes? The builder's greatest challenge is to make those structures strong enough to withstand extreme events. Builders have two options: Make the building stiffer or more flexible. Over time, they have figured out how to do both.

Robert Gannon explains, step by step, all of the pros and cons of different approaches. Gannon's writing secret is to *take his time*. He lets ideas unfold, one by one.

First, he identifies the problem. High-strength steel makes it possible to build skyscrapers. Tall buildings begin with a steel cage, which not only holds the building's load but also provides flexibility. Winds cause buildings to sway, rather than snap. That's all good, but there's a problem. When buildings sway too much, people get seasick. A swaying building can also cause "a mixing bowl of flying objects." When a building bends with the wind, elevators get jammed and interior spaces get damaged.

What to do? "One method of counteracting both seismic jiggles and wind sway is simply to build in additional stiffness," Gannon reports. But that can be both expensive and inefficient. Is there a better response? Yes, as a matter of fact: Anchor the building on "flexible moorings, which will bend, not break, in an earthquake."

Step by simple step, Gannon frames the problem. Then he explains, deliberately, two other solutions.

The first solution is a "tuned mass damper" (TMD), a 400-ton block at the base of the building. Gannon explains how this works at the 960-foot Citicorp Center. After a computerized system detects when the building's horizontal pressures exceeds 4 milli-gs (3/1,000 of the acceleration of gravity), a 400-ton damper shifts and glides along the floor. As the building's base moves, the building can shift too, without an excessive "lashing" effect.

The second solution distributes the effects of the wind along the height of the building. Gannon quotes an engineer: "A truly active system wouldn't simply have a mass floating around; it would have forces and sensors ... running along a tendon system." This tendon system is, essentially, a frame that sits atop a block and wraps around the building. When environmental disturbances occur, the block shifts and the frame absorbs the force of the shifts.

Gannon spends 11 paragraphs on the first solution and 16 on the second. In each case, he lets the ideas unfold. He deliberately breaks the problem down, issue by issue. He never rushes.

In another section, he describes the "shock absorbers" underneath the Foothill Community Law and Justice Center in Rancho Cucamonga, California, which lies on the San Andreas fault. In yet another section, he outlines eight distinct strategies to build steady buildings.

Gannon is a master teacher. He never rushes; he never gets too far ahead of the reader. He almost always uses ordinary language. When he uses a technical term, he explains it and tags it (e.g., TMD) before continuing. He uses technical language only when necessary to make his point.

◦◦

### And Another Thing . . .

PROGRESS COMES FROM SCIENTIFIC INQUIRY. Medicine, technology, machinery, transportation, space travel, psychology—all were made possible by the scientific mind.

In school, we learn the scientific method. We learn how to identify "variables" that may (or may not) be responsible for different phenomena. Do germs cause disease? Do chemical imbalances cause depression? Do standardized tests improve or impede learning?

But brain research shows us that we need to hear stories before we can explore abstract ideas and relationships. We cannot understand anything logically until we engage it emotionally.

Consider this experiment designed by Brian Knutson of Stanford and George Loewenstein of Yale. The researchers monitored the brain activity of students as they considered whether to buy consumer products—voice recorders, candy, Harry Potter books, and George Forman grills. The researchers watched what happened in the subjects' brains as they considered their purchases. Journalist Jonah Lehrer explains:

> When a subject was first exposed to an object, his nucleus accumbens was turned on. The NAcc is a crucial part of the dopamine reward pathway, and the intensity of the reaction was a reflection of the desire for the item. ...
>
> To explore desires, we must activate our desires. But then, before we succumb to those desires, we need to get critical.
>
> But then came the price tag. When the experimental subject was exposed to the cost of the product, the insula and prefrontal cortex were activated. The insula produces aversive feelings [and the prefrontal cortex] was computing the numbers, trying to figure out if the product was a good deal.

Nothing surprising about that. We experience that process every day. Your emotions say "I want that!" and your rationality says "But does that make sense?"

Try this. Daydream about a vacation in Hawaii ... or a new BMW in your driveway ... or meeting a hero ... or finding your soulmate. Or go negative by imagining the sudden death of a friend ... or becoming the target of identity theft ... or losing a job ... or getting a cancer diagnosis.

These reveries, positive and negative, arouse all kinds of emotions. Once we experience emotions, we need to put them on hold. We need to step back, analyze them, and figure out how to deal with them.

Whatever you want to understand or explain a topic, start with a story that arouses the emotions—then sort through those emotions. That's the work of analysis.

# 18

# MAKING A CASE

Put the argument into a concrete shape, into an image, some hard phrase, round and solid as a ball, which they can see and handle and carry home with them, and the cause is half won.

— RALPH WALDO EMERSON

P eople write to persuade.
Academics seek to persuade when they write a history of ancient Rome or explore the connection between protein and cancer. Politicians seek to persuade when they write a piece of legislation. Pundits seek to persuade when they handicap elections. Artists also seek to persuade. In *The Unbearable Lightness of Being*, Milan Kundera makes an argument about tyranny, survival, love, and living in truth. In "Mississippi Goddamn," Nina Simone makes an argument about racism.

Some writers state their theses clearly, like the loud guy in the front pew of church shouting "Amen!" They say, directly, *X causes Y*. The best researchers— in both the hard sciences and social sciences—state their arguments clearly. Look at these examples from academic journals:

Bacteria that attach to surfaces aggregate in a hydrated polymeric matrix of their own synthesis to form biofilms. Formation of these sessile communities and their inherent resistance to antimicrobial agents are at the root of many persistent and chronic bacterial infections.

In this book I attempt to state and test a theory of delinquency. The theory I advocate sees in the delinquent a person relatively free of the intimate attachments, the aspirations, and the moral beliefs that bind most people to a life within the law.

[O]ur analysis shows no apparent link between balance-of-payments and banking crises during the 1970s, when financial markets were highly regulated. In the 1980s, following the liberalization of financial markets across many parts of the world, banking and currency crises became closely entwined.

By stating their cases plainly, these scholars invite the reader to join ongoing debates. They stake their claim on a specific point of view, recognizing that other data or analyses might prove them wrong.

Popularizers of scientific research—Malcolm Gladwell, David Rock, Susan Blackmore, Lauren Slater, and Chip and Dan Heath, to name a handful—blend stories and academic analyses. They tell a story of a real-life example, then step back and generalize about what they see in the story. They yo-yo, back and forth, from scene to summary.

Give your reader the opportunity to discover the answer. Explain all the issues, provide scenes and evidence, and then stand back.

~

### Element 69
### Climb the 'Ladder of Abstraction'

IMAGINE CLIMBING a ladder that moves from the level of atoms all the way up to the most abstract thoughts. With every step, you reach ever more rarefied air, further from the rock-hard realities of ordinary life. Sometimes it gets disorienting at the top rungs. So then you move down a rung to get a clearer idea of the down-to-earth realities of life.

S.I. Hayakawa, a linguist who also served as a university president and U.S. senator, used this image to explain this range of ideas. At the lower rungs, we see lots of detailed information—specific people, places, actions, and results. At the higher rungs, we see abstract ideas—concepts like war, justice, fairness, and mind.

To think well, we need to move from the specific to the general. Hayakawa argues:

Interesting speech and writing, as well as clear thinking and psychological well-being, require the constant interplay of higher-level and lower-level abstractions, and the constant interplay of the verbal levels with the nonverbal ("object") levels. ... The interesting writer, the informative speaker, the accurate thinker, and the sane individual operate on all levels of the abstraction ladder, moving quickly and gracefully and in orderly fashion from higher to lower, from lower to higher, with minds as lithe and deft and beautiful as monkeys in a tree.

Whenever you struggle to understand a high-level concept, move down a rung or two. To understand relativity, Albert Einstein visualized lightening striking two trains as they passed each other at a station platform. He understood something abstract by making it concrete. Follow Einstein's example. When you need to understand a basic concept, think of concrete examples at the ladder's lower rungs. Once you have a concrete idea of an issue, climb to higher rungs of the ladder to explore whether there are recurring patterns.

Take a look at this graphic. The left refers to the different levels of abstraction. The right offers specific examples; track each example, up and down the ladder.

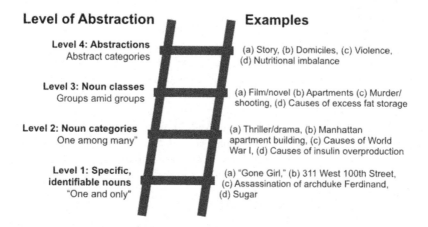

**Level of Abstraction**

**Level 4: Abstractions**
Abstract categories

**Level 3: Noun classes**
Groups amid groups

**Level 2: Noun categories**
One among many"

**Level 1: Specific,
identifiable nouns**
"One and only"

**Examples**

(a) Story, (b) Domiciles, (c) Violence,
(d) Nutritional imbalance

(a) Film/novel (b) Apartments (c) Murder/
shooting, (d) Causes of excess fat storage

(a) Thriller/drama, (b) Manhattan
apartment building, (c) Causes of World
War I, (d) Causes of insulin overproduction

(a) "Gone Girl," (b) 311 West 100th Street,
(c) Assassination of archduke Ferdinand,
(d) Sugar

At the lower rungs of the ladder, you will find evidence, examples, data. One of my high school teachers, a genial and brilliant man named Robert Leonard, used to call Rung 1 the level of "for-instances." If you want to understand your own struggle with weight, for example, track your consumption of meats, bread, vegetables, rice and potatoes, candies, cakes, and cookies.

As you climb to higher rungs, you find larger groups. At Rung 2, we begin to categorize specific things. To take the diet question, we look at meats, daily products, bread, vegetables, and starches. At Rung 3, we look even more broadly to understand what happens to the foods we eat. We might explore, for example, the causes of insulin overproduction in the body. This process might involve not just sugar consumption but also genetics, body type, and lack of exercise.

Finally, when we arrive at Rung 4, we find the biggest of all groups, which includes all of the categories of items below. Rung 4 is the most abstract level. Here, we have moved far away from the particularity of the bottom rung. In our case study of obesity, this top rung might include a concept like "nutritional imbalance."

Think of the rungs of the ladder this way: The lower the rung, the more concrete the topic, which enables you to visualize it; the higher the rung, the more abstract, symbolic, and general the topic. The bottom level is storytelling; the top level is theory.

To keep you mind nimble—and to explain even the most complex ideas to your reader—move up and down the ladder of abstraction.

**Case Study**
**Christopher Alexander's *A Pattern Language***

One of the great masterpieces of architecture, Christopher Alexander's *A Pattern Language*, offers 253 distinct strategies to create efficient, organic, and humane places.

Alexander's overriding goal is to make physical spaces "whole." In such a place, people live in harmony with their own needs and desires, with their friends and families and communities, and with nature. A whole place, complex and organic, results from countless actions by real human beings. Communities work best when they evolve, according to the basic needs of people and nature.

Alexander calls his strategies "patterns" because they take the same basic form in different places. For all 253 patterns—designs that accommodate basic human activities, e.g., eating, sleeping, working, playing, loving, tending, buying and selling—Alexander identifies specific strategies people can use to design their homes and communities.

Alexander starts at the top (general) of the ladder of abstraction, then moves down to the (specific) lower rungs. Take a look at the first cluster of his patterns, which take a grand view of the communities where people live:

1. Independent Regions
2. The Distribution of Towns
3. City Country Fingers
4. Agricultural Valleys
5. Lace of Country Streets
6. Country Towns
7. The Countryside

Now take a look at the last cluster of strategies, which zoom into the small details that makes places unique and intimate:

249. Ornament
250. Warm Colors
251. Different Chairs
252. Pools of Light
253. Things from Your Life

Let's map a handful of Alexander's strategies on the Ladder of Abstraction:

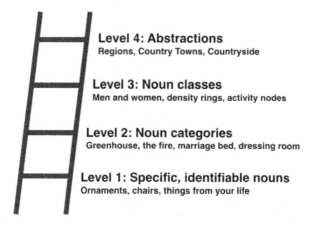

**Level 4: Abstractions**
Regions, Country Towns, Countryside

**Level 3: Noun classes**
Men and women, density rings, activity nodes

**Level 2: Noun categories**
Greenhouse, the fire, marriage bed, dressing room

**Level 1: Specific, identifiable nouns**
Ornaments, chairs, things from your life

Notice how general Alexander's strategies are at the beginning of the book (at the top of the ladder) ... and how they get more specific and detailed as he progresses (to the bottom of the ladder).

Consider, for example, Pattern 120—Paths and Goals. Alexander suggests setting a series of "goals" along a long, curving path:

> Arrange your walking process in such a way that you pick a temporary "goal"—some clearly visible landmark—which is more or less in the direction you want to take and then walk in a straight line toward it for a hundred yards, then, as you get close, pick another new goal, once more a hundred yards further on, and walk toward it. ... You do this so that in between, you can talk, think, daydream, smell the spring, without having to think about your walking directions every minute.

Here, Alexander wants us to both accomplish practical tasks (getting someplace) while having the time and space to live "in the moment."

This pattern nests inside more general patterns earlier in the book (e.g., 11—Local Transport Areas, 23—Parallel Roads, and 50—T Junctions). It also contains more specific patterns that come later in the book (e.g., 124—Activity Pockets, 174—Trellised Walk, and 191—The Shape of Indoor Space).

Throughout this work, when describing a pattern, Alexander refers to other patterns. Whatever pattern the reader explores, Alexander points backwards and forwards. Always, he wants the reader to climb up and down the ladder of abstraction. That way, we can truly understand how all of the patterns fit together to create a whole place.

～

### Element 70
### Identify and Operationalize Variables

ANALYSIS, as we noted before, is really a process of figuring out *what causes what.*

Scientists and mathematicians use the term *variables* to explain the many different factors involved in complex situations. For example, the Pythagorean theorem—

$$a^2 + b^2 = c^2$$

—has three variables, *a, b,* and *c.* When a variable on either side of the equal sign changes, a variable on the other side changes too.

To answer any complex question, you need to explore a wide range of possible explanations. What are the possible causes of the problem you seek to explain? What, for example, are the possible causes of wage stagnation? Of global warming? Of poverty? Of school performance? Make a list of all the possible factors that may explain the outcome you want to understand. Those are your variables.

To do their work, scientists usually talk about two kinds of variables:

- **Dependent variable**: The result, the effect, or the outcome. This is what you want to explain.
- **Independent variables**: All of the variables that might—or might not—explain the outcome. In other words, what factors contribute to a particular result. When analyzing a problem, your job is to "isolate" each variable while "controlling" the others.

Consider the simple question: *What causes a student's performance to decline?* The dependent variable—the result we want to explain—is student performance. For that we might use data for grade-point average, class rank, or test scores.

So what about independent variables? What factors might contribute to an academic decline? This list of possibilities is long. We might consider sleep, attendance, time spent on homework, teacher quality, family life, after-school activities, faith, workload, pressures outside of class, among others.

How might we gather data. In other words, how might we *operationalize* our variables? Some variables would be simple, some not. We can easily count the number of hours of sleep and minutes spent on homework. But we have to get clever to operationalize teacher quality, family life, and pressures outside class. To assess teacher quality, we might gather data from annual ratings or training. A family life score might require information about the presence of parents at home, the existence of home routines, the availability of books, and even whether the family eats meals together.

Let's explore operationalization in some detail. How can we find things to count? Consider just a few possibilities:

• **Existing statistics**: Organizations keep ungodly amounts of data on what they do. Business track labor costs, sales numbers, capital investment, productivity, debt, profits, stock prices, and more. Sports teams track player performances, fan bases, operating costs, and more. Schools track student grades, family backgrounds, faculty performance, and more. The government gathers data on every conceivable aspect of the population.

• **Surveys**: If you want to discover new information, you could conduct a survey. Find a representative group of people and ask a set of unbiased questions. You can ask about behavior, possessions, experience, attitudes, you name it. Surveys falter when people do not give accurate information—either when they lack the awareness to answer accurately or they are embarrassed to tell the truth. But well-worded questions can work around that problem.

- **Observation**: Watch what people do; record each relevant action in your log of data. Set up a time-lapse camera to record people's actions. Or just sit back, out of the way, and observe and count.

- **Experimental data**: Set up experiments to see how people—or even lab rats—respond to different situations. Devise situations where experiment subjects face two or more choices. Or create a situation where subjects must respond to a change in circumstances. Or ask subjects to participate in an activity and ask them questions afterwards. Be sure to get a big enough sample size to detect patterns.

- **Auto-counts**: In the information age, we count things automatically as we work, buy, watch, and surf. Every time you get online, your computer tracks you actions. Google keeps track of your searches—and therefore, your interests and obsessions. Amazon tracks your searches and purchases—not just your obsessions, but what you're willing to pay for. No major company, in fact, doesn't use these kinds of data. We now have so much data that we can measure every corner of human life.

Often, we create new statistics out of a set of smaller measures. Economists use the "Misery Index" (the sum of the unemployment rate and the inflation rate) to determine the strength of the economy. Baseball analysts use OPS (a combination of on-base percentage and slugging percentage) to determine the value of a hitter. Reading specialists use the Flesch Reading Ease Score (the average number of words per sentence minus the average number of syllables per word) to measure reading ease.

After we identify and operationalize independent variables, we would test each variable, one at a time. This is what researchers mean by "isolating the variable." To make sure that other variables don't distort the results, we will hold other variables "constant."

To assess what factors affect student performance, for example, we might start with data on how much students sleep. Then we might explore other possibilities. Maybe sleep doesn't matter as much as other variables, like alcohol use, kinds of classes, or peer influences.

Once you identify the variables, gather data on each one. Test the variables in different combinations. One by one, add variables to the equation. When one variable changes the equation more than another, we can conclude it's probably more important.

## Case Study
## Measuring Community Assets and Challenges

If research ultimately involves counting things, then what do we count?

Urban planners and policymakers face this challenge. Suppose you want to create an urban village—a community that's open, visible, with safe streets, and which bunches people together in creative clusters? How do you measure these and other qualities?

Here are some ways to operationalize some of the key variables to a vibrant urban community:

- *Access*: How many choices do people enjoy when going from Point A to Point B? How many places, in a given area, are accessible to people without permission? How many places have been outfitted to make it easier for people with physical and sight limitations?
- *Density*: How many people live in a square mile? How many people work in a square mile? How many people occupy such a space at different times of day? How do populations vary over the course of the day?
- *Visibility*: How much time is required to notice elements of a place, like street signs, buildings and front doors, sidewalks and pathways, parks, benches and other places to pause, facilities, and parking areas?
- *Land use mix*: How many different activities are permitted in a particular area, by zoning and other regulations? How many different activities actually take place in that area?
- *Street design*: How wide are vehicle lanes and sidewalks—separately and as a ratio? How many entryways offer access to buildings, parks, and passageways? How many spaces are available for people to stop or sit? What's the ratio of public (e.g., parks) to private (e.g., Starbucks) places?
- *Negative and positive space*: How much space is composed of "solids"

(mostly buildings) and how much by "voids" (streets and sidewalks, parks, parking surfaces)?

- *Heterogeneity*: How diverse is a community, by race, age, socioeconomic status, types of jobs, access to parks, and types of buildings?
- *Clusters/networks*: How many businesses are located in specific areas? How many businesses work in the same industries? How often do people from different businesses interact? How often do they buy and sell to each other? How often do they share information or equipment?
- *Inequality*: How evenly distributed are the incomes or wealth of a community? What's the ratio of incomes for the top and bottom deciles? What's the average income? The median income? What are the standard deviations?
- *Publicness/privateness*: What share of an area's places are available for use by everyone, like parks, squares, libraries, community centers? How many different activities do these places accommodate?

The challenge of research is to find statistics that can "stand for" the things we care about. To pursue the science of research, you need to master this tricky art.

~

### Element 71
### Crunch the Numbers

AFTER IDENTIFYING and operationalizing the variables, the next job is to gather data on each one.

Researchers use a number of different statistics to measure things. The statistical analysis you choose depends on what you're trying to understand.

Test the variables in different combinations. One by one, add variables to the equation. When one variable changes the equation more than another, we can conclude it's probably more important. We can even assign numbers to measure how important.

Statistical analysis, obviously, is beyond the scope of a book about writing. But let's look at a few maneuvers you can do with numbers.

To do so, let's explore the test scores in a hypothetical class. Suppose the 15 students in the class earn the following grades: 67, 72, 72, 73, 74, 77, 78, 79, 79, 84, 94, 95, 96, 98, 98. What we learn about the class, the teacher, and the students? Here's a short list of statistical measures to analyze issues:

- **Minimum, Maximum, and Range**: To start, consider the highest and lowest values and the gap between two. These figures tell you, without any hard labor, whether scores fit a short or long range.

The minimum score here is 67, the maximum 98, and the range 31—a full distribution of faster and slower learners. With a low score had been 88, we might wonder if the material is too easy. With a low score of 52, we might wonder whether some students don't belong or if the teacher struggles to speak at everyone's level.

• **Mean**: The average of all cases. When you want a simple measure of what's "normal," find the mean. The mean helps us make sense of cases both near (close to average) and far (deviation).

The average score—calculated by adding all of the scores (1,235) and dividing by the number of cases (15)—would be 82.4.

• **Median**: The midpoint for all cases. In cases with extremes, the median offers a useful way to find out what's normal. In cases with lots of extremes, the average might not reflect the norm for the group. The midpoint sometimes does a better job showing what's "normal" in a group.

In a set of 15 scores, the midpoint is the eighth case. And that score is 79. So half of all students scored 78 or lower and half scored 78 or better. This class was split; some did very well and some did very poorly. That poses a different challenge for the teacher than if, say, all students got an 84 or 85.

• **Mode**: The value that occurs most frequently in a sample. The mode helps to identify common values that might exert greater influence on the mean or median.

In this case the mode scores are 72, 79, and 98. This statistic captures the split performances in the class.

•**Standard deviation**: How much a particular cases differ from the mean. A low S.D. tells you that the scores lie close to the average; a high S.D tells you that the scores are far from the average. The lower the S.D., the more homogenous and predictable the scores are.

The standard deviation in this case is 10.86, which indicates very high variety and unpredictability among grades.

• **Correlation**: How a change in one variable relates to a change in another variable. Correlation shows how related two factors are. A positive correlation occurs when two variables move in the same direction; a perfect correlation would have a score of 1. A negative correlation happens when the variables move in opposite directions; a perfect negative correlation would have a score of –1. Two variables with no correlation would have a score of 0.

Correlation does not mean that X causes X *causes* Y, but it does suggest a relationship. Study time and test scores might be correlated, but we cannot assign causality without further inquiry.

In our case study, additional data might reveal that time spent studying correlates well to exam grades. We might find that TV time correlates negatively to test scores.

• **T-Test**: Whether the means of two groups are substantially different from each other. T-Tests offers a way to assess whether two groups are comparable.

They offer a way to see whether you're comparing apples with apples or apples with oranges.

Suppose we divided the class into two groups and the advanced students just happened to land in one group and the struggling students in the other. They would get a high T score. That would tell you that the two groups might need different approaches to teaching and learning.

Take care when using statistics. The nineteenth-century British Prime Minister Benjamin Disraeli warned against "lies, damned lies, and statistics." Bill James, the man who revolutionized baseball with exotic statistics, agrees. "Whenever we try to prove something by statistical analysis," James says, "we are at risk of going wrong in 6,000 ways."

## Case Study
### Edward Glaeser on Urban Vitality

To understand the role of cities in economic life, Harvard economist Edward Glaeser uses a wide range of variables. To explore economic vitality, for example, he looks at statistics for population, jobs, taxes, investment, and new firms. To explore housing markets, he looks at rents, new- and old-home sales prices, vacancy rates, permits, and construction costs and times

Then he gets clever. He compares regional economic data with the temperatures of different cities in winter months. Why temperatures? He wants to see whether a preference for warm weather communities gives the Sunbelt an advantage over the Frostbelt.

So let's plot the growth rates of 20 American cities from 1950 to 2000 against the average temperature for the cities in February.

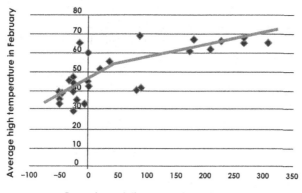

Now, let's organize the cities into groups. Let's put all the cities with

average February temperatures in the 20s and 30s, 40s, 50s, and 60s. What population trends do we see for all of the cities in those groups?

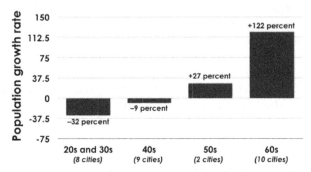

**Average February temperatures**

Cold-weather cities, we see clearly, lose population in this period; warm weather cities gain population.

The upshot? To compete, cities in frigid climes need to mobilize other resources.

Like what? To figure it out, Glaeser offers two other clever measurements—statistics on car ownership and college degrees. Car ownership offers a proxy measure for regional sprawl since people need cars more in spread-out communities. And college degrees offer a good proxy measure for the education levels of the workforce. After crunching the numbers, Glaeser concludes that "sun, sprawl, and skills" are the three leading variables for metropolitan economic growth.

At their best, statistics identify not just what variables *contribute* to an outcome, but *how much*. So Glaeser, through his statistical analysis, shows the importance of three variables to economic vitality. In this example, Glaeser can provide measures of simple correlation to make his point. To go deeper, he could determine the standard deviation to show just how much, say, growth rates varied in warm-weather cities than in cold-weather cities. He could also do a T-test to compare the averages in different groups.

So if we're creating an economic development strategy for a city, we can set priorities. If we're in a warm-weather area, we can emphasize the comfort of living there. If we live in a cold-weather region, like Boston or Minneapolis, we need to develop our smarts. Wherever we are, we might consider how to make housing available throughout the area.

Often the simplest numbers do the job. Matthew Gallagher, a top policy advisor to Maryland's Governor Martin O'Malley, says the state's vaunted statistical approach to policy analysis often began and ended with simple counting:

modestly, state your conclusion. Remember to make it causal: X, combined with certain other variables but not others, causes Y.

Throughout the process, you are playing the game of halves. You expand and contract your questions, possible answers, variables, measures for variables, and answers. Like the back of the shampoo bottle says, you need to "rinse and repeat," over and over.

### Case Study
### Anna Lee Sexenian's 'Inside-Out'

For generations, politicians and policymakers have asked how they can create jobs—or, even better, *middle-class jobs*. When the employment rates rise, they claim credit. When the unemployment rates rise, they get punished.

But no politician creates jobs. At best, government can create the *conditions* that allow private companies, large and small, to grow. When those companies grow, they often need workers to meet their demand. That's where jobs come from.

Let's explore this question. Let's start with a broad view of the problem, then, step by step, sharpen our focus.

**Step 1: Brainstorm all the possibilities**. Sorting the factors that cause company growth—which, in turn, create demand for new workers—can get messy. In fact, lots of factors promote business growth and jobs. A partial list includes these factors:

- Education
- Space for growth
- Comfortable climate
- Infrastructure, including ports, roads, utilities, public transportation
- Linkages to regional, national, and global economies
- A creative class
- A dominant industry that spurs spinoff businesses
- Location near crossroads of commerce
- Diverse populations
- Cultural attractions
- Housing and accommodations
- Diverse businesses
- Waves of immigrants

**Step 2: Sort those variables, in different ways**. A list of important variables, though, only gets us so far. We need to sort them and then consider how they relate to each other. Then we can create a number of categories. So what categories best consolidate these ideas?

We might begin with the textbook inputs of a market economy:

- **Land**: Space for growth, comfortable climate, infrastructure, linkages of external economies, and housing.
- **Labor**: Diverse populations, waves of immigrants, education, and creative classes.
- **Capital**: The availability of capital and equipment and dominant industries.

This approach helps us to narrow our focus, but it offers little insight about the city or region. All of these factors could describe a rural or sprawling economy—or even an online economy.

Maybe, then, we should consider Louis Wirth's classic elements of a city:

- **Size**: Vast population, including wave after wave of immigrants and others coming to the city to "seek their fortune." Enough population to support extensive economic and social activity and infrastructure and other systems.
- **Density**: Enough people and businesses to pack people in tightly, so they feed off each other, master social arts from collaboration to conflict.
- **Heterogeneity**: Enough different kinds of people and businesses so that no one group dominates—and diverse cultural activities result.

**Step 3: Home in on a key variable**: Exploring size, density, and heterogeneity offers a useful way to sort these variables. Cities are all about people packing close together. Not all cities need the density of New York or London or Hong Kong; robust activity is possible in low-density areas too. But cities allow—even demand—people to interact in a spontaneous, continuous way.

So density matters. But why and how?

For years, urban economists have extolled the virtues of "clusters"—the concentration of diverse but related activities in small areas. Clusters seem to arise spontaneously. Like-minded people settle in an area to take advantage of its real estate, transportation, labor, and proximity to related businesses. The existence of a few related companies attracts others. Soon a "critical mass" has gathered, sparking demand for related businesses.

**Step 4: Sharpen understanding of that variable.** But what kinds of concentrations are we talking about? Lots of cities and regions concentrate related activities, but they experience different outcomes. Consider, for example, two of the great centers of technology in the second have of the twentieth century. The Route 128 corridor, outside Boston, spawned the most dynamic companies of the 1980s—DEC, Wang, Data General, and Prime. Silicon Valley, near San Francisco, spawned an ever-richer collection of companies—Apple, Hewlett Packard, Sun, and Silicon Graphics.

After years of growth, Route 128 faltered while Silicon Valley thrived. The two areas had the same employment levels in 1975, but the Valley generated three times as many jobs from 1975 to 1990. In 1990, the Valley exported $11 billion in electronics products while Route 128 exported $4.6 billion in products. Why?

**Step 5: Analyze key distinctions**. AnnaLee Saxenian has explored this riddle. She begins by eliminating some obvious possibilities. "Silicon Valley's superior performance cannot be attributed to differentials in real estate costs, wages, or tax levels," she says. "Nor can the differences be traced to patterns of defense spending." She also disproves the idea that the Valley gained an advantage when companies began outsourcing production. Outsourcing took place in both tech centers.

Then she makes a distinction between *clusters* and *networks*. In clusters, companies located close to each other do not necessarily share ideas or products. In networks, companies share everything—ideas, products, processes, workers, financing. This difference can be traced to the cultures of the companies that locate in the two areas:

> DEC maintained clear boundaries between itself and other companies or institutions in the region. This was, in part, a result of extensive vertical integration period… HP was both less dominant in Silicon Valley and more open to the surrounding economy…. DEC's Palo Alto lab contributed more to Silicon Valley firms such as Sun and MIPS than it did to DEC, because its findings were quick quickly diffused through technical papers and local industry forums.

Company cultures were shaped by regional cultures. "Engineers who worked at both locations emphasize how differently the two were," Sexenian writes. "DEC East was internally focused, whereas DEC Palo Alto was well integrated into Silicon Valley social and technical networks." DEC's Silicon Valley operation enjoyed autonomy from its headquarters in Massachusetts. One DEC manager in the Valley explains:

> It would be very difficult for me to do what I'm doing here within DEC on the east coast. I'm a fairly autonomous business manager out here, with all the functions necessary to success reporting to me and the freedom to use outside suppliers. Back east, I would have to rely on DEC's internal suppliers and functional groups for everything. We're like a start up organization here.

Local cultures, then, influenced the openness of the company cultures.

Back to the jobs question. How can policymakers create jobs? Fostering density—tightknit clusters of related businesses—is a start. But it's not enough. Somehow, the local economy needs to encourage *networks* to share ideas, equipment, expertise, intellectual property, and even workers. Without sharing, neighboring companies might as well be hundreds of miles away.

～

**And Another Thing . . .**

THE WORD ANALYSIS comes from the Greek *analusis*, from *ana* (meaning "up" or "throughout") and *lysis* (meaning "a loosening"). Analysis, in other words, is about breaking things up to see how they fit together.

Whatever we study, we want to figure out what causes things to come together and break apart.

What makes the elements of a larger entity work—separately and together? What causes bonding, connection, commonality? What creates splits, dissonances, tensions? How are these connecting and separating influences change over time?

How do relationships work? What are their basic elements? What about businesses? Nations? Political alliances? Schools? Neighborhoods? And what about less tangible things, like patriotism and prejudice, tolerance and manners, determination and patience?

How do health epidemics occur? What are their elements? How do they come together and break apart? How about the ecosystems of rain forests? Polar icecaps?

The next challenge is to show how all these pieces work together. When you do—when you add analysis to your foundation of storytelling and mechanics—you will be a complete writer.

and get ready for work, then put yourself in a different frame of mind for the morning commute. You greet friends as you arrive, then retreat to review email or meet with your assistant. You huddle with colleagues to debate the best strategies for a common challenge, then work quietly at your desk. You have a lively dinner with your kids, then everyone scatters to do chores or homework.

Physiologically, we all need action and sensuality, to experience what it feels like to move, to engage, to change. We need excitement. But we cannot experience movement and excitement all the time. We also need time to recover, sit back, ponder, and get background information. And then we need more action.

I use the term yo-yo to describe this shift, back and forth, from action to inaction. Your writing should offer the same kind of movement.

In one passage, describe action. Show your characters as they move around, interact with others, struggle against barriers. Zoom in on characters at critical moments. Place obstacles in front of them. Show how they act and react. Show conflict. Get sensual. Excite readers with sounds and sights and physical sensations. Take the reader on a journey. Show change.

Then, in the next passage, take a break from the action. Offer background information about the characters and the story, about the issues, about the community and place and time. Give the reader enough to appreciate the action—not just what happened, but also what lies ahead.

Yo-yo back and forth. Depict more action ... then offer more summary or background information ... then move to action again ... then summary. Yo-yo back and forth, from scene to summary.

To use the yo-yo format in drafts, give scenes and scenes and summaries distinctive markers. Note the scenes and summaries with headers. Or simply place a symbol at the beginning of each section. You might mark scenes with a hashtag and summaries with asterisks. Whatever you do, make it easy to see whether you are yo-yoing. Then, as you prepare your final draft, delete the markers.

Whatever you write—stories or articles or books, even emails and memos —yo-yo back and forth from scene to summary. Arouse your readers with vivid, action-packed scenes, then allow them to put the scenes into context with summary information.

## Case Study
### David Guterson's 'Enclosed, Encyclopedic, Endured'

When you enter a strange new world—especially when that world is big and overwhelming—the tendency is to get lost. So when David Guterson visited the Mall of America, which is big enough to contain seven Yankee Stadiums, he probably stood with his mouth agape, telling himself: *Huge ... so huge ... endless ... wow ... huuuge ...*

But of course simply expressing awe would not convey anything interesting. To explain this strange hypermall, Guterson zoomed into human experiences. He offers scenes like this:

> On this evening a few thousand young people had descended on the mall in pursuit of alcohol and entertainment. They had come to Gators, Hooters, and Knuckleheads, Puzzles, Fat Tuesday, and Ltl Ditty's. At Players, a sports bar, the woman beside me introduced herself as "the pregnant wife of an Iowa pig farmer" and explained that she had driven five hours with friends to "do the mall party scene together." She left and was replaced by Kathleen from Minnetonka, who claimed to have "a real shopping thing—I can't go a week without buying new clothes. I'm not fulfilled until I buy something."
>
> Later a woman named Laura arrived, with whom Kathleen was acquainted. "I *am* the mall," she announced ecstatically upon discovering I was a reporter. "I'd move in here if I could bring my dog," she added. "This place is heaven, it's a mecca."
>
> "We egg each other on," explained Kathleen, calmly puffing on a cigarette. "It's like, sort of, an addiction."
>
> "You want the truth?" Laura asked. "I'm constantly suffering from megamall withdrawal. I come here all the time."
>
> Kathleen: "It's a sickness. It's like cocaine or something; it's a drug."

Like a scene from a movie, this vignette offers a glimpse of just a handful of the 40 million people who visit the mall every year. For these characters, shopping is not just a necessity; it's a passion. The Mall of America may be like nothing else, physically and architecturally. But it gets its character from the people who go there.

So what does it all mean? Guterson steps away from this scene to reflect on the larger phenomenon of shopping:

> There is, of course, nothing naturally abhorrent in the human impulse to dwell in marketplaces or the urge to buy, sell, and trade. Rural Americans traditionally looked forward to the excitement and sensuality of market day; Native Americans traveled long distances to barter and trade at sprawling, festive encampments. In Persian bazaars and in the ancient Greek agoras the very soul of the community was preserved and could be seen, felt, heard, and smelled as it might be nowhere else. All over the planet the humblest of people have always gone to market with hope in their hearts and in expectation of something beyond mere goods—seeking a place where humanity is temporarily in ascendance, a palette for the senses, one another.

Guterson makes sense of the Mall of America by yo-yoing back and forth, from scene to summary. He offers an intimate side of the Mall of America, bringing readers into the middle of a scene. Then he steps away, so we can assess the larger context.

∼

### And Another Thing . . .

LIKE THE BEATS in a movie or song, every phrase or sentence should respond to what happened before and set up what follows. Every passage should offer something new, even surprising.

Whatever you write, beats create tempo and move the journey forward. You nudge the reader toward X, and then surprise him with an assertion of Y. You look at Y in a new light, then surprise him with Z.

Beats also offer a useful way to test writing. If a beat—a movement, a sound, a look—changes a story in useful ways, it belongs. If it doesn't, cut it. Apply this beat test to all aspects of your writing. Does the quotation add to the story—*change* the story—in a useful way? Does a statistic? A piece of historic background? A detail about a character's appearance or mannerisms?

If a beat adds useful insight, keep it; if it doesn't, let it go.

# WORDPLAY

Genius is play, and man's capacity for achieving genius is infinite, and many may achieve genius only through play.

— WILLIAM SAROYAN

Think of children playing with trains or dolls, animals chasing each other in a park, athletes clashing on a field, teenagers teasing and flirting at a mall, or improv actors discovering their lines as they speak them.

Each is a form of play. Each is a joyful activity that takes place not for a "rational" purpose but to take delight in living. Play is a pervasive—and essential—part of the experience of all animals. When we play, as when we dream, we release thoughts and emotions that otherwise get suppressed. By playing, we make discoveries.

Ironically, play requires rules. Think of kids playing ad-hoc street games like Capture the Flag or Kick the Can. Before the games, they earnestly set ground rules. With the rules set, they can play with abandon. Or think of kids playing make-believe. When someone plays out of character, other players get upset. To enter the special "space" of play, we need special rules.

Now think of the playful things writers do with words. Think of the jazz-like riffing of Will Shakespeare or Walt Whitman or Herman Melville or James Joyce. Think of the quips of Gertrude Stein or Mae West or the clever puns of a Marx Brothers movie. Here's Groucho Marx in *Animal Crackers*:

One morning I shot an elephant in my pajamas. How he got in my pajamas, I don't know. Then we tried to remove the tusks. The tusks. That's not so easy to say. Tusks. You try it some time. As I say, we tried to remove the tusks. But they were embedded so firmly we couldn't budge them. Of course, in Alabama the Tuscaloosa, but that is entirely ir-elephant to what I was talking about.

Wordplay requires the reader to do more work. Readers need to think through the puns and the twists, the odd couplings and the irregular sounds.

When you master wordplay, magic happens. With the right rhythm and cadence, sounds and smells and sights and touches, words send readers' imaginations into unpredictable spins. Writing does more than simply communicate. It *changes* thinking and feeling.

To get the reader to play along, create a rhythmic groove. Ancient literature, like Homer's *Odyssey* and *Iliad,* took the form of verse. In an oral tradition, without written records, storytellers used a distinctive meter, melody, wordplay, and imagery to remember the lines of the epic tales.

Too much wordplay, though, taxes readers' patience. So mix your wordplay with simple language. Put on a display of linguistic pyrotechnics, then back off and give your reader a chance to absorb the fireworks.

To test your pacing—*is it too fast? too slow? too wordy? too simple?*—read your drafts aloud. If the words sound sprightly moving from the left to the right side of the page, you're probably on the right track. When you hear awkward phrases and exhausting references, figure out what blocks the flow.

~

### Element 76
### Tap Into Life's Everyday Rhythms

OUR LIVES RHYME. Without trying, we create cadences in our language. We use rhythm first to emphasize points—and just because it sounds pleasing. When we please people with the cadences of our speech, we want to do it again. Even the simplest conversations hop along rhythmically, like this exchange I heard before the 2015 Super Bowl:

> "You like the *Patriots*! I *hate* the Patriots! Tom Brady is such a *fake*! And Bill Belichick? Give me a *break*!"
>
> "Hey, the Patriots are the *best team*! You're for the *Jets*? All you can do is *dream*!"

In fact, we find speech without rhythm annoying. People who speak in monotones sound robotic. Their flat and unrhythmic speech lacks life. It's sometimes hard to know what they think—even when they *say* what they think—because they don't emphasize any words or ideas.

Shared, rhythmic movements create a "we" feeling. Well-paced writing engages readers, word by word, phrase by phrase, sentence by sentence, and paragraph by paragraph. When we spend a lot of time with someone, we start to move and talk and even breathe the same way. Almost as soon as we gather, we mimic each other. You do this, I follow; I do that, you follow.

Rhymes reinforce ideas. In an experiment at the University of Texas, researchers asked volunteers to read a collection of aphorisms. Some of the aphorisms rhymed and others did not. The volunteers remembered the rhyming aphorisms more than the others. Why? The rhymes could be absorbed whole, without much effort. The rhythm, pace, and sounds give them "handles" that make them easy to grasp and hold.

Consider one notorious example. In the O.J. Simpson murder trial, his attorney, Johnny Cochran, told jurors: "If the gloves don't fit, you must acquit." Cochran was wrong, of course. But it didn't matter. Jurors remembered the phrase in their deliberations. Despite overwhelming evidence against Simpson, the jury acquitted him.

Why do rhymes affect people's hearts and minds? Every rhyme brings a sense of closure, wholeness. Compare two simple rhymes. First: "Roses are red, violets are blue, it's Valentine's Day, and I love you." Then: "Rose are red, violets are blue, some poems rhyme, but this one doesn't." Because the first ends in a rhyme, it sounds complete. Because the second one doesn't, it feels like a violation.

A century ago, a literary scholar named Abram Lipsky set out to understand the rhythm of prose. He gathered 1,000-word samples from 35 acclaimed literary works. Then he counted the number of unaccented syllables between accented syllables. These works contained an average of 330 segments. Here's an overview of these passages:

| Number of unaccented syllables between accented syllables | 0 | 1 | 2 | 3 | 4 | 5 | 6 |
|---|---|---|---|---|---|---|---|
| Average instances per 1,000-word fragments | 26.9 | 98.5 | 99.0 | 66.8 | 27.5 | 8.8 | 2.1 |
| Percent of total sample | 8% | 30% | 30% | 20% | 9% | 3% | 1% |

Source: Abram Lipsky, "Rhythm as a Distinguishing Characteristic of Prose Style," *Columbia University Contributions to Philosophy and Psychology*, June 1907. Note: Percentages do not add up to 100 because of rounding.

Almost 60 percent of these segments had either one (DUM-da-DUM) or two (DUM-da-da-DUM) unaccented syllables between accented syllables.

The lesson? *Step lively*. Keep the pace of your words brisk. Don't overwhelm the reader with long stretches between accented syllables.

To understand rhythm, listen to it, line by line. Find a passage from a great writer. Read sentences aloud, with rhythm. See how the rhythm draws you in and holds your attention? Now, compose your own passage. Write one sentence per line, using the Landscape View. Then read whatever you just wrote. When you stumble—or get bored or confused—revise and rewrite.

With a regular pulse, you can carry the reader smoothly through any story or essay. Get into the rhythm, delivering images and ideas with the steady pace of a heartbeat. Then you will engage the reader on the deepest possible levels. Then, the occasional deviation will surprise and delight the reader.

### Case Study
### Mike Greenberg's *The Poetics of Cities*

Goethe famously called architecture "frozen music." The best buildings suggest a kind of grace that we experience with music—simple patterns, repeated with variations; different shapes, with different lengths of phrasing; and illusions of light and weight and texture.

Actually, as Mike Greenberg argues, buildings move as much as the people who see or use them. People walking past the Empire State Building or the Eiffel Tower, for example, do not see it whole or in a fixed view. They see the building's elements shift with views. The beauty of architecture, in fact, lies in the way structures dance on the stages of their cities and towns, as Greenberg writes here:

> As we walk, our perception of the present moment is conditioned by our field of vision and the tempo and length of our gait. One can't quantify how physiology conditions our perception of the present. As Cooper and Mayer say, "Rhythmic grouping is a mental fact, not a physical one." The general principle is that the present—however defined—must contain a sufficient number of ordered events to establish consciousness of rhythm, and that rhythm must propel the listener/walker to the next (and overlapping) present.

Do you see the rhythms of Greenberg's writing? It might help to break up the paragraph, as we might read the passages aloud:

As we walk,
our perception of the present moment
is conditioned
by our field of vision
and the tempo and length of our gait.
One can't quantify
how physiology conditions
our perception of the present.
As Cooper and Mayer say,
"Rhythmic grouping is a mental fact,
not a physical one."
The general principle is that the present
—however defined—
must contain
a sufficient number of ordered events

> to establish consciousness of rhythm,
> and that rhythm must propel
> the listener / walker
> to the next (and overlapping)
> present.

Greenberg writes unusually long sentences for a journalist. In this two-paragraph passage, the sentences were 24, 11, 15, and 35 words in the first paragraph, and 7, 20, 59, 9, 38, 46, 1, and 8 in the second paragraph. If his prose lacked rhythm, Greenberg would probably lose the audience.

You can create the same kind of rhythms in your writing. Just pay close attention to the phrase-chunks that you create, as you make your journey from the start to the end of each sentence.

~

### Element 77
### Use Metaphors and Similes to Orient and Disorient

WE MAKE sense of the world by saying one thing *is* something else—or is *like* something else—even when it isn't. When two things share similar shapes, textures, or sounds, we use metaphors and similes to make the connection.

The metaphor says X *equals* Y; the simile says X *resembles* Y. So what's the difference? "Metaphors are forceful," Poet Laureate Ted Kooser notes. "Similes are, like, casual." A metaphor insists that a leader is a lion; a simile suggests, more tentatively, that the man acts *like* a lion. A metaphor says X=Y. A simile, on the other hand, says X≈Y.

Both metaphors and similes work by orienting and disorienting the reader at the same time. They make the familiar unfamiliar and the unfamiliar familiar. Unfamiliarity makes us curious; familiarity helps us to understand. Put the two together and you get insight.

Suppose I tell you that the X-1 rocket—something that most people reading this have never seen—has a needle for a nose. You will know what I am talking about, right? The familiar idea helps us conjure an image of something unfamiliar. Likewise, if I tell you that megachurches are like a floating crap game, you'd get the idea.

Take a look at Michael Oakeschott's metaphor for the possibilities and limits of politics:

> In political activity, then, men sail a boundless and bottomless sea; there is neither harbor for shelter nor floor for anchorage, neither starting-place nor appointed destination. The enterprise is to keep afloat on an even keel; the sea is both friend and enemy; and the seamanship consists in using the resources of a

traditional manner of behavior in order to make a friend of every hostile occasion.

Now look at the simile that C.S. Lewis uses in his memoir of grieving his late wife:

Grief is like a long valley, a winding valley where any bend may reveal a totally new landscape. ... Sometimes the surprise is the opposite one; you are presented with exactly the same sort of country you thought you had left behind miles ago. This is when you wonder whether the valley isn't a circular trench.

Notice how Lewis's similes drift into metaphors. We humans just cannot help speaking in metaphors. Over time, expressions that originate as metaphors become part of ordinary speech.

As both of these passages show, metaphors and smiles come to life with movement. Both take the reader on journeys—Oakeshott to some unknowable place, Lewis's back home to familiar terrain. Both images work because they take us, the readers, to new insights.

Metaphors distort our judgment. Consider two experiments. As they pretended to struggle with piles of folders, researchers at Yale and Colorado asked subjects to hold their cup of coffee. When asked to describe a person later, subjects holding warmer cups gave warmer descriptions; subjects holding cooler cups gave cooler descriptions. In another experiment, a Yale researcher asked subjects to describe a person based on a resume held in a clipboard. Subjects holding heavier clipboards described the person in more serious terms than those holding lighter clipboards. Objects (coffee and clipboards) become metaphors for something completely separate (people).

The power of metaphor extends far and wide. That, ultimately, is the work of all language—to engage us completely to express ideas and feelings.

## Case Study
### The Chicago Schools' Urban Ecology

For more than a century, the University of Chicago has been one of the great centers of urban study. At the heart of the Chicago School's early work was the idea that urban life mimics natural ecology.

The Chicago School included such seminal theorists as Robert Park, Louis Wirth, and Ernest Burgess. In a landmark essay, Burgess marvels at the city's growth in the late 1800s and early 1900s. With this growth, populations shifted rapidly from old city centers into new suburbs.

Those population shifts resembled the movements of different species in nature, Burgess says. Like plant and animal species, he says, people often shift from place to place. When an area becomes crowded or when the struggle for resources becomes too intense, people move.

Burgess uses the ecological term "invasion and succession" to make his point. In a forest, the growth of hardwood trees can cast a shadow over red pines, which need the sun to grow. The two kinds of trees battle for dominance of the territory. Likewise, in cities, different populations battle over neighborhoods. A neighborhood dominated by a particular group—say, black families or white ethnics—struggles to survive when new groups "discover" it, buy and renovate property, and drive up costs.

To illustrate this process in the city, Burgess drew a series of concentric rings, with the Loop (or downtown) in the center, surrounded by a factory zone, a zone of transition, zone of workingmen's homes, residential zone, and commuters zone. Then he asked: How do people find their place in this sprawling community?

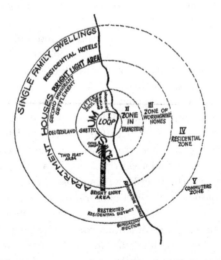

Cities, Burgess and the other members of the Chicago School argued, have a distinctive "metabolism," a self-regulating process that organizes the species in that space and promote homeostasis.

Urban ecology appropriates a variety of concepts from natural ecology, including symbiosis (the idea that different populations offer each other value), dominance (which group dominates the territory), gradient growth (gradual development of areas), superordination and subordination (a hierarchy of power in the territory). Ecological theories also use a multiple nuclei model, which indicates that an area contains multiple levels of centers.

The ecological model offers a dynamic view of the city. As the model suggests, urbanites often move to different parts of the city, according to their abilities, tribal loyalties, levels of education, professions. With the ecology model, battles over space and resources in the city seem natural, inevitable, and even beneficial to all. People live in different places, under this understanding, because they are best suited to those places. Blacks live in ghettos, laborers in the ring around the center, and more affluent populations in the Gold Coast and suburbs because they naturally *belong* there. Likewise, different kinds of activities—office buildings, industrial concerns, worker housing, middle-class communities—find their natural and appropriate habitats.

The ecology metaphor, alas, neglects many important aspects of urban life —the power of business coalitions, investments in infrastructure from transit to utilities, technologies that allow new kinds of construction, access to energy grids, racism and segregation, the police role in enforcing territory, violence and arson, vast economic cycles, government programs, demographic patterns, and much more.

Metaphors like urban ecology both giveth and taketh. They offer compelling ways to simplify complex realities. With the ecology metaphor, we can see patterns underneath the seeming chaos of urban life. But these metaphors also avert our attention from important processes that shape our world.

∾

**Element 78**
**Riff by Playing with Words**

RIFFING—THE jazzlike styling of scenes and ideas, which seems to follow no rules and bends whatever rules are even acknowledged—is actually the product of extraordinary care and discipline.

When I think of riffing, I think of Christopher Columbus zigging and zagging across the ocean blue in 1492, using his sextant but not really knowing where he was going. Columbus thought he was taking his rowdy crew to India —he worked it all out, based on this crazy idea that the earth was round—but he ended up in Hispaniola. His discovery of the New World was an accident, but an accident that only a master seaman could have achieved.

Working on a good theory but bad data—but prepared with all the skills needed for that five-week journey across the Atlantic Ocean—Columbus commanded ships under the direst of conditions. He coaxed and prodded his crew to work together and stay on course. In the end, he discovered things he couldn't have imagined.

That's what riffing is all about. Riffing requires some vision, a willingness to take chances, and lots of improvisation, all supported by mastery of all the basic skills of the trade. In the end, you discover things you could not have imagined.

Let's check out three essential parts of riffing, one by one:

**(1) Create a sensual experience.** Start off by looking for vivid details. Describe those details with precision. As you construct a scene, think of all the ways that we see things—their colors, brightness, and shadows; their shapes, size, and scale; and their arrangements and alignments. Then pick the ones that most casual observers would miss.

See how Robert Penn Warren, in *All the King's Men*, introduces us to the heat and monotony of highways in Louisiana, the kingdom of the corrupt governor Willie Stark:

> You look up the highway and it is straight for miles, coming at you, with the black line down the center coming at you, black and slick and tarry-shining against the white of the slab, and the heat dazzles up from the white slab so that only the black line is clear, coming at you with the whine of the tires, and if you don't quit staring at that line and don't take a few deep breaths and slap yourself hard on the back of the next you'll hypnotize yourself and you'll come to at just the moment when the right wheel hooks over into the black dirt shoulder off the slab, and you'll try to jerk her back on but you can't because the slab is high like a curb, and maybe you'll try to turn off the ignition just as she starts the dive.

This stream-of-consciousness passage—146 words in one sentence—puts the reader in the car on one of those endless, mind-numbing trips that define the politician's life. We feel the heat, hear the sounds, experience the monotonous blur of stripes on the highways, and feel the car drifting as the driver dozes off in boredom.

To evoke sounds, play with onomatopoeia, words that sound like what they're describing. *The bus hissed away from the curb. The ball smashed the window. He told her to shush. The snake slithered through the grass.*

Alliteration, the repetition of the same constant sounds, also engages the reader and produces memorable phrases. Consider the work of masters like Shakespeare ("I grant I never saw a goddess go") or Robert Frost ("I have stood still and stopped the sound of feet") or Alfred Lord Tennyson ("Fly o'er waste fens and windy fields") or George Manley Hopkins ("swift, slow; sweet, sour; adazzle, dim"). Politics and mass media—professions dedicated to selling ideas and products—use alliteration too. Remember Spiro Agnew's attack on liberals as "nattering nabobs of negativism"? Or commercials for Reese's ("rich rushing butter cups") or Fila ("Functional, Fashionable, Formidable")?

Don't just get the sounds right, but the unusual ways they come together. In his portrait of the elder George Bush, Richard Ben Cramer imitates Bush's whiny, fractured, faux-folksy (*fauxsy*?) voice to reveal Bush's evasions over the Iran-Contra scandal.

> Jeezus! What did they want? They wanted an answer on Iran-contra: *What did Bush know ... and when did he know it?*
>
> For more than a year, ever since late '86, Bush had been holding the line: *I did what I did ... I told the President what I told the President. ... And honor forbids me to*

*say more*. Bush had said that so many times, he was frustrated. He thought he had answered *every conceivable nuance*. Of course, he never actually said anything.

But once he'd made his point ... well, anyone who insisted on bringing it up was just *rehashing* ... try'na make him *look bad*.

They were, you know, acting like bullies. And the old school code treats a bully with ... contempt. That's why he couldn't believe—wouldn't hear it!—when his white men warned that Dan Rather was going to jump him ... . "No," said the Veep. "Dan's a friend." (He'd known Rather since Texas—Dan was just a local newsman, Bush was in the oil bidness ... Jeez, it'd been more than 20 years!)

Cramer merges his own voice with Bush's to capture the vice president's impatient, calculating, *fauxsy* voice—*Jeezus, try'na, bidness, Jeez*. But notice that Cramer doesn't overdo it. He uses ordinary expressions to pad the jazzy, funky phrasing that demands more of the reader's attention.

**(2) Speculate, with real information**. When in doubt about details, speculate about them. Even when you cannot answer a question definitively, you can still offer possibilities. We don't know what Washington experienced as he crossed the Delaware River, what Civil War soldiers felt as they saw a brother die, or how athletes felt when they won an Olympic medal. But we can explore plausible scenarios. When we do, we excite the reader's imagination.

Look at *The Big Bam*, Leigh Montville's biography of Babe Ruth. As much as we know of America's most famous athlete, we know few basic facts about his early years. So Montville uses what he *doesn't know* to create intimate images of young George Herman Ruth:

Behind that moon face with those small eyes, that fat nose, those big lips that will be captured in any instantly recognizable portrait in a blue New York Yankees cap, the boy will forever hide. He is only a shape, glimpsed here, glimpsed there, lost again. No one has found that boy at the beginning of it all, touched him, gotten to know him. No one ever will. If the right questions ever were asked, the answers never were given. Time has finished the job. There is no one to talk to now. No one is around.

By riffing about unknown facts, Montville helps us see, better than ever, this unknowable boy. Montville allows us to join in the speculation. Montville turns a deficit of information to his advantage. When he suggests possibilities, he invites the reader to project their own images and ideas into the scene.

**(3) Put everything into action**. Show people doing things. Action speaks louder than description. If we pay close attention to everyday actions, and describe them in detail, we see just how complex and surprising life can be.

Tom Wolfe, the master of modern nonfiction riffing, uses action to explore abstract ideas. In *From Bauhaus to Our House*, Wolfe describes the absurdities of modernist architecture. In 155 words, he shows how elites embrace modernism

—and then, alarmed at its sterility, spare no expense to cover it up. See how Wolfe uses movement to make his point:

> Every great law firm in New York moves without a sputter of protest into a glass-box office building with concrete slab floors and seven-foot-ten-inch-high concrete slab ceilings and plasterboard walls and pygmy corridors—and then hires a decorator and gives him a budget of hundreds of thousands of dollars to turn these mean cubes and grids into a horizontal fantasy of a Restoration townhouse. I have seen the carpenters and cabinetmakers and search-and-acquire girls hauling in more cornices, covings, pilasters, carved moldings, and recessed domes, more linenfold paneling, more (fireless) fireplaces with festoons of fruit carved in mahogany on the mantels, more chandeliers, sconces, girandoles, chestnut leather sofas, and chiming clocks than Wren, Inigo Jones, the brothers Adam, Lord Burlington, and the Dilettanti, working in concert, could have dreamed of.

Wolfe puts details into motion. Rather than *explaining* the buyer's remorse of Modernism, he shows people scrambling to replace Modernist foofaraw with classic materials. Read that passage again and mark the action verbs and precise verbs. If brevity is the soul of wit, as Shakespeare once remarked, then specificity is the soul of riffing.

One last point. Once you've composed a riff—once you've departed from straightforward description and decided to dazzle your audience—make sure the passage reads well. Riffs pull the reader out of familiar paths and rhythms. That can be jarring, in a good way. Just make sure your wordplay does not become a distraction. Read everything aloud. If it sounds right, you might —*might*—have something worth keeping.

Riffing requires discipline. That's the most important lesson of all: Play all you want, but then work hard to make sure the play engages, rather than distracts, the reader.

### Case Study
### James Howard Kunstler's *The Geography of Nowhere*

No one has written angrier or more passionate screeds against regional sprawl than James Howard Kunstler. And his critiques have proved valid over the years. Consider this 111-word sentence:

> Eighty percent of everything ever built in America has been built in the last 50 years, and most of it is depressing, brutal, ugly, unhealthy, and spiritually degrading —the jive-plastic commuter tract home wastelands, the Potemkin village shopping plazas with their vast parking lagoons, the Lego-block hotel complexes, the "gourmet mansardic" junk-food joints, the Orwellian office "parks" featuring buildings sheathed in the same reflective glass as the

sunglasses worn by chain-gang guards, the particle-board garden apartments rising up in every meadow and cornfield, the freeway loops around every big and little city with their clusters of discount merchandise marts—the whole destructive, wasteful, toxic, agoraphobia-inducing spectacle that politicians proudly call "growth."

Normally, I preach against sentences that get anywhere close to 111 words. But Kunstler wants to overwhelm the reader with the complete awfulness of the fake landscape that we all inhabit. To do so, Kunstler creates a mad rush of images and ideas. For most authors, such a mad rush would create mad confusion. But Kunstler holds the reader's attention. How? By making sure that every piece of his sentence—every phrase—offers a clear image or idea. To see how, let's break up the passage into discrete parts.

> Eighty percent
> of everything ever built in America
> has been built in the last 50 years,
> and most of it is depressing, brutal, ugly, unhealthy, and
>     spiritually configuing—
> the jive-plastic commuter tract home wastelands,
> the Potemkin village shopping plazas
> with their vast parking lagoons,
> the Lego-block hotel complexes,
> the "gourmet mansardic" junk-food joints,
> the Orwellian office "parks"
> featuring buildings sheathed
> in the same reflective glass
> as the sunglasses worn
> by chain-gang guards,
> the particle-board garden apartments
> rising up in every meadow and cornfield,
> the freeway loops
> around every big and little city
> with their clusters
> of discount merchandise marts—
> the whole destructive, wasteful, toxic, agoraphobia-inducing
>     spectacle
> that politicians proudly call "growth."

Had Kunstler faltered even once, he would have lost us. But every phrase, every cluster of words, carries us along in this dystopian journey. The rush of images and ideas is, in fact, a little overwhelming. But the reader follows every step of the way.

~

## Element 79
### Remember that Good is Great

EVERY COMPLEX THING is really a collection of simple things. "Nature is pleased with simplicity," Isaac Newton said. "And nature is no dummy." Everything— every great structure, work of art, scientific proof, business plan—contains a set of basic elements.

Remember the Periodic Table of Elements, which organizes 118 basic chemical elements according to their atomic number, electron configurations, and recurring properties. Everything in nature is comprised of some combination of these elements. From a limited number of inputs, nature creates unfathomable complexity.

Complex writing works like that. Every great sentence and paragraph, every great passage, is really a combination of simple pieces:

- Specific (and, if possible, unusual) subjects and verbs.
- Prepositional phrases that modify things and actions.
- Precise, sensual details that evoke images, sounds, and feelings.
- Rhyme, alliteration, onomatopoeia, consonance, anaphora, parallels, and other poetic devices.
- Terms that refer to shared knowledge and ideas.

Gather these pieces, one by one. Pay close attention to the character, place, or scene. Then record and arrange those details in ways that pull the reader, moment by moment.

In fact, all *great* writing is just a collection of *good* elements. So when you want to create great language, remember this: *Good is great.*

To capture anything cleverly—whether it's a look, a movement, a feeling, a sound, a smell, or an idea—gather small observations. Mull them. Think metaphorically. Look for *unexpected* images and sounds and ideas.

And then put the pieces together, one by one. String those phrases together in unusual ways, like Charlie Parker or Miles Davis. Combine shapes together like Picasso and use colors like Monet. Do the little things well and you'll surprise yourself.

### Case Study
#### Tom Wolfe's *From Bauhaus to Our House*

Look once again at Tom Wolfe's screed against modernist architecture (contained in the previous section on riffing). Now look at the passage, broken this passage into pieces:

> Every great law firm in New York
> moves without a sputter of protest
> into a glass-box office building
> with concrete slab floors
> and seven-foot-ten-inch-high concrete slab ceilings
> and plasterboard walls
> and pygmy corridors
> —and then hires a decorator,
> gives him a budget of hundreds of thousands of dollars
> to turn these mean cubes and grids
> into a horizontal fantasy
> of a Restoration townhouse.

And so on. Look at the passage, line by line. What do you see? Simple phrases, each with a precise image or action. Separately, each of these lines is simple. Added together, they are anything but simple.

Wolfe achieves something great, with simple goodness, line by line.

∼

### And Another Thing . . .

PLAYING with words takes you places you could never imagine before the journey.

Rather than following a linear path, the reader jumps around. Ideas and images bloom and fly in strange, even surreal, ways. The reader makes associations that challenge the normal ways of thinking.

When jazz musicians improvise, they move into a dreamlike trance; they turn off their inhibitions and self-censorship. At the same time, they rev up the parts of the brain that allow for free expression. Riffing—in music or writing—is a wild process of discovery. It's a literary Mardi Gras—exuberant, creative, wild, sometimes out of control.

Still, even the wildest riffing requires some basic rhythm and beat and even melody to work. The riff is the crazy counterpoint to the main line. Listen to Willis Conover, the host of a jazz program on Voice of America for 41 years. "Jazz is a cross between total discipline and anarchy," Conover told an interviewer. "The musicians agree on tempo, key, and chord structure but beyond this everyone is free to express himself. This is jazz. And this is America. That's what gives this music validity." Riffing is freedom, and it works with just enough discipline to put the listener on a track.

Get the words and rhythm, the sounds and the cadences, right. For one moment, forget about rules and restrictions. Let loose with the riff.

As long as you pull together the brilliant pieces afterwards—and throw away the garbage—you have great fun.

# AND ANOTHER THING . . .

## WRITING IS LIFE

At the beginning of our journey, I offered the Golden Rule of Writing. If you follow this rule, I promised, you will write well every time—every sentence, paragraph, story, chapter, essay, report, book, you name it. It's so simple, and it yields powerful results instantly, but it takes real effort to make it automatic.

Then I offered a number of specific skills—strategies and tactics you can deploy to build on the Golden Rule. We explored how to develop characters, the world of the story, action and beats, and details. We looked at sentences and paragraphs, verbs and other word choices, grammar and editing. We concluded with a strategy of analysis—using stories, asking questions, framing problems, finding and organizing evidence, and deploying models.

I think of this process as a modern form of apprenticeship.

Throughout history, novices learned skills by working as apprentices. The apprentice worked side by side with a master craftsman. The master talked the apprentice through the process, demonstrated how to use tools, and then invited the apprentice to try his hand. The apprentice tried and failed until he mastered the skills. Over time, he came to understand the logic and theory behind the work.

So I have tried to work with you, side by side. I have shown you the flow of the process, from beginning to middle to end. I have shown you how to take the pieces apart and put them back together again. And I have shown you how to step back and make sense of a complex, abstract issue.

As you embark on your journey, I want you to celebrate your work. Writing, you see, is not just an intellectual or emotional enterprise. Writing touches the deepest aspects of human life.

Writing is teaching. Writing is learning.

Writing is showing. Writing is telling.

Writing is disclosure. Writing is concealment.
Writing is raw. Writing is polished.
Writing is wild. Writing is disciplined.
Writing is intimate. Writing is universal.
Writing is intellectual. Writing is spiritual.
Writing is struggle. Writing is triumph.
Writing is power. Writing is humility.
Writing is a royal pain. Writing is a joy.
Writing is complex. Writing is simple.
Writing is everything we can think of. Writing is life itself.

Writing is, of course, ultimately a journey. We don't always know where we're going, or what we need to do to get there. The destination may change. Our feelings might change along the way. We always find surprises. And at the end of the process, if we do all the little things right, we're better for the experience.

In these times of change—when journalism, publishing, schools, work, and everything, in fact, involving the production and consumption of words, has changed—one truth remains. That truth is that writing matters, and always will.

Our job is to seize the dizzying new opportunities of writing. If we do that, we can all create great gifts, wherever we are, whatever we do.

# ACKNOWLEDGMENTS

This book is the product of hundreds of conversations with fellow writers and teachers, students, people in business and government, and friends and family. I would like to thank a handful of the most important of those people.

Students in my writing classes at Yale University joined me in another terrific conversation about writing. I make suggestions, the students try them out, and we explore what worked and what did not. I have never known as open and curious bunch as these young men and women. For the content of this book, I owe them more than anyone else. I would also like to acknowledge Fred Strebeigh and my other colleagues at Yale, who offered potent advice about both writing and teaching in our many meetings over the years.

Richard Chenoweth, a gifted architect and artist, not only provided the inspiration for the discussion of the narrative arc. He also created the gorgeous art that graces the cover. The image depicts the Hall of the House of Representatives, the "most beautiful room in the world." Richard's vision and talents helped to recreate this masterpiece, long lost to history.

A number of people read drafts of this book. Marsha Rabe gave an early draft a careful proofreading and improved it immeasurably. Donna Baer Stein and Isabel Chenoweth also offered careful readings and saved me from a slew of embarrassing typoes and repetitions and repetitions. Myra Brown, Katie Hafner, and Aaron Ritzenberg also offered invaluable advice.

I presented early versions of this book in seminars at Vanderbilt University, The Graduate Institute, the Met School of Providence, the National Education Association of New Hampshire, the New Haven Free Public Library, the Utah Humanities Book Festival, the International Book Fair, the State University of New York at Purchase, Hamden Hall Country Day School, Gen Re, the Eli Whitney Museum, Christian Community Action of New Haven, Codman

Square Health Center in Boston, Richmond Events, NetCom Learning, Amneal Pharmaceuticals, Sandler Training, Oxford University Press, and a number of smaller groups.

Finally, Isabel Chenoweth and her children, Walker and Leila, offered their love and support throughout the process of writing this book. I cannot imagine life without the three of them.

You could not get in our house, except by passing through the main gate controlled by Ahmed the doorkeeper. But you could get out a second way, by using the roof-level terrace. You could jump from our terrace to the neighbors' next door, and then go out to the street through their door. Officially, our terrace key was kept in Lalla Mani's possession, with Ahmed turning off the lights to the stairs after sunset. But because the terrace was constantly being used for all kinds of domestic activities throughout the day, from retrieving olives that were stored in big jars up there, to washing and drying clothes, the key was often left with Aunt Habiba, who lived in the room right next to the terrace.

Each sentence raises a new issue—a problem to be solved, a possible response, and new wrinkles to the problem or solution.

- **Access restricted**: You could not get in our house, except by passing through the main gate controlled by Ahmed the doorkeeper.
- **But there is a second way**: But you could get out a second way, by using the roof-level terrace.
- **It's a lot of work**: You could jump from our terrace to the neighbors' next door, and then go out to the street through their door.
- **The keeper of the key**: Officially, our terrace key was kept in Lalla Mani's possession, with Ahmed turning off the lights to the stairs after sunset.
- **A second keeper of the key**: Because the terrace was constantly being used for all kinds of domestic activities throughout the day, Aunt Habiba often held it in the room right next to the terrace.

The paragraph moves briskly, like snappy dialogue. Every sentence responds to something, then moves the story forward.

Mernissi could have said: "Access to the house was restricted, but we found secret passages in and out of the house." But then she would lose the larger story of people discovering clever ways to maneuver in a mysterious and forbidden place. And she would lose the bigger story of how the house shapes the family's life.

Instead, Mernissi raises a problem—restricted access to the house—and deals with it by exploring a sequence of aspects of the matter, one by one.

~

### Element 75
### Yo-Yo Scene and Summary

THINK about a typical day in your life, about what happens in your home, school, or workplace. Think about how you interact with family and friends.

Your day alternates between action and repose. You quietly eat breakfast

To describe something—a person, place, thing, action, or idea—break it into pieces. Pretend you are giving the reader a guided tour: *First notice this ... then look over there ... then see that ... now watch this ...*

Think of your description as a kind of dialogue. One moment raises a question, the next moment answers the question and raises another, a third detail answers the second question and raises another, and so on.

In this way, we can create drama out of mere description. Part by part, as we move through a description, details take on greater importance. Each detail —*each beat*—raises the stakes of the description. In this way, your description will resemble an Aristotelian drama, with every moment increasing tension but also bringing us closer to a resolution.

When we examine an image, part by part, we actually imitate our eye's actions. Our eyes flit, in microseconds, from one small part of the image to another. These movements are called saccades. Our eyes see only a small piece of any scene at a time. When look at something, we make a series of these tiny observations, from which our mind constructs a whole image.

Try this exercise. Make a list of the things and qualities of a person, place, or thing, moving from one part to another. Record everything you can see— along with your thoughts about these observations—in detail. Using those notes, write a passage describes these details.

Now identify some idea you want to develop. It could be from any field— science, politics, psychology, economics, sports, the arts, or any other field. Pick a concept or debate, like global warming, terrorism, the effects of technology on human relations, the causes and effects of consumer debt, the reasons for chronic sports injuries, or Balanchine's revolution in dance, to offer a few examples. Now, with your topic, list the issues that matter most to understand this issue.

Move back and forth from one aspect of the idea to its opposite—and then on to the next logical idea and its opposite, and so on. Create a kind of double helix of ideas and their opposites.

When you do that, you'll be using beats for description. As we will see later, you can follow the same process to make an argument.

## Case Study
### Fatima Mernissi's *Dreams of Trespass*

What would it be like to grow up in a brothel? Could it be normal? Could it be healthy? How would you find positive influences? What kinds of relationships could a child have with buyers and sellers of flesh? What kinds of private refuge could a child find—and what kinds of open, playful activities could the child explore outside?

These are some of the questions of Fatima Mernissi's *Dreams of Trespass*, the memoir of a girl's life from age five to ten years in a brothel in Morocco. Take a look at this passage, which describes the layers of identity and meaning:

moved the project toward completion…. The residents resorted to the one resource they had left: the media. They staged publicity demonstrations; the residents hounded Mayor [John] Lindsay even down to Florida…

The publicity campaign scared City Hall. … Mayor Lindsay assigned Mario Cuomo the role of fact finder and independent judge… He observed, talked, and debated; he drew up a compromise favorable to Forest Hills. … But these practical gains had by that time ceased to matter to the community. …

On September 14 Cuomo records the way the rise of "sandbagging" works. A community group had gotten word to the mayor that it could accept a compromise if the mayor could first commit himself to it; the community board then would work covertly on the other members of the board on which the mayor sits to get them to vote against the compromise. In this way the mayor would be tricked into supporting something that no one else supported; he would appear isolated and extreme; he would be humiliated. It was, Cuomo concludes, "a classic case of fraud in the inducement."

See how the beats work in this story? Let's map the distinct moments that move the story forward. The more positive beats are above; the more negative ones are below.

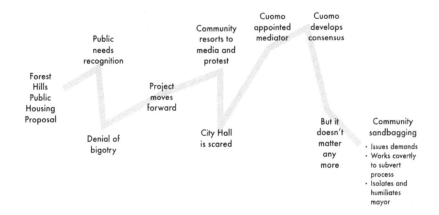

Beats give stories energy. The constant back-and-forth tempo, from positive and negative developments, keeps everyone engaged. Every moment matters.

～

### Element 74
### Use Beats For Descriptions

BEATS NOT ONLY PACE ACTION, from one moment to the next. Beats also pace *description*. To observe something, look at it moment by moment, beat by beat.

the second or third chapter it absolutely must go off," the Russian playwright Anton Chekhov once said. "If it's not going to be fired, it shouldn't be hanging there." Unnecessary details distract and confuse the audience.

You might wonder how to *pace* beats. How fast should this exchange take? How quickly should the characters act? How briskly should the story move from scene to scene? The answer is simple: As fast as necessary to move the scene forward, maintaining the mood of the scene, without leaving the audience behind.

Writers in all genres—stories, speeches and sermons, journalism, even corporate reports and analyses—would benefit from the use of beats. Just remember: *Keep things moving with brisk exchanges—and make every moment matter.* If you do that, you will always hold the reader's attention.

## Case Study
### Richard Sennett's *The Fall of Public Man*

A specter haunts America's cities, towns, and suburbs—the specter of the loss of public life.

In healthy, creative communities, people have access to a wide variety of public spaces. In parks, city squares, streets, libraries, public buildings, community centers, union halls, even bars and ballparks, people can gather, spontaneously, to explore, debate, and even contest their values and priorities as a community. But in recent generations, the civic life of our common places has declined. Even when our civic life has not disappeared, it has become managed and "corporatized."

Without vibrant public places for strangers to meet and interact, people lose their ability to engage in public conflict. They become snowflakes, unable to respond to even minor disturbances. Public debate withers. Even cities, which are best equipped to foster civic engagement, have seen their public life wither.

To illustrate this argument, Richard Sennett describes the battle over public housing in Forest Hills, a predominantly Jewish and middle-class neighborhood in Queens, New York. In the early 1970s, City Hall decided to locate new public housing developments in the neighborhood. For years, people in the area had felt neglected by city government. Now they feared that public housing would undermine the stability of their community. Here's how Sennett describes the controversy:

> For the people of Forest Hills, recognition by the city that they had legitimate objections was especially important. We are not racist bigots, they insisted; slum families have a high incidence of crime; we are afraid for our children; physically our neighborhood will be destroyed.
>
> The more concerned the people of Forest Hills became, the closer the city machinery of community consultation, Board of Estimate hearings, and the like

They know that if they don't catch their flaws, someone else will. They also know that discovering flaws can point the way to truth.

Scientists take a deliberate, step-by-step process to move from information to insight. I suggest a simple process that moves through the following stages: *steep, spill, show and tell, cluster, cut, test, scale,* and *close.*

- **Steep**: Start by investigating your subject by reading books and articles, exploring archives and data, and interviewing people. Find out what experts say about the subject. Stand on the shoulders of others.
- **Spill**: This is brainstorming. Using all your resources—research materials, prior knowledge, logical leaps, educated guesses, wild speculation—spill all kinds of information in one space. In our discussion of brainstorming, I suggested getting a tabloid-size sheet (11 inches by 17 inches) for your purposes. Spill everything you know, think, guess, or wonder—onto that sheet.
- **Show and Tell**: Now take a stab at a story. Find one instance of your subject and spin a tale. See if you can identify the "characters" in your analysis, how they interact, and how they move from one state of being to another. Don't try to be exact. This is an exercise in imagination. Be speculative. Find real stories that suggest possibilities. Look for what's common and what's different in those stories. Once you tell the story one way, try another way. If you think economic interests cause war, tell a story that makes that argument. Then argue against it. Tell a story that makes something else—ideology, religious values, greed, fear—the key motivation for your characters.
- **Cluster**: Once you express your ideas, get another 11x17 sheet and cluster them into different categories. Organize the mass of loosely related ideas into categories. Don't try to fit every idea under a category. Lots of ideas won't fit anywhere; they're "outliers." But hold on to them. Keep them close by, just in case you might need them later.
- **Test**: You are almost there! Now you need to test your variables. Operationalize your variables. Find something to count. Then test the variables, one by one.
- **Scale**: Almost always, you need to expand and contract the "universe" of possibilities. A computer analyst, for example, needs to zoom out to explore all the possible coding options—or zoom in to find the algorithm that works best for a particular need. A social scientist needs explore topics like war, peace, wealth, poverty, or group formation as broadly as possible—then zoom into the aspects of those issues that hold the greatest explanatory value.
- **Close**: Now decide what the evidence shows you. Boldly, but also

I think you can get pretty far with addition, subtraction, multiplication, and division. And the vast majority of the analysis that we did fell into eighth-grade math skills. ... In one meeting I said something along the lines of, 'You know, we ought to do a regression analysis on these five data series.' And there were probably 50 people in the room and it just went way over everybody's head. Honestly, there wasn't like a huge appetite for that level of analysis.

Like all aspects of life, sometimes getting the simple things right goes a long way toward understanding.

~

### Element 72
### Play the Game of Halves

A MUSIC DIRECTOR was talking about the tricks he uses to find the right voices for his community choir—and how to eliminate the off-key voices.

"I give them a simple song that they all know, like 'Twinkle Twinkle, Little Star.' I tell them to sing with gusto. And then I listen."

When he hears a discordant voice, he cannot always tell who is responsible. But he knows, roughly, the location of the off-key sound. So he cuts the group in half. "OK, just the tenors now!" he says. Or: "Everyone on the right side of the room, sing out!"

Halving the voices might not be enough to spot the wayward warbler. So he breaks the group in half again—and a third time, too, if necessary. Quickly, though, he identifies the problem.

As the director proceeds, he double-checks and triple-checks his assumptions. "The last thing I want to do is lose a good voice," he says. "I like to be wrong when I think I had found a bad voice. Maybe the bad-sounding singer was affected by someone nearby. Maybe he wasn't breathing right. Maybe he grew up in a family of bad singers. With some coaching, he might help the choir. So I want to prove my suspicions wrong."

Doing analysis works like that. You start with a big "universe" of possibilities, then deliberately break those possibilities into parts. Eventually you identify the two or three factors that might answer your question. Then you test them.

The Greek philosopher Democritus called this approach the "game of halves." What would happen, Democritus wondered, if he could break a piece of matter in half, again and again? How long would it take to get to the smallest piece? Would the makeup of the pieces change when taken apart? What about when they're put together in different combinations?

When isolating variables, to separate "the signal from the noise," scientists look for ways they might be wrong. They seek to "disprove the hypothesis." Good scientists are actually happy when they discover flaws in their argument.

"take delight when a skillful musician violates the expectation in an interesting way—a sort of musical joke that we're all in on."

Other forms of expression follow music's rhythms and beats. Dance creates patterns of bodily movement in space. Visual art deploys patterns of color, shape, and solids and voids over surfaces. Language deploys patterns of sound and pacing in the spoken and written word. Stories have their own patterns, from the Aristotelian arc to the moment-by-moment beats of speech and action.

∿

### Element 73
### Use Beats to Move Stories Forward

A BEAT IS, the Hollywood script doctor Robert McKee tells us, "the smallest element" of all stories.

A beat is a moment of change. A person acts, changing the trajectory of the story. If the beat happens, the story moves in one direction; if it doesn't happen, the story moves in a different direction.

Of course, beats demand responses. I do this, you do that; I advance, you retreat; I ask a question, you answer; I make an offer, you counter; I make a gesture, you respond.

To give a scene movement, intrigue, and verve, depict a series of beats. When one character does something, get another to respond. Move back and forth—with a series of actions and responses—throughout the scene. In a well-constructed scene, every action raises a question; every answer, in turn, raises a new question. Each of those movements is a beat, creating a scene that looks like this:

Problem/ → Answer/ → Answer/ → Answer/ → Answer/ →
Question    Question    Question    Question    Question

Every worthwhile piece of dialogue, action, gesture, description, and detail acts like a beat. Each beat offers new information and new possibilities. *Each beat changes the trajectory of the story.*

In fact, the best way to assess whether to use something in a story—an action, a response, a detail, a thought—is to ask whether it advances the story. In a well-constructed story, every beat matters. If a beat does not somehow advance the story, we should cut it from the story.

If you could remove an action, response, detail, or thought from a passage without changing the trajectory of the passage, do so. If it does not contribute to the story's progress, delete it.

If you use details that do not advance your pieces you confuse the audience. "If you say in the first chapter that there is a rifle hanging on the wall, in

# RHYTHM AND BEATS

How can we know the dancer from the dance?

— WILLIAM BUTLER YEATS

E very part of our world moves with tempo. We follow the pace of the seasons, months, weeks, and days. We follow the circadian cycles of light and darkness, the monthly cycles of the tides, and the annual changes of seasons. We synchronize our actions to our rates of breathing and the tick-tock of the clock. We feel our pulse quicken in moments of stress or exertion.

Life has evolved for 3 billion years. Every animal and plant developed within the cycles set by world's daily revolution and annual trip around the sun. Even in the absence of light, the internal clocks of animals and plants follow those rhythms, which have become part of life's cellular structure. "Animals and plants that charter same ecological niche must coordinate the biological rhythms," says J.T. Fraser, a philosopher of time. "There must be a chasing time, and eating time, and drinking, mating, and building times."

It only stands to reason that the arts reflect the rhythms of nature. To give writing flow, we mimic the regularity of waves lapping on the shore. And then, to break through the monotony of such regular flows, we interrupt the rhythm.

Music offers the best example of creative rhythms. Music's tempo pulls us into a flow. Then the tempo changes and we are surprised—and more alert. "Our brains are keeping track of how many times particular notes are sounded, where they appear in terms of strong versus weak beats, and how long they last," Dan Levitan writes in *This Is Your Brain on Music*. Listeners

# PRAISE FOR THE ELEMENTS OF WRITING

*The Elements Of Writing*, the basis of this book, has won praise from teachers and writers alike:

> *The Elements of Writing* is an essential reference for writers and storytellers. I use it myself and recommend it to my students. The classic literary examples are extremely helpful. I feel smarter just having this book by my bedside, and I discover new insights every time I pick it up.
>
> — LEE-SEAN HUANG, COFOUNDER AND CREATIVE DIRECTOR OF FOOSA

The rare writer's handbook that is both useful and a pleasure to read. The book's structure is original and smart; aspiring writers can read the book cover to cover or can look up specific issues. Besides articulating his own "tricks of the trade," Euchner offers a huge, wonderful array of examples. In clear, lucid terms, Charlie Euchner explains and shows what makes for strong prose.

— AARON RITZENBERG, DEPARTMENT OF ENGLISH, COLUMBIA UNIVERSITY

This book offers a great way to get everybody from students to practicing professionals excited about the skills, knowledge, and work habits that go into the composition of clear, solid prose. Too often, this information gets presented in a way that turns people off or triggers anxiety, making the challenge of writing well seem far more daunting than it really is. Charlie Euchner's approach gets the job done with just the right blend of rigor, encouragement, and fun.

— ALEX HEARD, EDITORIAL DIRECTOR OF OUTSIDE
MAGAZINE AND AUTHOR OF THE EYES OF WILLIE MCGEE

Charles Euchner is the rare talent who can both write and teach. As I struggled to write my first book, he pulled me back to reality and explained the tricks of the trade. With brilliant simplicity, he explained all the big—and little—things that lead to a successful book. Remember what you are trying to say. Open each story with a strong lead. Use stories to explain your analysis and concepts. Help the reader see, feel, and smell the situation. Within a month, I had learned what I needed to write a book. Euchner has now codified his wisdom. This book which teaches all the skills you need to become a strong writer. Trust me, it works.

— FORMER AMBASSADOR NANCY E. SODERBERG, AUTHOR OF
THE SUPERPOWER MYTH

Writer and educator Charles Euchner provides a simple, intuitive, skill—based approach to writing in all genres. I've incorporated the approach in my classroom to help my students write their autobiographies. It is difficult to write about one's life, but this book helps students to find the right words, in the right order, to construct their personal narrative. It's a must read for all educators who are serious about guiding the young authors to unlock their unique voices and develop as both writers and thinkers.

— DAVID CASS, TEACHER/ADVISOR AT THE MET SCHOOL,
PROVIDENCE, R.I.

Lots of people, especially writers in business, know what they want to say but are not sure how to get it down in a comprehensible and simple fashion. Euchner has a dead simple tool that will help in composing and editing any written work.

— GERRY LANTZ, PRESIDENT OF STORIES THAT WORK

# FOR MORE INFORMATION

You can transform writing in your organization—your business, school, agency, or other group—with just one seminar.

Books are great. You can immerse yourself for hours in a book, and you can go back to check facts or do exercise.

But seminars offer a more dynamic setting. As questions arise, you can ask them. You can work on projects as a group—creating stories, developing characters, showing action, building sentences, editing drafts, making arguments. Students not only learn from the seminar leader, but also reform each other. The sparks from one student creates new learning possibilities for others. In a seminar, you engage all the senses. You encounter surprises.

Consider bringing Charles Euchner, the author of *The Elements Of Writing*, to your organization. Euchner will not only teach you the simple, intuitive skills of writing—in his breakthrough story-to-construction-to-analysis sequence—but will give you strategies to put your new skills to work right away.

The payoff—faster, better writing, with more opportunity for creative and rigorous thought—comes right away.

Charles Euchner's seminars have been praised for their fast-paced but relaxed style and the breadth and depth of information. Participants in seminars get workbooks and other supplemental materials to master all the skills of writing on the spot.

Email charlie@theelementsofwriting.com or call (203) 645-6112.

# ABOUT THE AUTHOR

Charles Euchner, a longtime college teacher and author, is the creator of The Elements of Writing, the only comprehensive learning system for writing in all fields.

Euchner (pronounced *Ike*-ner) has taught and directed research institutes at a number of premier universities, including Harvard, Yale, Columbia, Penn, Holy Cross, Northeastern, and St. Mary's. He was educated at Vanderbilt and Johns Hopkins.

He is the author or editor of ten books. Critics have praised *Nobody Turn Me Around: A People's History of the 1963 March on Washington* (Beacon Press, 2010) as a dramatic reinterpretation of the civil rights movement. *Kirkus Reviews* calls it "dynamic ... sharp, riveting." Juan Williams, author of *Eyes on the Prize*, calls it "compelling and dramatic." Curtis Wilkie, a longtime chronicler of civil rights, says the book provides "a panorama of vivid characters." Roger Wilkins, a former White House aide in the civil rights era, said it "brings it all back in vivid detail." A short documentary based on the book, written by Euchner, won the award for best writing and editing at the 2011 Re-Image Film Festival and has aired on PBS stations.

Euchner's other books include works on the state of sports in modern America (*Playing the Field, The Last Nine Innings,* and *Little League, Big Dreams*), grassroots politics (*Urban Policy Reconsidered* and *Extraordinary Politics*), presidential politics (*Selecting the President* and *The President and the Public*), and regional politics (the two-part *Governing Greater Boston* project).

Euchner delivers writing seminars and keynote addresses all over the United States. His topics include writing, civil rights, sports, and urban politics and planning. To learn more, email charleseuchner@gmail.com.

In addition to his career in academe, Euchner has also been a reporter for *Education Week* and the coordinator of Boston's citywide master planning process. He has contributed to major newspapers and magazines including *The New York Times, The Boston Globe, The American,* and *Commonwealth,* and has been interviewed for hundreds of media outlets including "Nightline," "All Things Considered," "The Diane Rehm Show," "Talk of the Nation," "NBC Nightly News," and more.

For information about Writing Code seminars, call (203) 645-6112 or email charlie@theelementsofwriting.com.

www.theelementsofwriting.com
charlie@theelementsofwriting.com